AF702539

8087 Applications and Programming for the IBM PC, XT, and AT Revised and Expanded

Richard Startz

A BRADY BOOK
Published by Prentice Hall Press
New York, NY 10023

8087 Applications and Programming for the IBM PC, XT, and AT—Revised and Expanded

Copyright © 1985 by Brady Communications Company, Inc.

All rights reserved
including the right of reproduction
in whole or in part in any form

A Brady Book
Published by Prentice Hall Press
A Division of Simon & Schuster, Inc.
Gulf + Western Building
One Gulf + Western Plaza
New York, NY 10023

Library of Congress Cataloging in Publication Data

Startz, Richard, 1952–
8087 applications and programming for the IBM PC, XT, and AT.

Includes index.
1. Intel 8087 (Microprocessor) 2. IBM Personal Computer—Programming. 3. IBM Personal Computer XT—Programming. 4. IBM Personal Computer AT—Programming. 5. Assembler language (Computer program language) I. Title. II. Title: Eight thousand eighty-seven applications and programming for the IBM PC, XT, and AT. III. Title: Eight thousand and eighty-seven applications and programming for the IBM PC, XT, and AT.
QA76.8.I2923S8 1985 001.64′2 85-11387

ISBN 0-89303-485-1

Printed in the United States of America

86 87 88 89 90 91 92 93 94 95 2 3 4 5 6 7 8 9 10

Acquisitions Editor: Terrell Anderson
Production Editor: Roberta Glencer
Text Designer: Michael Rogers
Art Director/Cover Design: Don Sellers
Assistant Art Director: Bernard Vervin
Manufacturing Director: John Komsa

Indexer: William Lively
Typesetter: Harper Graphics, Waldorf, MD
Printer: R.R. Donnelley & Sons, Harrisonburg, VA

CONTENTS

About The Diskette

The diskette, which is available as an option with the book, contains all the programs listed in The Cookbook. Each program appears in three forms: as an assembly language source program (e.g., PROG.ASM); as an already assembled object module (e.g., PROG.OBJ); and as a file ready to be BLOADed into BASIC (e.g., PROG.SAV). In several cases, a number of programs have been combined into a single module for ease. For instance, the most important matrix manipulation routines are combined in files MATRIX.ASM, MATRIX.OBJ, and MATRIX.SAV. The programs are supplied on a standard single-sided, 5.25 inch diskette formatted on an IBM Personal Computer running PC-DOS 1.1. A copy of the diskette documentation appears at the end of the book.

Preface to the Second Edition

Do you know the two elements required for a publisher to request a new edition of a book? They are:

1. There has to be something new to say.
2. Quite a few people have to have bought the first edition.

Something New

Nearly two years have passed since I finished the manuscript for the first edition of *8087 Applications and Programming*. In that time, use of the 8087 has boomed, and the introduction of powerful new personal computers based on Intel's 286 and 287 chips, notably the IBM AT, has greatly expanded the range of computing available on a desktop.

This new edition of *8087 Applications and Programming* covers all the news about the 287 co-processor. The good news for 8087 users is that the 8087 and 287 are about 99.44 percent compatible. (This edition covers the remaining 0.56 percent difference, too.)

For Old Friends

In addition to new material, I've fixed several bugs and typos in the text in program listings. (There were only about half a dozen errors in the first edition, which, to be perfectly honest, left me feeling pretty smug.) Almost all the corrections are due to alert readers. To these friends and helpers around the country, many, many thanks.

Dick Startz
Seattle, Washington

Trademarks

The following trademarks are used in this book:

- IBM, IBM Personal Computer, IBM PC, IBM AT and PC-DOS are trademarks of International Business Machines Corporation
- 8086, 8087, 8088, 186, 188, 286, Numeric Data Processor, and iAPX are trademarks of Intel Corporation. The 8087 and 8088 instruction mnemonics are copyrighted by Intel.
- Microsoft and MS-DOS are trademarks of Microsoft Corporation.
- Apple II+ is a trademark of Apple Computer.
- DEC-2060 and VAX are trademarks of Digital Equipment Corporation.
- IMSL is a trademark of IMSL Inc.
- Turbo Pascal is a trademark of Borland International.

Acknowledgments

I've decided that the only reason a book ever reaches print is that about the time the author runs out of steam someone else comes along and gives the project a boost. At least that's certainly been true for this book.

The people at the Brady Communications Company, editors and staff, have been a pleasure to work with.

Books are reviewed for style and accuracy before going to press. I've been fortunate in having three reviewers make substantial contributions to the final product. Many thanks are due to Peter Norton, Leo Scanlon, and Andy Verhalen.

Intel has been most generous in allowing the use of copyrighted material and in supplying technical information. The authoritative source on the 8087 is Intel's *iAPX 86, 88 User's Manual,* from which I have borrowed liberally.

My wife, Shelly Lundberg, a performed a final inspection of the manuscript. As always, I get my best suggestions from my best friend.

Before I let anyone else see the initial manuscript, I sent it to my sister, Barbara Startz, for editing. Barbara knows a little about computers and a great deal about writing. I haven't quite figured out how she found the time to repair my writing after 90 hours a week at her own job, but I'm awfully glad she did.

It should go without saying that all the people named above are entitled to credit for things you like in the book, but that I alone remain responsible for any remaining inaccuracy or awkwardism.

Limits of Liability and Disclaimer of Warranty

The author and publisher of this book have used their best efforts in preparing this book and the programs contained in it. These efforts include the development, research, and testing of the theories and programs to determine their effectiveness. The author and publisher make no warranty of any kind, expressed or implied, with regard to these programs or the documentation contained in this book. The author and publisher shall not be liable in any event for incidental or consequential damages in connection with, or arising out of, the furnishing, performance, or use of these programs.

Note to Authors

Have you written a book related to personal computers? Do you have an idea for developing such a project? If so, we would like to hear from you. Brady produces a complete range of books for the personal computer market. We invite you to write to Terrell Anderson, Senior Editor, Simon&Schuster, General Reference Group, 1230 Avenue of the Americas, New York, NY 10020.

Introduction

Let me explain why I'm excited about the 8087. I've used large computers for many years as a tool for professional research. When I bought my personal computer, I found I could do many things far more conveniently than on these larger machines. But I quickly discovered that my machine wasn't fast enough for large scale numerical computing.

Having an 8087 means that now I can solve many large problems on my personal computer. While some problems still belong on big machines (and always will), my personal computing horizon has expanded tenfold.

The 8087 isn't just fast; it's very easy to use. Whether you are mostly a "program user" or mostly a "program writer," you will find that the 8087 is a remarkable device. I hope you will find *8087 Applications and Programming* an enjoyable, as well as an educational, introduction.

Who is This Book For?

- People who want to know what the 8087 will do (especially Part I, Chapters 1-4).
- People who want to learn how to program the 8087 (especially Part II, Chapters 5–8 and Chapter 12 in Part III).
- People who want prepared programs for number crunching applications on their personal computer (especially Part III, Chapters 9–15).

Part I describes the capabilities of the 8087 at a fairly non-technical level. If you are considering buying an 8087 and want to know about 8087-compatible hardware and software, Part I is for you.

Parts II and III are for the more technically inclined reader. While we "begin at the beginning," some prior programming experience is helpful. You needn't be an expert by any means, but this book isn't an Introduction to Computers.

Part II (Chapters 5–8) provides an in-depth description of the 8087's instructions. We also discuss some of the fundamentals of assembly language programming for the 8088. We pay special attention to linking assembly language and BASIC programs, including a blow-by-blow interactive session in which we link an assembly language program with both interpreted and compiled BASIC.

Part III concentrates on applications. We develop many useful 8087 assembly language routines in Part III. You can use these programs as examples, to learn more about 8087 programming, or you can use the programs "cookbook" fashion. (Part III also includes, in Chapter 12, an explanation of some of the 8087's most advanced instructions.

How to Read This Book

I've taken care to write so that you can skip around from one section to the next as suits your mood. Please don't feel constrained to read from beginning to end.

Most readers will probably find Part I informative and easy reading. If you want to write 8087 assembly language programs, concentrate on Part II. (If you are an experienced 8087 programmer, you can skip Part II and move on to the applications in Part III.) If you are interested in applications, but don't care about intimate programming details, read Part III. You can always flip back to Part II if you need to check something.

Finally, you can use the programs here "cookbook" style. You don't need to know why a program was written in a certain way or how it operates internally, if you just want to get a fast answer. Go ahead and use the programs. If a program is useful enough that you want to modify it or write a similar one yourself, you can return later for the "how and why."

The Cookbook

Several chapters begin with an introductory paragraph and then a sign that says

The Cookbook

Under this sign, you will find a list of the programs appearing in the chapter, together with a brief description of the purpose of the program and the input and output required. Use the cookbook when you want to find a program in a hurry. We spend quite a bit of time discussing why certain things are done in certain ways. If you want to run programs, but not build your own, you don't need to read the "how and why" material. Do scan the material which describes the information you need to pass to the programs.

Strategic Number Crunching

In addition to a great deal of detail about the 8087 and about numerical programming, this book presents a strategic approach to serious computational work. Our strategy grows from two programming maxims:

- *10 percent of program code accounts for 90 percent of program execution time.*
- *The cost of creating a working program is proportional to the square of the length of code, regardless of the power of the programming language being used.*

Serious programmers sometimes go to great effort, mistakenly, to write "efficient programs." A far better strategy is to identify the 10 percent of the code that has 90 percent of the computational burden. Re-write the 10 percent for maximum efficiency; write the other 90 percent for maximum clarity.

The search for efficiency often leads to writing programs in assembly language. Because assembly code can be 10 times the length of equivalent BASIC code, assembly language programs can be 100 times harder to debug. It (almost) never makes sense to write an entire program in assembly language. It does make sense to code the *critical routines* in assembly language. In this way, we get almost the entire advantage of assembly language speed at a small fraction of the cost of assembly language programming.

We can actually do even better by recognizing that many numerical programming problems use the same underlying subroutines. An 8087 assembly language program to add up an array is somewhat more complicated than a FOR/NEXT loop in BASIC. But we only need to write and debug the 8087 program once. Having done so, using the subroutine over and over is probably easier than writing a FOR/NEXT loop every time we need to add up an array. Computer scientists call this planned reuse of subroutines "modular programming." For an example of the convenience and power of modular 8087 subroutines, take a look at the statistical package in Chapter 14.

You can actually do *even* better. 8087 routines for many numerical computing needs appear in this book (and on the optional diskette). While we hope you decide to learn about all the capabilities of the 8087 and to write your own special subroutines, you're more than welcome to begin by lifting the subroutines bodily from these pages and putting them to use in your 8087-equipped personal computer.

Hardware and Software Requirements

The programs in this book run on computers based on the Intel 8087 Numeric Data Processor and the 8088,8086 family of Intel microprocessors. In addition to the 8088 and 8086, this family includes the 188, 186, and 286 microprocessors and the associated versions of the 8087. The programs were all developed and tested on an IBM Personal Computer. All timing assumes the processor is a 5 megahertz 8088. Timings are only approximate. (For example, the IBM PC runs about five percent slower than the stated timings. An 8086-based machine will be somewhat faster.) Timings given for BASIC programs refer to interpreted BASIC without an 8087, unless otherwise qualified.

The 8087 assembly language programs can be called as subroutines from programs written in either interpreted Microsoft BASIC or compiled Microsoft BASIC, as available on the IBM Personal Computer. The programs assume that data is stored in 8087-compatible format. (See Chapter 3 for an extensive discussion of 8087-compatible software.) The programs will run with pre-8087 versions of BASIC, but you will need to add the Microsoft-to- Intel conversion programs in the appendix.

In order to assemble the programs in the book, you will need an assembler that recognizes the full set of Intel mnemonic instructions. (Be warned that version 1.0 of the IBM Personal Computer MACRO Assembler does not recognize 8087 instruction mnemonics, though it will generate 8087 instructions. You can still use this assembler if you are willing to re-code the 8087 mnemonics into the 8088 ESCape instruction. On the optional diskette, we have already re-coded the mnemonics, so you can use the IBM Macro Assembler.) Since BASIC is the dominant personal language, we've written all the programs to be called from BASIC instead of FORTRAN or some other language more common on large computers. If you want to combine the programs with a language that uses different internal conventions BASIC, you may have to re-write a few instructions. The programs all work under Microsoft BASIC using version 1.1 of the PC-DOS operating system on the IBM Personal Computer. If you are using another computer or different software, some minor details may be different.

1

Turning Minutes Into Seconds

The 8087-equipped personal computer has three nice features: it's *easy*, *accurate*, and *fast*. Everything you need to apply 8087 power to practical computational problems is in this book. This first chapter describes the 8087 and its use at the broadest level.

Throughout the book, we try to take a scientific and analytical approach to understanding the 8087. Wherever possible, we discuss general principles—the "why" of programming—along with the hundred-and-one technical details needed to make a computer work. To keep the discussion concrete, each general principle is illustrated with a practical application. The 8087 is powerful, yet easy to use. We hope this book will be occasionally mind-stretching—and fun as well.

How Easy Is Easy?

The 8087 has been designed to emphasize ease of use as much as raw computational power. Your first step as an 8087 user is especially easy. Just add an 8087 to a personal computer and run your programs as usual. (You will need software intended for use with the 8087.) Without any further effort, you can expect to see improvements in execution speed ranging from about 20 percent to as much as a factor of 10.

If you want the maximum advantage from the 8087's hardware power, you will need software specifically designed for the 8087. There is an extended discussion in Chapter 3 of what to look for—and what to look out for—when purchasing software for the 8087. Here we give a quick overview.

The most important piece of knowledge about 8087 compatible software is really a statement about hardware. The 8087 *extends* the capabilities of existing processors without interfering with the processors' usual operations. Therefore, any software designed "pre- 8087" should continue to operate normally when the 8087 is present.

Such 100 percent "upward compatibility" is a great advantage, but it does have a flip side. When you add an 8087 to a system, programs using "pre-8087" software do not speed up at all. For example, you can add an 8087 to the original IBM Personal Computer in a minute or two. (I added one to my IBM PC in order to write the programs for this book.) All your interpreted BASIC or compiled BASIC programs will run correctly, but no faster. So when we make statements about the speed advantage from adding an 8087, there is also an implicit statement made about using 8087 compatible software.

(With a little reprogramming, you can use the 8087 with pre-8087 versions of BASIC and other software. We discuss this problem in Chapter 3, but if you'd like a little reassurance, all the programs in this book were written using pre-8087 software.)

You should be aware of one potential trap in buying software for use with the 8087. It is possible, though unlikely, that you will get into trouble by mixing software designed to take advantage of the 8087 with pre-8087 software. See Chapter 3 for more discussion.

Assuming you have the versions of BASIC or other programming languages intended for use with the 8087, you can run all your usual programs. Programs that do a great deal of numerical computing will race when compared to pre-8087 performance. If you are a really heavy number cruncher, you will eventually want to use a library of specially written high-speed 8087 subroutines.

Part III of this book (Chapters 9–15) includes the most important subroutines for numerical computing. All you need do is read the explanation of how to use each subroutine, enter them into the computer, and combine them with your BASIC programs. (On the diskette available with this book, the subroutines have been typed in and assembled for you.) When compared to pre-8087 BASIC, the use of these subroutines increases execution speed by a factor of 10 to 200. (In rare cases, improvement factors as high as 500 have been noted.)

Part II of this book (Chapter 5–8) prepares you for the most advanced stage of 8087 use: writing your own subroutines. As you will see in the examples throughout this book, programming the 8087 in assembly language is relatively simple because of the 8087's elegant design. When you've seen the examples and instructions here, you'll have no trouble writing your own special purpose programs.

How Accurate Is Accurate?

Easily written, fast-executing programs are no great trick—if you don't care about getting the right answer. The most important attribute of the

8087 is its remarkable accuracy. The 8087 has three accuracy-enhancing features:

- Internal calculations yield 11 more bits of accuracy than BASIC double precision numbers. That's worth three extra decimal places.
- Internal calculations have an extremely wide range. The 8087 can represent numbers as large as 10^{4932} and as small as 10^{-4932}. As a result, calculations rarely overflow or underflow during intermediate steps. In fact, both the precision and range of numbers are greater than those found on most traditional mainframe computers.
- The 8087 is designed to handle a wide range of error conditions and make an automatic, and graceful, recovery. As a result, simple "paper and pencil" algorithms are much more likely to work. And when something goes wrong, the 8087 follows well- behaved rules instead of producing the wrong answer.

How Fast Is Fast?

Just how fast is an 8087-equipped PC? A good comparison can be made to either a standard mainframe computer or to a microcomputer without an 8087.

Perhaps the most remarkable statement to be made about the 8087 is that it actually makes sense to compare its speed to that of a mainframe computer costing hundreds of thousands of dollars. The 8087 is several times slower than a half million-dollar machine—but then it's more than several times cheaper.

Exact comparisons are always risky, but a few numbers can give you a feeling for the speed of the 8087. Moderate speed mainframe computers require from about one to five microseconds to multiply two numbers. A supermini might require one microsecond. A $50,000 table-top mini might require about 3 microseconds. Efficient 8088 software uses about 400 microseconds to multiply two numbers (about 900 microseconds for double precision). The 8087, which is an inexpensive add-on to a personal computer, uses 20 to 30 microseconds for the same task.

For the very first time, a microcomputer is a cost-effective alternative to number crunching on large computers. The PC with an 8087 has ¼ to 1/20 the speed of a large computer at 1/10 to 1/100 of the large machine's cost. While large machines will always be more cost-effective than micros for some tasks, the 8087-equipped personal computer is the first micro to compete economically with its larger cousins.

Most PC owners care more about how the 8087 will speed up their personal computing than about comparisons to large central computer facilities. The speed advantage of adding an 8087 to a PC depends on the application and on how you use the 8087. (Having read through this book, you'll know the methods for attaining the greatest possible advantage.) The central point to understand is that the 8087 is a *Numeric Data Processor*. The 8087 only speeds up programs involving numerical computation. If you only use the PC for word processing, the 8087 is about 99 percent irrelevant. But if you crunch the occasional number, adding an 8087 is like trading a sparkler for the Fourth of July fireworks display.

The speed advantage of the 8087 depends very much on how you use it, but as an overall guide:

The 8087 turns minutes into seconds.

Specific Speed Comparisons

Just how much you get out of an 8087 depends on the software you use as well as the 8087's hardware speed. Speed is discussed extensively in Chapter 4. We give a preliminary discussion here.

What the 8087 will do for you depends on how much time your software spends on various "overhead" tasks versus how much time is spent in numerical calculations. The 8087 speeds up the numerical calculations but does little or nothing about the time spent on overhead. Table 1-1 shows what kind of results you can expect when you combine the 8087 with low-overhead, high-speed routines.

Table 1-1. BASIC versus 8087 speed benchmarks (time in seconds).

Program	*50 by 50 matrix multiplication*	*5,000 square roots*
BASIC	1148	53
8087 routine	8	0.38

The times in Table 1-1 compare (pre-8087) BASIC to special 8087 routines which you will find later in this book. The improvement is typical of what the combination of the 8087 and good software can do. Depending on the application, the 8087 hardware produces an improvement in speed by a factor of about 10 to 50—the rest is due to the low-overhead software. You won't see nearly as good an improvement if you use the 8087 with high-overhead software. (The BASIC interpreters built into a computer are, of necessity, high-overhead software.) Since the 8087 only speeds up numerical calculations, and such software spends relatively little time on numerical calculation, the sum of overhead time and numerical calculation time won't fall by nearly the amount shown in the table above. The improvement will be impressive, nonetheless.

What Equipment Do You Need to Use an 8087?

You need an 8087, of course. You can get an 8087 either as part of the original equipment of your personal computer or by adding it to an existing machine. You can probably add an 8087 to any PC based on the Intel 8088 or 8086 family. The degree of difficulty of adding an 8087 depends on whether the manufacturer provided a place for the 8087 when designing the computer. Even if no provision was made, it is probably possible to add an 8087. However, doing so requires quite a bit of technical expertise.

The good news is that a number of manufacturers did provide a place for the 8087. In particular, when IBM (and those companies making compatible personal computers) introduced its first PC, it left an empty socket on the main circuit board expressly for the 8087. To add an 8087, you need only plug an 8087 into this empty socket. Plugging it in is easy (I installed my 8087 without help from anyone); easier, in fact, than adding a printed circuit board to one of the "expansion slots" inside the computer. (If you really know nothing at all about the inside of your computer, get someone to help you. Your computer is, after all, a fairly expensive piece of equipment.)

If you add an 8087 yourself, be sure to buy the version of the 8087 appropriate for your machine. For example, an 8087-3 runs at a speed of 5 megahertz and is suitable for an IBM PC. An 8087-2 runs at 8 megahertz and should be used in some fast "PC-compatibles." If you have an IBM AT, or another computer based on the Intel 80286, you need the version of the 8087 called an 80287. Any competent dealer will be able to guide you to the right chip.

What about folks who own a personal computer that is not based on the Intel 8088, 8086 family. Can they take advantage of the speed of the 8087? The answer, unfortunately, is a qualified "no." The 8087 works only with the Intel family. However, because the Intel family is so popular, several enterprising companies now sell circuit boards, carrying an Intel processor, that fit into Apple and some other computers. Some of these boards include an 8087 or make provision for one to be added. These boards won't speed up programs executed on your original processor, but they do allow you to make use of the programs in this book and other 8087-compatible software.

2

The Intel 8087 Chip

Processors and Co-processors

The "brain" of any computer is its "CPU," or central processing unit. For the IBM PC, and many other "second generation" personal computers, the "brain" is an Intel 8088. A complete, general purpose central processing unit built into a single chip, the 8088 has a complete instruction set for 8- and 16-bit integer arithmetic, programming logic, and input and output. Like most microprocessors, the 8088 lacks the advanced mathematical instructions found in large, mainframe computers.

The Intel 8087 Numeric Data Processor extends the instruction set of the Intel 8088 by adding sophisticated new mathematical instructions. The 8087 high-speed hardware carries out mathematical operations which would require thousands of lines of code if implemented in software. The 8087 hardware can operate 10 to 200 times faster than equivalent software.

From a programmer's viewpoint, the 8087 adds additional instructions to the 8088's repertoire and makes available additional processor registers. Why not include all the capabilities on one chip, rather than create an add-on device? There are several reasons:

- The 8087 is an extraordinarily sophisticated computational device, including 75,000 transistors on a single chip. Even though the 8087 is "limited" to numerical processing, it is much more complex (and more expensive) than the general-purpose 8088. Building two separate chips holds down development costs and allows users and system manufacturers to tailor-fit systems for different uses.
- The 8088 (and its 16-bit bus sibling, the 8086) were available to the general market for several years before the first delivery of the 8087. In designing 16-bit personal computers, several manufacturers left an open socket, labeled the "co-processor socket" on the IBM PC, so that machines could be upgraded easily when the 8087 became available.

- Because the 8087 and 8088 are two devices, they execute instructions simultaneously. As a practical programming matter, this means that while the 8087 completes one numerical computation, the 8088 prepares the next.

In the remainder of this chapter, we describe the capabilities of the 8087 in a general way. Chapter 5 provides a much more detailed technical discussion.

A Growing Family of Hardware

The 8088 and 8086 were the first two members of Intel's family of 16-bit microprocessors. Today, three newer chips have joined the first two. The 188 and 186 are newer versions of the 8088 and the 8086. These chips were designed to reduce computer design costs by including extra electronic functions right on the main microprocessor chip. These chips are also somewhat faster than the 8088 and 8086 and include several new instructions. From the user's viewpoint, the 188 and 186 are pretty much identical with the 8088, including in their use of the 8087.

The really important new family member is the 286, which is used in the IBM AT. The 286 can run in either "real mode" or "protected mode." In real mode, you can safely think of the 286 as a *very* fast 8088. Protected mode gives the 286 powers rather more like a minicomputer than a personal computer. However, protected mode is only partially compatible with the 8088. The version of the 8087 used with the 286 is 287. (You will sometimes see the individual chips referred to as 80286 and 80287.)

You'll be pretty safe in assuming everything we say about 8087 programming applies to the 287 (in real mode) as well. The rare exception is covered explicitly.

Overview of the 8087

The 8087 serves as a *co-processor* with the 8088. The 8087 "watches" instructions as they are received by the 8088. The 8087 processes its own instructions, while allowing 8088 instructions to pass by. The 8088 also watches all instructions, processing its own, while allowing 8087 instructions to pass by. The 8088 does provide one important service for the 8087. On seeing an 8087 instruction, the 8088 calculates any necessary memory address and makes the address available to the 8087. The 8088 then proceeds immediately to the next instruction. In this way, the co-processor design allows the 8087 and 8088 to execute instructions simultaneously, thus considerably enhancing total system performance.

The central feature of the 8087's architecture is eight 80-bit data registers. These registers are organized as a classic "pushdown stack," an organizational technique that leads both to fast vector operations and to efficient code generation by high-level language compilers. (Chapter 5 includes an extensive discussion on the operation of the pushdown stack.) The 80-bit register width allows the 8087 to perform extremely accurate calculations. While the 8087 instruction set recognizes seven different data types in memory, all data is automatically converted to an 80-bit internal representation when brought into the 8087. This frees the programmer from most worries about converting between data types.

Instruction Classes

Each of the 8087's 68 instructions fall into one of six classes. (The classification scheme is a convenient way of describing the capabilities of the 8087. You needn't remember the classifications in order to use the 8087.) The six classes are:

Data transfer (discussed in Chapter 6). These instructions move data back and forth between the 8087 and memory and shuffle data internally among the 8087 registers.

Arithmetic (discussed in Chapter 6). At the heart of the 8087 instruction set are the operations for addition, subtraction, multiplication, and division—plus some extras such as square root and absolute value.

Transcendental (discussed in Chapter 12). The 8087 hardware has built-in capabilities for computing logarithms and trigonometric functions. (These instructions are rarely found even on large-scale mainframes.)

Constants (discussed in Chapters 6 and 12). Seven of the most frequently used constants, such as 0, 1, and pi, are built into the 8087.

Comparison (discussed in Chapters 6 and 7). These instructions are used for making less than/equal to/greater than, and other similar tests.

Processor control (discussed in Chapter 12). This class of instructions gives the programmer total control over the behavior of the 8087. Some of these instructions are also used in conjunction with the comparison instructions and 8088 branching instructions to control program flow.

Data Types

The seven regular 8087 data types are examined in depth in Chapter 5. However, for most ordinary 8087 programming considerations, only a few facts are really important. The only data types directly available in BASIC are integer, single precision, and double precision. Generally, only the latter two are used to hold numerical data. If your principal use of the 8087 is scientific programming, you need remember only three facts about data types:

1. *Single precision* numbers (called *short real* in 8087 terminology) have six or seven decimal digits of accuracy and occupy four bytes of memory.
2. *Double precision* numbers (called *long real* in 8087 terminology) have 15 or 16 decimal digits of accuracy and occupy eight bytes of memory.
3. *Temporary real* numbers are used internally by the 8087 for all calculations. They retain better than 18 decimal digits of accuracy. When stored in memory, a temporary real occupies 10 bytes.

If you are primarily a number cruncher, these three data types will probably account for 95 percent of your use. However, the 8087 recognizes four additional data types:

1. *Integer* numbers (called *word integer* in 8087 terminology) occupy two bytes of storage and are used principally to index arrays and other data structures. BASIC and the 8087 use the same representation for integer data.
2. A *short integer* occupies four bytes. While the largest (signed) word integer is 32,768, a short integer can be as large as two billion.
3. A *long integer* occupies eight bytes. A long integer has two or three more digits of accuracy than a double precision real number and can hold values as large as 10^{18}.
4. *Packed decimal* representation is used for business and data processing operations. A packed decimal uses 10 bytes of memory and holds 18 decimal digits. Unlike the three preceding data types, the packed decimal form uses decimal rather than binary representation. Each of the digits 0—9 is represented by four binary bits. These decimal digits are then "packed" two to a byte.

By way of contrast, the types of data recognized by the 8088 hardware are limited to one- and two-byte binary integers and short packed decimal values. All the numerical processing in pre-8087 BASIC and other high-level languages is performed by software created from operations on integers. The 8087 eliminates the need for such software. Not only are 8087-based systems faster, but programs use up much less space and numerical results are more reliable.

How Does My Computer Access the Power of the 8087?

In the next chapter we discuss software for the 8087. In order to understand why some software is 8087-compatible—and why some isn't—it helps to review the basics of the 8088/8087 co-operative set-up.

The instruction set for the 8088 was designed to be extended at a later date. One of the 8088's instructions is called the *escape* instruction. The 8088 knows that the escape instruction really calls for an operation on the 8087, so it essentially ignores this instruction and allows the 8087 to process it. The instructions used by the 8087 are different varieties of the 8088 escape.

When both the 8088 and 8087 are installed, we can think of the combination as one large computer with expanded capability. Software which uses the escape instruction internally must have an 8087 present in order to operate correctly. Software built "pre-8087" simply does not use the escape instruction and therefore does not take advantage of the new capacity.

If you are writing your own programs at the machine language level, you'll know whether or not you've used the escape instruction. Most of the time you use a computer, such intimate internal detail isn't under your control. In the next chapter, we discuss some of the varieties of 8087-compatible—and incompatible—software.

3

Buying and Building 8087-Compatible Software

What special considerations apply when buying or building software for use with the 8087? Your first question will always be, "What software works?" Your second question, "How well?" In this chapter, we break our analysis of software compatibility into three parts. In the first part, we discuss some important technical details about compatibility. In the second section, we analyze why some software produces very fast programs—and why some does not. In the chapter's last section, we discuss the merits of various types of software in terms of programming convenience and calculation speed.

Compatibility—The Technical Details

Suppose we could look at a program that had been translated into our computer's "machine language." The program uses either the machine language instructions that drive the 8087, the "escape instructions" mentioned in the last chapter, or it doesn't. If it doesn't use these instructions, then the 8087 is irrelevant. The program will run with or without an 8087 and will run at the same speed either way. If the program does use 8087 instructions, then the 8087 must be present, of course.

As it turns out, there is a second issue, equally important for compatibility, which hinges on a detail of software design. All computers represent numbers internally as particular patterns of 0's and 1's. Different computers use different patterns for the same number. For the most part, we don't care which pattern the computer uses, since we don't see the individual 0's and 1's anyway. The important thing is that the computer's hardware knows how to interpret its own patterns. (As it happens, the representation used on the 8087 has been proposed as an industry standard. For the curious, we show what the 8087's representation looks like in Chapter 5.)

Until the introduction of the 8087, personal computers based on the 8088 family had hardware for integer arithmetic only. Since there was no hardware "with an opinion" on how non-integers should be represented, each software designer was free to choose his or her own patterns. In practice, this meant that whoever built translators for programming languages (compilers, interpreters, and assemblers) made the decision for everyone using a particular language. Since Microsoft has been the principal supplier of programming languages for 16-bit computers, the vast bulk of software uses the patterns chosen by Microsoft.

Unfortunately, *the Microsoft pattern and the Intel 8087 pattern are different.*

The result of this conflict is that pre-8087 software and 8087- compatible software cannot trade data represented in their respective internal formats. With your 8087 in place, you can safely use either pre-8087 or 8087-compatible software. If you try to combine programs produced with pre-8087 and 8087-compatible translators, you will usually get garbage. Further, if you try to exchange data between such programs you will get garbage if the data was stored using the computer's internal format. If the data is not stored in the internal format, then the programs can probably exchange data.

There is no general rule as to whether a conflict will occur between two pieces of software; you need to know the particulars of each program. In the third section of this chapter, we give some examples of where to look for trouble.

What Makes a Program Fast or Slow?

Three basics determine a program's speed: the way you solve the problem (what computer scientists call the "algorithm"); your hardware's speed; and the behavior of the programming language translator. The first is always the most important. There is no computer so fast that it cannot be slowed to a crawl by a sufficiently bad way to solve a problem. The applications chapters of Part III supply high-speed solution techniques to many problems in numerical programming.

The question of hardware speed you solve, of course, when you get an 8087. If hardware were the only determinant, your program execution time would be cut by a factor of 10 to 50!

But hardware isn't the only determinant. Depending on how your program is translated into instructions the computer can understand, using an 8087 may drop execution time by only a few percent or speed up execution by a factor of 200. For this reason, and because you can exercise a fair amount of control over which translator you use, we concentrate on this third factor.

Translating the Source Program

Suppose we instruct the computer to add variables A and B and to save the result in variable C. A typical command might look like this:

C=A+B

The process of going from command to answer is composed of three phases:

- Translation time
- Invocation time
- Calculation time

Translation time is the time the computer takes to figure out what to do. For example, every time the BASIC interpreter sees "C=A+B," it has to translate this to mean "find the variable A in memory and then find the variable B, next add the two, and finally place the sum in variable C." The BASIC compiler makes the same translation as the interpreter, but only once, rather than every time a line is executed. Interpreted programs spend a lot of time in the translation phase while compiled programs spend none at all.

Invocation time is the time it takes the computer to calculate the addresses of the variables and to call the appropriate internal subroutine. For example, the BASIC ROM includes a floating-point addition subroutine. The interpreter calls this subroutine to add A and B. Code produced by the BASIC compiler calls a similar routine in the run-time library.

Calculation time is the time the computer spends doing the actual addition. All the direct advantage of the 8087 hardware comes from improvement in this phase.

Since the 8087 speeds up only this last phase, programs in which most of the time is spent in calculation get a big boost. Programs which spend most of their time in translation or invocation get only a small boost. Reduction of translation and invocation time depends on the appropriate choice of a program translator.

You might think that we would always choose the translator that gives the fastest results. However, there are some tradeoffs involved. For example, compilers produce faster programs than interpreters, but interpreters are more convenient to use. And, as a practical matter, almost every personal computer comes with a built-in BASIC interpreter, but not everyone has a compiler.

So how important is each phase? The answer depends on the problem. In Chapter 1, we presented some representative timings for a matrix multiplication problem and for taking 5,000 square roots. I've made some estimates of the time spent in each phase for pre-8087 interpreted BASIC, for an 8087-compatible compiler, and for an 8087 assembly language program. Table 3-1 shows the time in microseconds for a single addition and multiplication (for the matrix program), and for taking the square root of one element of a vector. I do have to warn you that Table 3-1 is much less accurate than other timings given in this book. Nonetheless, it gives a rough guide as to the trade-offs involved.

Table 3-1. Execution-time speed breakdowns (time in microseconds).

	Matrix Problem			*Square Root*		
	(translate	*invoke*	*calculate)*	*(translate*	*invoke*	*calculate)*
interpreter	(8400)		1200	(3600)		6800
compiler	0	135	56	0	66	70
assembly language	0	10	56	0	0	70

We will refer back to Table 3-1 several times in our discussions in the next section. While the table shows the speed advantage of assembly language, it does not reveal the extra work generally involved in writing assembly language programs rather than BASIC. As a rule of thumb, an assembly language program requires ten times the amount of code as one written in BASIC.

The bulk of numerical computing uses what are called "linear operations." A small family of programs, such as matrix multiplication, can be put together to solve all sorts of different linear problems. With a library of these routines, such as the library put together in this book, you can solve most problems without having to write any subroutines yourself.

The square root example is somewhat different. "Non-linear" operations are all different; there isn't a small family of routines that you can re-arrange as needed for your own problems. As a result, non-linear problems require more custom programming. The more programming required, the more we will want to favor programming convenience over calculation speed.

Both the matrix multiplication routine and the square root routine appear, in assembly language, in later chapters. As assembly language programs go, neither is very difficult to write. (. . . and of course you needn't write these particular programs, since we've already done so.)

Computational Accuracy

Accuracy deserves as much attention as does speed. The 8087 is extremely accurate, but most translators don't allow you to access the 8087's 80-bit registers. Assembly language allows full use of 8087 accuracy, as do a few compilers (notably, those developed at Intel) intended specifically for use with the 8087. These compilers, which provide for operations on 80-bit data, are not, at present, in common use.

For some problems, the extra accuracy of 80 bits is worth any amount of programming inconvenience, but for "every day" use most of us will settle for double precision accuracy. The assembly language routines in this book use 80-bit data in the "delicate" part of calculations and the usual single and double precision data types elsewhere.

8087-Compatible Software

In this section we discuss a number of different approaches to buying and building 8087-compatible software. For each approach, we discuss the trade-offs between programming convenience and execution speed. The approaches discussed are:

- *Using packaged programs*
- *8087 hardware with pre-8087 software*
- *Interpreted BASIC*
- *Compiler with 8087 floating point library*
- *Compiler for 8087 "native code"*
- *Assembly language modules for BASIC*
- *Pure assembly language code*

Using Packaged Programs

How much advantage the 8087 gives you with a "canned" program depends on how well the program is written. A really well-written canned program will take better advantage of the 8087 than any program you write. Not because the programmer knew anything about the 8087 that you won't discover in this book, but because for a program that sells thousands of copies, a programmer can afford to spend time squeezing out every last microsecond. Unfortunately, there is no real satisfactory way of knowing how good a canned program is short of "field testing" it. Also, unfortunately, software manuals almost never say anything about execution speed.

You will find three kinds of packages being advertised (with respect to 8087 compatibility).

First, there are programs intended to run only with the 8087, which make no attempt at compatibility with earlier software or non-8087 machines. Many applied problems cannot be solved on a microcomputer (in a reasonable amount of time) without an 8087. For programs that solve such problems, compatibility is not an issue. In fact, the speed of the 8087 is so critical for some applications that enterprising software houses began to market 8087-only packages before the manufacturers of personal computers had begun to sell the 8087!

Second, there are programs that will run either with or without the 8087. Some software comes in a single version that will run either way. Other programs come in two versions: one explicitly for the 8087 and one that does not use the 8087.

Third, there are programs that ignore the 8087.

A warning about canned programs. Many high-efficiency programs save information on disk in what are called "binary" files. Binary files store data using the computer's internal representation of numbers rather than the "ASCII" representation more commonly used for disk storage. (This scheme allows programs to avoid conversions between internal and external formats and thus makes data storage and retrieval much, much faster.) As discussed above, the 8087 uses a different internal representation for numbers than does most pre-8087 software. For this reason, pre-8087 and 8087-compatible binary files are incompatible.

If you use a pre-8087 program that saves binary files on disk and then switch to 8087-compatible software, you will be unable to read the files back in. Further, since you usually do not have access to a description of the file format, it may be impossible for you to convert the files yourself. To protect yourself when using a canned program with binary files, use the program to convert the files into an ASCII representation *while you are still using the pre-8087 software* and then convert them back to binary later.

8087 Hardware with Pre-8087 Software

It would be awfully nice if we could get the benefit of the 8087 without attention to software. For reasons we've discussed, this isn't possible. For example, if you add an 8087 to a machine with a pre-8087 BASIC interpreter, your BASIC programs will run, but they won't make any use of the 8087. This is not much of an option.

Understand, however, that it's the *translator* not the *program* that needs to be 8087-compatible. If you have an 8087-compatible BASIC interpreter, or some other 8087-compatible translator, your old BASIC programs will run and will take advantage of the 8087. (This illustrates an important reason for using BASIC or another standard "high-level language." If the hardware changes, as is the case when an 8087 is added, you need only obtain a new translator and usually do not need to re-write your applications programs.)

It is possible to combine 8087-compatible software with pre-8087 software by explicitly converting data back and forth between the Intel and Microsoft formats. (Conversion programs appear in the appendix.) For example, you can use the 8087 programs in this book with the original BASIC interpreter supplied with the IBM Personal Computer, but you will have to do a little bit of extra BASIC programming.

Interpreted BASIC

The Microsoft BASIC interpreter included with most personal computers completely ignores the 8087 (at least as of early 1985). You can safely combine your own assembly language programs, such as the ones in this book, with BASIC programs as long as you pay careful attention to converting data between the Microsoft and 8087 formats. There are also BASIC interpreters that use the 8087 directly, but they may or may not be fully compatible with standard Microsoft BASIC.

Here's an important warning about using an 8087 version of BASIC. No matter what you may be told, the 8087 and non-8087 versions of BASIC are not fully compatible (though they are close). Because floating point numbers are represented differently, there is no way to make them fully compatible. Two fundamentally irresolvable problems exist.

First, the two floating point representations differ slightly in their precision and range. In particular, for double precision the Intel format trades about one decimal place less precision for a substantially increased range for the exponent. On rare occasions, programs that worked on the original BASIC interpreter will give incorrect answers when used on the 8087 version because of round-off error. Somewhat more frequently, programs that run under the new version will have overflow errors if used on a personal computer with the old BASIC. Fortunately, such problems are rare, and quite unlikely to be a major concern for most users.

Second, some programs use the BASIC functions MKS$, MKD$, CVS, and CVD to convert back and forth between floating point numbers and strings. Typically, this is done in order to store numbers on a disk file in their binary representation. The functions work in both versions of BASIC. But if you store numbers on the disk in one version and retrieve them in the other, you will get garbage data without getting any indications of error. If you use binary-representation files for storage between program runs, be absolutely certain to convert the files as part of the process of changing from one version of BASIC to the other.

Compiler with 8087 Floating Point Library

A compiler differs from an interpreter in that it translates the source language program only once, rather than every time a line of code is executed. Compilers have some disadvantages: they take a relatively long time to translate a program; they usually generate code that takes up more space than does an interpreted program; they slow the business of debugging programs; and they can be expensive. But they have one undeniable advantage over an interpreter: they eliminate the translation phase from program execution, and thereby reduce execution time enormously.

Many of the compilers used on personal computers handle floating point operations in the following way. Whenever a floating point operation is needed, the compiler generates a CALL to the appropriate subroutine. After the program is compiled, the LINK program is used to combine the compiler output with a library of subroutines that includes all the floating point operations. IBM's BASIC compiler works this way.

Compilers that use floating point libraries can be converted to 8087 operation by substituting a new library for the one originally supplied with the compiler. The original IBM BASIC compiler can be converted in this manner. Using a compiler with an 8087 library not only eliminates the translation phase, but also brings the calculation phase up to 8087 speed. However, the invocation phase remains unchanged. Referring back to Table 3-1, we see that such a compiler might be 50 times as fast as pre-8087 BASIC in the matrix multiplication example and about 75 times as fast on square roots.

(You should be warned that the effectiveness of this approach to making a compiler 8087-compatible varies. Some implementations do not do nearly as well as the speed improvements suggested in the previous paragraph.)

On linear problems, the combination of the 8087 and a compiler is very, very good. (Even if it doesn't quite reach our goal of "turning minutes into seconds.") On non-linear problems the combination is truly excellent.

Compiler for 8087 "In-Line" Code

Compilers on mainframe computers, and on minicomputers with floating point hardware, directly generate floating point instructions instead of generating calls to a subroutine library. This technique eliminates most of the invocation time. Some mainframe "optimizing" compilers are so good that the code they generate is almost as fast as assembly code. Equally good compilers for personal computers are only beginning to appear and are not currently in widespread use. You may want to look for 8087 "in-line" or "native" code compilers as they come on the market, since such a compiler provides the best combination of execution speed and programming convenience.

Assembly Language Modules for BASIC

Assembly language is at the bottom of the list when it comes to programming convenience, but at the top of the list when it comes to speed. Fortunately, assembly language routines are easily combined with either interpreted or compiled BASIC, as well as with programs written in other high-level languages. In fact, preparing assembly language modules for frequently used tasks can be more convenient than writing the same code over and over again in BASIC. (It is very inconvenient to write re-usable modules in BASIC.)

In a typical program, almost all the work takes place in a very small fraction of the code. Optimally, we use assembly language modules to replace this fraction of the code, while leaving the remainder of the program intact. This strategy leaves the bulk of the writing in a convenient programming language and the bulk of the computation in a high speed routine.

Assembly language remains the undisputed speed champion. The assembly language matrix multiplication routine which appears in Chapter 10 is about 150 times faster than pre-8087 BASIC. The square root routine also beats BASIC by about 150-to-1.

Pure Assembly Language Code

Early versions of the IBM PC assembler did not explicitly handle the 8087 instruction set. Newer versions of the IBM assembler (version 2.0 and later) or Microsoft assembler do handle 8087 instructions automatically. It is possible to program the 8087 with an old version of the assembler by judicious use of the Escape mnemonic. There are even third-party software products to do this for you. In fact, the first edition of this book was developed using one such product. (You can see the use of the Escape mnemonics on the optional diskette.) If you plan to do more than minimal amounts of assembly language programming, the newer, and more expensive, versions of the assembler are worth the money.

When does it pay to write an entire number crunching program in assembly language? In my opinion, never. For linear problems, writing the entire program in assembly language has no significant speed advantage over using a small number of strategically chosen assembly language modules. (This is the approach we follow in the second and third parts of the book.) For non-linear problems, where isolating re-usable modules is difficult, writing special assembly language programs does increase speed over using a compiler, but only at an unreasonable cost in terms of programming effort.

Two final conclusions:

- *If most of your number crunching is on linear operations—and most of the world's is—your best overall bet is probably an interpreter and a small set of assembly language routines, either the routines appearing in Parts II (Chapters 5–8) and III (Chapter 9–15) or another subroutine package you purchase commercially.*
- *If a good part of your number crunching is non-linear, your best bet is probably the combination of a compiler and the 8087. While assembly language routines are still substantially faster than programs written in higher-level languages, higher-level languages are far more convenient.*

On to Chapter 4

Just how does the 8087 stack up against other computers? In the next chapter we insert a few of our strategic modules in BASIC programs and run some timing tests.

4

Benchmarks

With the advent of the 8087, moderate-to-large scale numerical computing can now be done on a microcomputer. The 8087 increases the computational range of the microcomputer by one to two orders of magnitude.

The 8087 brings the "minimum-efficient-scale" of computing down to the personal level. In the past, a mainframe computer that cost 100 times more than a personal computer would have been thousands or tens of thousands times faster. While the 8087 remains several times slower than powerful mainframes, an 8087-equipped PC also costs tens or hundreds of times less. So today, the 8087 has made the personal computer a cost effective number cruncher.

Historically, large computers have always been more cost efficient, in terms of raw computational power, than smaller computers. Very large mainframes are more cost efficient than minis; minis are more cost efficient than micros. Just as the advent of "super-mini" computers a few years ago closed most of the gap between minicomputers and mainframes, the 8087 closes most of the gap between personal and minicomputers. To help you draw your own conclusions, speed benchmarks for a range of machines appear below.

Comparing Benchmarks

Speed and accuracy ratings are presented below for a number of different combinations of hardware and software. Before you start drawing conclusions, understand what benchmarks do and do not tell us.

Benchmark programs are used to compare various combinations of software and hardware by executing the same program under controlled conditions. We've continued here with the timing of the two problems examined in Chapter 1. The first benchmark program multiplies two 50 by 50 matrices in order to illustrate the 8087's power in linear operations. The second benchmark program, taking 5,000 square roots, illustrates the 8087's non-linear calculations. Please realize that benchmark comparisons have some limitations.

First, these benchmark problems are not intended to be "fair." I picked two problems which show off the capabilities of the 8087. They show the kind of results the "number crunching" user can reasonably expect, which aren't necessarily the results a "typical" user might expect and are totally unrelated to what a "word processing" user will see.

Second, our benchmark programs are "tuned" to be efficient on the 8087. For example, we've run most of the comparison programs in BASIC because BASIC is the dominant language on personal computers. On a larger computer, Fortran or APL or some other computer language may be more efficient than BASIC. If we were starting on one of these machines, we might well program in a language other than BASIC.

Even if not totally "fair," these benchmarks do give a pretty good idea of what the 8087 will do. The first set of benchmarks below, compares timings on an IBM Personal Computer with and without the 8087. The second and third benchmarks demonstrate 287-based IBM AT performance as compared to 8087-based PC performance. The fourth set of benchmarks compares the 8087 to several other micro, mini, and mainframe computers.

IBM Personal Computer Benchmarks

The IBM PC is the most popular of the "second generation," 16-bit personal computers. Internally, the PC uses an Intel 8088 microprocessor running at a "clock speed" of 4.77 megahertz. It is worth knowing for purposes of comparison that some of the 8088-based personal computers on the market run at a 5 megahertz "clock," and are just a little bit faster. Also, computers based on the 8088's "big brother," the 8086, are quite a bit faster.

For this benchmark, we've taken Table 1-1 from Chapter 1 and added a third alternative, the IBM BASIC compiler. Table 4-1 shows execution speeds for both matrix multiplication and the square root problem using IBM's pre-8087 BASIC interpreter, IBM's pre-8087 BASIC compiler, and our own assembly language modules.

Table 4-1. BASIC versus 8087 speed benchmarks (time in seconds).

Program	*50 by 50 matrix multiplication*	*5,000 square roots*
BASIC interpreter	1148	53
BASIC compiler	140	6
8087 routine	8	0.38

The first two rows show why people turn to compilers. The IBM BASIC compiler beats the BASIC interpreter by around eight to one. Our 8087 routines beat the compiler times by a factor of 20!

8087 (PC) versus 80287 (AT) Benchmarks

In 1982, the only option for high-speed number crunching on an IBM PC or compatible was to add in the 8087 co-processor. As a new alternative, you can buy a more powerful computer than the original PC. The newer IBM AT is much faster than the PC and as an option can be equipped with its own version of the 8087 co-processor, the 80287.

In 1982, BASIC completely dominated the PC programming world. Today you have many alternatives, although BASIC continues to be used more than any other single language. Two of the most popular languages are FORTRAN and Pascal. The next two tables show benchmark timings for the Microsoft implementation of FORTRAN (version 3.2) and Borland International's popular, low-cost, Turbo Pascal (version 2.0).

These benchmarks illustrate the incredible variety in speed that results from different combinations of hardware and software. You should remember that speed is not the only criterion for choosing between computers or programming languages. In fact, ease of use, price, and accuracy may all be more important than raw speed.

Note several differences between the programs benchmarked below.

- **8087 routine**—These assembly language routines show the maximum possible speed of the machine.
- **BASIC interpreter**—The programs use the version of Microsoft BASIC supplied with the IBM PC.
- **Turbo Pascal** uses six byte numbers for programs without the co-processor and eight byte (double precision) numbers for programs with the co-processor. So the Pascal benchmarks are somewhat more accurate than the other programs shown.
- **Microsoft FORTRAN** actually operates in three different modes. In default ("straight out of the box") mode, FORTRAN uses the 8087 if present and uses software to emulate the co-processor if the 8087 is absent. In this way, a default mode program can be used on a PC whether or not there is an 8087 present. In "8087 mode," FORTRAN programs will work *only* when a co-processor is onboard. In "alt-math mode," FORTRAN programs ignore the co-processor completely. Alt-math mode programs may be very slightly less accurate than programs using either of the two previous modes.

In the following tables, the lines marked "FORTRAN (flexible)," show the default mode results. The lines marked "FORTRAN (optimized)," use the alt-math and 8087 mode results.

We now have two benchmark programs, several languages, two different personal computers, and comparisons with and without use of the co-processor. To keep things under control, I've split the benchmarks into two tables. Table 4-2 shows the results for the matrix multiplication. Table 4-3 shows parallel results for the square root problem.

Table 4-2. PC and AT speed benchmarks for 50 by 50 matrix multiplication (time in seconds).

	PC		*AT*	
Program	*no-8087*	*8087*	*no-80287*	*80287*
8087 routine	—	8	—	10
BASIC interpreter	1148	—	438	—
Pascal	489	74	203	41
FORTRAN (flexible)	167	44	58	20
FORTRAN (optimized)	78	36	25	19

Table 4-3. PC and AT speed benchmarks for 5,000 square roots (time in seconds).

	PC		*AT*	
Program	*no-8087*	*8087*	*no-80287*	*80287*
8087 routine	—	0.38	—	0.48
BASIC interpreter	53	—	20	—
Pascal	217	1.5	48	1.00
FORTRAN (flexible)	22	1.5	7.1	0.96
FORTRAN (optimized)	3	1.5	0.65	0.96

Those last couple of numbers in Table 4.3 are not misprints! On the AT, the optimized no-co-processor version of FORTRAN runs faster than the optimized co-processor version, although the assembly language 8087 routine is faster yet. However, the no-co-processor version computes results accurate to 32 bits while the co-processor versions are accurate to 80 bits.

Kilo-FLOPS

It has become customary to rate number-crunchers according to "K-FLOPS", thousands ("*K*") of *F*loating *P*oint *OP*erations per *S*econd. Figure 4.1 rates the various combinations of hardware and software in terms of K-FLOPS. (Figure 4.1 is really just another way of looking at Table 4.2.)

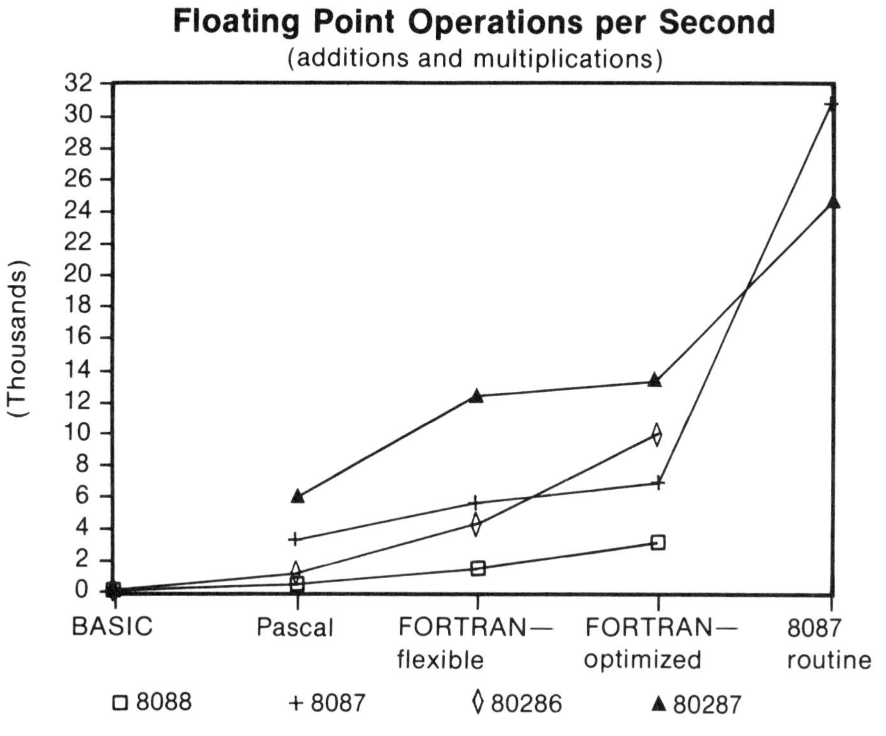

Figure 4.1.

Using the 8087, moving from a PC to an AT, and choosing efficient software all contribute to number-crunching speed.

A Note About Raw Machine Speed

As time passes, computers become faster! The benchmarks here were calculated on an IBM PC and an IBM AT circa early 1985. The IBM PC runs both the 8088 and the 8087 at speeds just under 5 megahertz. Some PC compatibles run both the 8088 (or 8086) and the 8087 at 8 megahertz. So these machines should produce about 60 percent more K-FLOPS than the figures above. The IBM AT runs its 80286 at about 6 megahertz and its 80287 at about 4 megahertz. (The last explains why the raw 8087 timings are faster than the raw 80287 timings.) Faster versions of the IBM

AT will be available eventually. Of particular interest is that we can expect 8 megahertz versions of the 80287 one day, so the raw co-processor speed on the AT will double!

"Outsider" Benchmarks

How does an 8087-equipped personal computer compare with "other people's" equipment? The comparisons below repeat our benchmarks on several popular combinations of hardware and software.

Please don't read these comparisons as "better" or "worse." The hardware used runs from an Apple II+ to an IBM 3081. The Apple isn't as fast as the PC, but then it doesn't cost as much. An IBM 3081 is faster than the PC, but it won't fit on your desk.

The comparisons are run on four machines:

- **Apple II+**—Many people's favorite first-generation personal computer. Both programs used the Apple's built-in Applesoft BASIC interpreter.
- **DEC 2060**—A moderate size mainframe computer used by many universities to provide time-sharing services. (Manufactured by Digital Equipment Corporation.) Both programs were executed using compiled BASIC. DEC-2060 BASIC includes a matrix multiplication function which we used for the first program.
- **VAX 780**—A 32-bit "super-mini" computer, very popular for moderate size number crunching applications. (Manufactured by Digital Equipment Corporation.) These test programs were written in the popular scientific language FORTRAN, and executed using the VAX's optimizing compiler.
- **IBM 3081**—The IBM 3081 is a very large mainframe computer costing millions of dollars. Both programs were written using the "Stanford BASIC" interpreter. We again used a built-in matrix multiplication function for the first program.

The benchmark results appear in Table 4-4.

Table 4-4. Micro, mini, and mainframe speed benchmarks (time in seconds).

Program/Computer	*50 by 50 matrix multiplication*	*5,000 square roots*
8087 routine	8	0.35
Apple II+ BASIC	1796	130
DEC 2060 BASIC	5.2	0.40
VAX 780 FORTRAN	1.6	0.20
IBM 3081 BASIC	0.11	0.26

As we cautioned above, you need to be careful about benchmarks. The 8087 routines make optimal use of the 8087's potential. (The 8087 routines appear in later chapters, so you can examine their innards if you wish.) The programs on the other machines use standard programming techniques, and so make moderate to excellent use of the hardware's potential.

Caveats notwithstanding, Table 4-4 tells us quite a bit about how to classify an 8087-equipped personal computer. When it comes to number crunching, the 8087 doesn't just make a fast micro—it creates the equivalent of a slow super-mini or a slow mainframe computer!

5

Introduction to 8087 Architecture

This chapter provides a detailed, technical description of 8087 architecture. The 8087 instruction set is described in Chapters 6 and 12. (For hardware and electronic details about the 8087, see Intel's *iAPX 86,88 User's Manual,* the definitive source on the 8087. For hardware and electronic details about the 287, see Intel's *iAPX 286 Programmer's Reference Manual.*)

More detail is given in this chapter than the typical 8087 user need be concerned with. You may want to browse through this chapter and then proceed directly to the description of the simple instruction set in Chapter 6.

Co-processor Organization

The 8087 is designed as a *co-processor* for the 8088 CPU. Both the 8087 and 8088 "look" at each instruction fetched from memory. The 8087 acts on its own instructions and ignores those belonging to the 8088. When the 8088 sees an 8087 instruction, which is an 8088 ESCape instruction, it calculates the address of any data referenced by the instruction and reads—but ignores—one byte of data from this address. Otherwise, the 8088 treats the 8087 instruction as a null operation. The 8087 copies the address calculated by the 8088 and uses it to store or fetch data to and from memory. In this way, the co-processor design allows the 8087 and the 8088 to execute simultaneously, considerably enhancing total system performance.

To ensure properly coordinated parallel operation, 8087/8088 programs must follow the following synchronization rules:

- The 8088 must not change a memory location referenced by an 8087 instruction until the 8087 is finished. The 8088 is free to change its own internal registers and flags.

- A second 8087 instruction must not be fetched until the current operation is complete. (Under special circumstances it is possible to safely violate this rule, but such circumstances do not generally occur in application programs.)

These synchronization rules are implemented slightly differently on the 8087 and the 287. We'll cover the 8087 first.

Synchronization, obedience to both rules of the 8087, is achieved through judicious use of the 8088 WAIT instruction. The WAIT instruction tells the 8088 to suspend processing until the TEST line becomes active. (The 8088 checks the TEST line status once every microsecond.) When the 8087 begins an instruction, it sets the TEST line to inactive. It then resets the TEST line to active when the instruction is complete.

The programmer has responsibility for seeing that the first rule is obeyed. To ensure synchronization, code an FWAIT instruction after an 8087 instruction and before an 8088 instruction whenever the two instructions access the same memory location. (Except that the FWAIT may be omitted if neither instruction changes the memory location.) FWAIT generates an 8088 WAIT instruction. (Use of the mnemonic "FWAIT," for "floating wait," is a software convention.) FWAIT holds the 8088 until the 8087 operation is complete, thus preventing violation of the first rule.

Responsibility for implementing the second rule is left to the assembler. The assembler automatically places a WAIT instruction in front of every 8087 instruction. (Except those few instructions mnemonics that explicitly indicate "no-wait." These mnemonics begin with "FN" rather than "F.") Thus the 8088 will suspend processing and not fetch another 8087 instruction so long as a previous 8087 instruction is still being executed.

Programs violating either of the two rules will have unpredictable results. Possible outcomes include the computer coming to a dead halt (if you are lucky), and having random numbers presented as final results (if you are not so lucky).

Synchronizing the 287

Synchronization of the 287 is more completely automatic than on the 8087. The 286 takes responsibility for the second synchronization rule. The 286 checks electronically to see if the 287 is busy before sending it an instruction. (Processor control instructions are an exception. See Chapter 12.) Therefore, unlike 8087 systems, the assembler need not code a WAIT instruction before a 287 instruction. Omission of the WAIT instruction increases efficiency in two small ways. First, memory is saved because every WAIT omitted saves one byte of code. Second, executing a WAIT takes three "clock cycles," so, on a 6 megahertz IBM AT, each WAIT omitted saves about half a microsecond. Note that the programmer retains responsibility for implementing the first synchronization rule through judicious application of the FWAIT instruction.

If you want your programs to run on both 8087 and 287 systems, you have to follow the 8087 synchronization rules. For this reason, the IBM Macro Assembler, version 2.0, always obeys the 8087 synchronization rules and produces the WAIT instructions for you. Thus the Macro Assembler wastes a half microsecond here and there on the IBM AT in return for staying compatible with a few million PCs, XTs, and compatibles. Some non-IBM assemblers, notably Intel's ASM286, omit the "extra" WAIT instructions.

Internal 8087 Registers

Five internal data areas are accessible by the 8087 programmer. These are the *register stack*, the *status word*, the *control word*, the *tag word*, and the *exception pointers*.

8087 computation is organized around eight 80-bit data registers. These registers form a pushdown stack, called the *register stack*. The register at the top of the stack is referred to as ST or ST(0); the register immediately below the top is ST(1); and so forth through ST(7). Many 8087 instructions implicitly reference ST(0) or both ST(0) and ST(1). Many instructions also push data onto or pop data off of the stack. (The stack is actually organized as a chain, so that ST(0) is "below" ST(7). It is the programmer's responsibility to prevent stack overflow.) Stack operations are described in detail in Chapter 6.

The 16-bit *status word* shows the current state of 8087 operations. We make extensive use of the *condition code* bits in the status word, which indicate the result of 8087 comparison operations. The status word also shows whether any exceptions (computational errors) have occurred, whether the 8087 is busy, whether the 8087 has requested to interrupt the 8088, and which of the eight stack registers is currently the top of the stack. These elements are primarily used for systems programming. Figure 5.1 shows the layout of the status word.

The 16-bit *control word* allows a number of 8087 options, described below under "control options," to be set under program control. These include the exception and interrupt-enable masks, which are primarily of interest to systems programmers. Other options, defining rounding, infinity, and precision controls, are occasionally used to control the results of numerical operations. Figure 5.2 shows the layout of the control word.

The *tag word* has two bits for each stack register to indicate whether the contents of the register are valid, zero, special, or empty. The *exception pointers* show the current instruction and operand. Neither the tag word

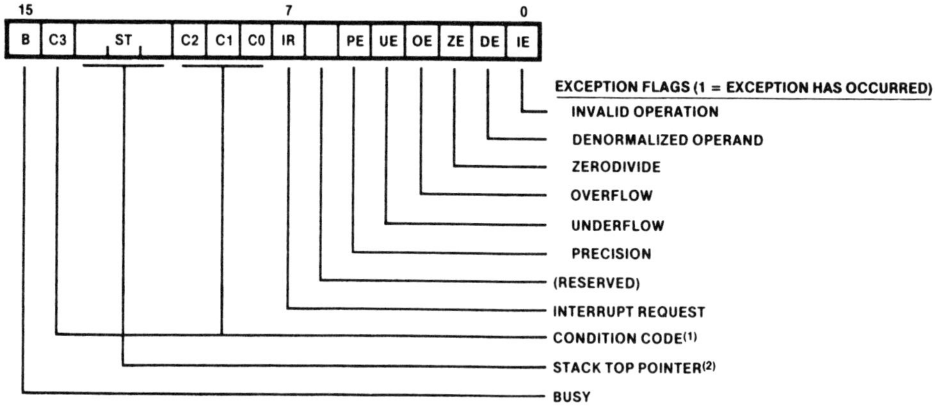

(1) See descriptions of compare, test, examine and remainder instructions for condition code interpretation.

(2) ST values:
000 = register 0 is stack top
001 = register 1 is stack top
•
•
•
111 = register 7 is stack top

Figure 5.1. (Used with permission of Intel Corporation.)

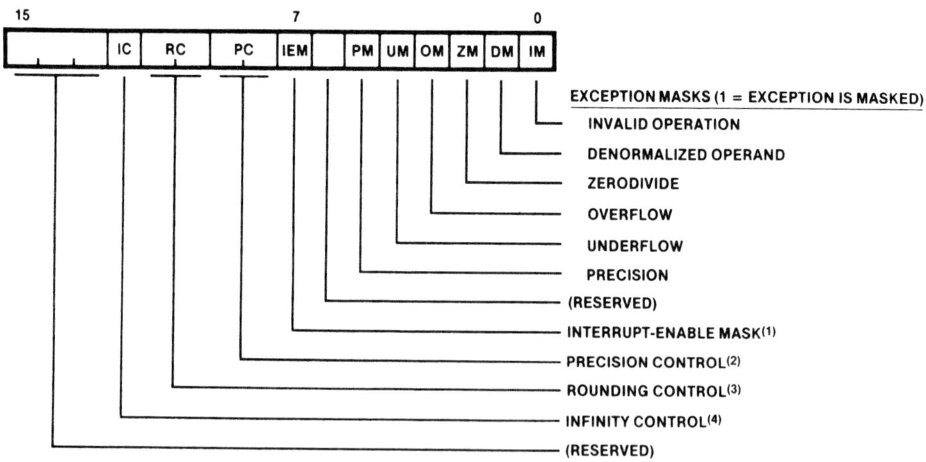

(1) Interrupt-Enable Mask:
0 = Interrupts Enabled
1 = Interrupts Disabled (Masked)

(2) Precision Control:
00 = 24 bits
01 = (reserved)
10 = 53 bits
11 = 64 bits

(3) Rounding Control:
00 = Round to Nearest or Even
01 = Round Down (toward $-\infty$)
10 = Round Up (toward $+\infty$)
11 = Chop (Truncate Toward Zero)

(4) Infinity Control:
0 = Projective
1 = Affine

Figure 5.2. (Used with permission of Intel Corporation.)

nor exception pointers are normally of any interest to application programmers.

Control Options

By manipulating the control word, you can change the way the 8087 handles rounding, infinity, and precision.

The 8087 offers four methods of rounding off answers that cannot be represented exactly in the available number of bits. The options are *round to nearest*, *round down* (toward minus infinity), *round up* (toward infinity), and *chop* (truncate toward zero). *Round to nearest* is the default.

The 8087, unlike most computers, has a well-defined representation of infinity. The 8087 produces the proper result when calculating mathematical functions with infinite arguments, at least when a mathematically well-defined result exists. For example, 5/infinity yields zero. Both positive and negative infinity may be represented.

Two modes of "infinity control" are offered on the 8087: *affine closure* and *projective closure*. Under affine closure, positive and negative infinity are regarded as being at opposite "ends" of the number line. Under projective closure, positive and negative infinity are considered equal, as if the two "ends" of the number line bent around and came together. Relative comparisons between finite numbers and infinity are permitted under affine closure, but not under projective closure. Projective closure is the default.

Precision on the 8087 can be set to 64, 53, or 24 bits of accuracy, corresponding to the temporary real, double precision, and single precision data types. This option is offered so that the 8087 may comply with certain industry standards which offer only reduced accuracy, and so that 8087 computation can be made compatible with less accurate computers. Aside from the compatibility issue, the only value in using less than the full 64 bits of accuracy is the educational value of learning that more accuracy is better. Default precision is 64 bits.

Exception Masking

Various important computational errors are trapped by the 8087. When such an error occurs, the 8087 raises an *exception* condition. Exceptions may be *unmasked* ("unmasked" means exposed to the 8088), in which case a program interrupt occurs to permit user supplied exception handling software to take control. Usually, however, exceptions are *masked* (hidden from the 8088). The 8087 holds onto any masked exception and executes an internal error correction procedure. For example, if your program attempts to divide a number by zero, the 8087 will set the answer to infinity under exception masking.

Table 5-1 presents the six exceptions and the most common masked response. Note that execution is never halted by a masked response. As a default, all exceptions are masked. See Appendix 2 for a full description of the masked responses to each exception.

Table 5-1. Common masked response to 8087 exceptions.

Exception	Most Common Masked Response
Zerodivide	Return properly signed infinity
Overflow	Return properly signed infinity
Underflow	Denormalize result
Denormalized	Memory operand—proceed as usual Register operand—convert to unnormal
Precision	Round result

Note: The terms "denormal" and "unnormal" are defined under Special Data Types, below.

Number Systems

The 8087 "understands" floating point, integer, and packed decimal numbers. For number crunching, floating point numbers are by far the most important.

Floating Point Numbers

In order to accommodate a wide range of values, computers store numbers in a "floating point" or "real" representation. Essentially, floating point is the computer's version of scientific notation. For example, in standard scientific notation the fraction "negative one-half" can be written out as

$$-5.0 \times 10^{-1}$$

Scientific notation splits the representation of a number into three sections. The "sign field" tells us the sign of the number, in the case above the leading "−" indicates a negative number. Next, the "significand field," 5.0 above, gives the number's significant digits. (The significand field is also called the "mantissa.") The third section is the "exponent" field. The "$^{-1}$" above tells us to multiply the significand by ten to the minus one power, or, equivalently, to shift the decimal point one place to the left.

The 8087 stores floating point numbers in a form of scientific notation. The exact bit patterns used are laid out for the computer's convenience so they are a little less than obvious to humans. Fortunately, we almost never need concern ourselves with such minute detail. While exact bit patterns are covered below, there are really three facts to know about each data type:

1. How many bytes of memory are used up to store a number?
2. How many digits of accuracy are retained in a number?
3. How wide is the range of numbers which can be represented? That is, how large an exponent can be used?

The answers to 1 through 3 are shown in Table 5-2.

Data Types

The seven regular 8087 data types are shown in Table 5-2. A brief discussion of the use of each type appears below.

Table 5-2. 8087 data types.

Data Type	*Bits*	*Significant Digits*	*Range*
Word Integer (BASIC Integer)	16	4	−32,768 to 32,767
Short Integer	32	9	-2×10^{9} to $2\text{x}10^{9}$
Long Integer	64	18	-9×10^{18} to 9×10^{18}
Packed Decimal	80	18	18 decimal digits + sign
Short Real (BASIC Single Precision)	32	6 or 7	10^{-37} to 10^{38}
Long Real (BASIC Double Precision)	64	15 or 16	10^{-307} to 10^{308}
Temporary Real	80	19	10^{-4932} to 10^{4932}

Short real. Short real corresponds to BASIC's single precision data type. Micros have less storage than mainframe computers. Since real-world data rarely has more than six or seven digits of accuracy, this data type is commonly used for economical storage of basic input data.

Long real. Long real corresponds to BASIC's double precision data type. As a rule, most calculations should be done in double precision in order to minimize the effect of round-off error in intermediate steps.

Temporary real. Whatever the data type in memory, the 8087 converts all numbers to the temporary real format for internal use. The significand of the temporary real format holds 64 bits, so that every other data type can be loaded into a temporary real without loss of precision.

By designing the 8087 around the temporary real concept, Intel has simplified the application programmer's life in several important ways:

- Since all data types are converted to temporary real by the hardware, the programmer rarely need worry about explicit type conversions.

It is just as easy for the programmer to multiply a double precision floating point number by a packed decimal number as it is to multiply two integers. (Of course, when storing a number back in memory, the programmer remains responsible for ensuring that the destination data type is large enough to hold the result being stored.)

- The range for temporary reals is (almost) infinite. The exponent range is 10 to the ±4932. As a result, overflows and underflows are almost always caused by a bug in either the data or the program, and only rarely indicate a numerical computing error.
- The temporary real has 19 significant digits. Even when a long series of intermediate calculations produces significant cumulative round-off error, the loss of 3 or 4 digits of accuracy still leaves an accurate double precision answer. With the 8087 onboard, an IBM Personal Computer is more accurate than the standard IBM mainframe!

Word integer. Word integer corresponds to BASIC's integer data type. A word integer occupies two bytes of storage and is principally used to index arrays and other data structures.

Short integer. A four-byte integer. Not usually used in numerical programming.

Long integer. An eight-byte integer. Not usually used in numerical programming.

Packed decimal. Packed decimal representation is used for business and data processing operations. A packed decimal uses 10 bytes of memory and contains 18 decimal digits. Unlike the three preceding data types, the packed decimal form uses a decimal rather than a binary representation. Each of the decimals 0—9 is represented by four binary bits. These decimal digits are then "packed" two to a byte.

Business and data processing programs generally spend much more time converting data between external (ASCII) and internal (binary) representation than doing arithmetic. Conversion between ASCII and packed decimal representation is quite easy. (Also, some data processing languages, such as COBOL, use packed decimal representation as a standard data type.)

Data Type Hardware Representations

The 8087 knows exactly where each and every little bit goes. This is fortunate, because the physical and logical orders in which numbers are placed in memory differ. It is fairly easy for this difference to confuse us human types. However, the physical layout is easier for the machinery to handle and isn't relevant to programmers, except, on occasion, when trying to debug a machine language program. The description of the exact hardware representations is included here for the sake of completeness.

Logically, all the data types are laid out left to right. The left-most bit is the most significant. Thus, a 16-bit integer is represented by a string of 16 bits running from the high-order bit 15 on the left to the low-order bit 0 on the right. Each of the seven data types is laid out in this way, as illustrated by Figure 5.3.

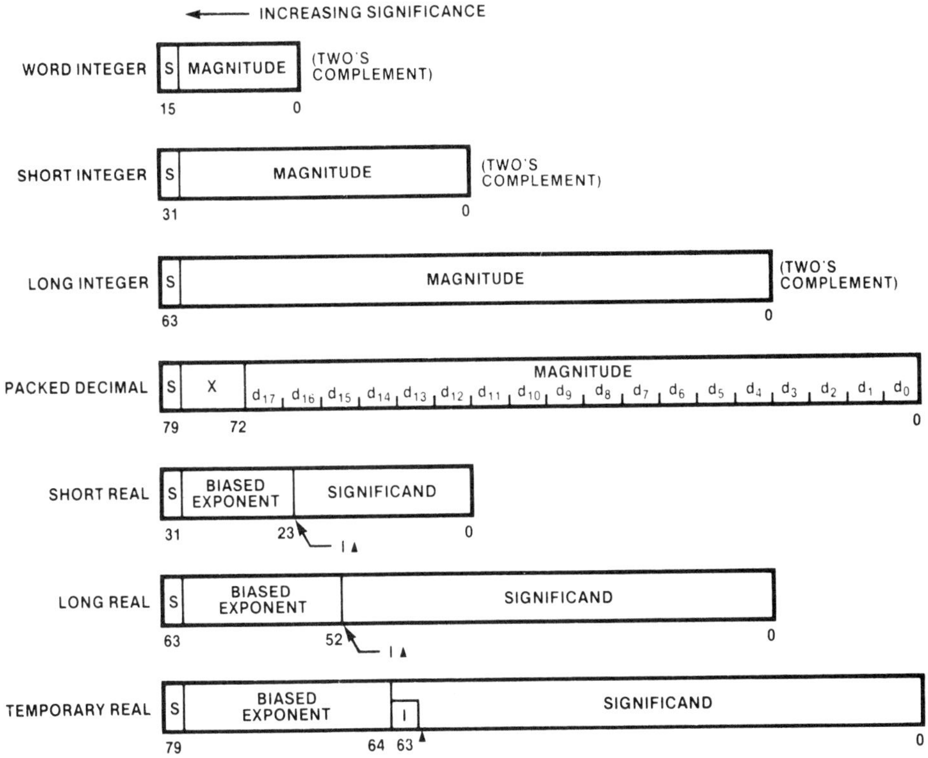

NOTES:
S = Sign bit (0 = positive, 1 = negative)
d_n = Decimal digit (two per byte)
X = Bits have no significance; 8087 ignores when loading, zeros when storing.
▲ = Position of implicit binary point
I = Integer bit of significand; stored in temporary real, implicit in short and long real
Exponent Bias (normalized values):
Short Real: 127 (7FH)
Long Real: 1023 (3FFH)
Temporary Real: 16383 (3FFFH)

Figure 5.3. 8087 data type bit patterns. (Used with permission of Intel Corporation.)

Physically, the right-most logical byte comes first. For example, suppose a 16-bit integer is stored in memory locations 100 and 101. The low-order bits, 7-0, are in byte 100, and the high-order bits, 15-8, are in byte 101. The same "reversal" holds for all the data types. This format is used throughout the 8088/8086 family and is common to many microprocessors. See Figure 5.4.

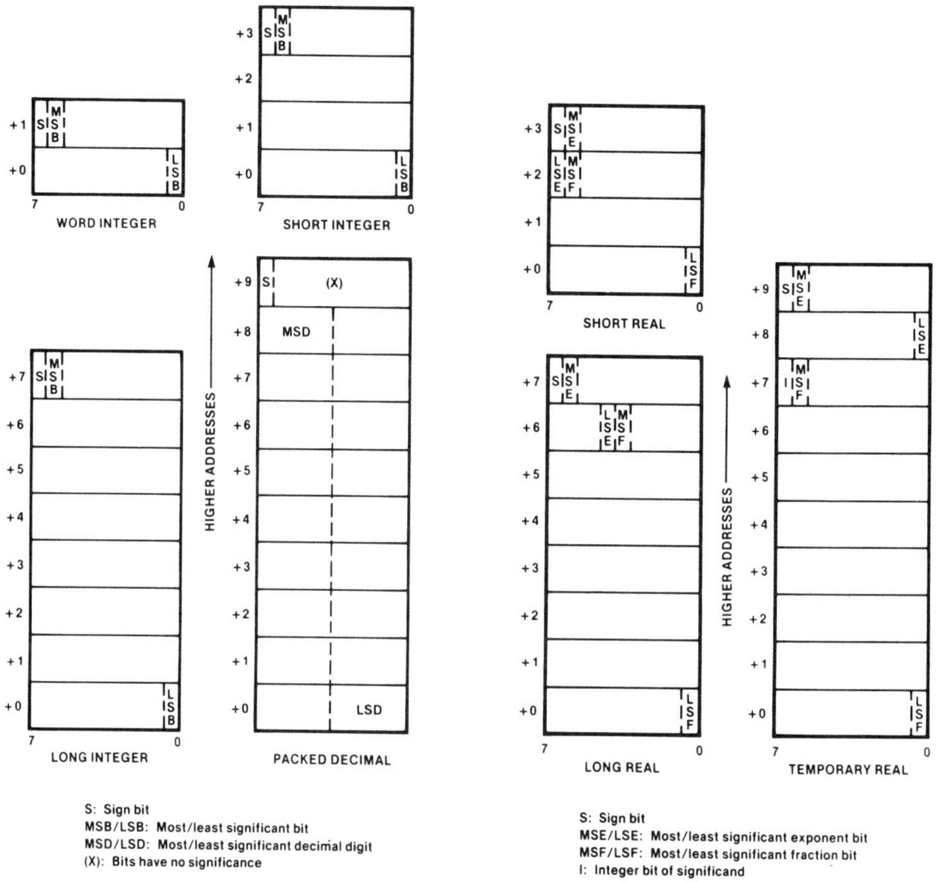

Figure 5.4. 8087 data type byte patterns. (Used with permission of Intel Corporation.)

Floating Point Representation

8087 floating point representation makes a number of concessions to the computer's convenience.

- Numbers are represented, unsurprisingly, by a string of binary bits rather than decimal numbers.
- The position of the "binary point" is implicit. Since computer memory contains only zeros and ones, there is no convenient way to explicitly write in a decimal point. In ordinary scientific usage we write 153.7 as 1.537E2. (Computers typically use "E" in this context to indicate multiplication by a power of ten.) If our type font had no period, we might agree to write 153.7 as 1537E2 and agree that a decimal point is implicit after the first digit. On the 8087, the binary point is assumed to appear immediately to the right of the most significant bit of the significand.

- Floating point numbers are represented in a "normalized" format. The leading bit of a floating point number is always a one. The computer shifts the significand left or right, while decreasing or increasing the exponent, in order to maintain this format. (However, see *Special Data Types*, below, for some exceptions.)
- Since single and double precision numbers are always normalized, the leading bit is always a one and therefore needn't be stored. It isn't. The leading bit *is* stored in the 80-bit temporary real format.
- Exponents in scientific notation can be either positive or negative. Rather than store an explicit sign bit for exponents, the 8087 uses a "biased exponent." The exponent field holds the sum of the true exponent and a positive constant. For example, the exponent stored in a single precision real number is the true exponent plus 127. The exponent bias, chosen to provide the widest possible range given the number of bits assigned to hold the exponent, is 127 for single precision, 1023 for double precision, and 16383 for temporary real.
  To illustrate floating point representation, the significand of 2.0 is "[1]00 . . ." (where the "[1]" indicates the leading 1 is assumed but not stored and "00 . . ." indicates enough zeros to fill out the rest of the significand field). The exponent of 2.0, for single precision, is 128. Examples of significand and exponent fields for other numbers are: ½ is "[1]00 . . ." and 126; 3.0 is "[1]10 . . ." and 128; and 4.0 is "[1]00 . . ." and 129.
- Zero is represented by all exponent and significand bits set to zero. (The sign bit may be either positive or negative, without significance for any arithmetic or comparison operation.)

Integer Representation

The three integer types are represented in "two's complement" format. Positive numbers are simply binary integers. Negative numbers are represented in the following way: If X is a positive integer, then −X is written as (NOT X)+1. The left-most bit of an integer is always a one for negative integers and 0 for zero or a positive integer.

Packed Decimal Representation

Packed decimal numbers are integers represented with a sign and exactly 18 decimal digits. Bits 0-3 hold the least significant digit, that is, the "one's place." Bits 4-7 hold the "ten's place," and so forth. Bits 72-78 are unused. (If an additional digit were stored here, it would not always be possible to convert a packed decimal number into an eight-byte integer.) The high-order bit, bit 79, holds the sign. If a decimal digit is not in the required range 0-9, the result of using the packed decimal number is undefined.

As an exercise, try writing out a number in each of the seven formats. Figure 5.5 gives the hexadecimal representation of −127 for each format. (Note that 127 is 01111111 in binary or 7F in hexadecimal.)

WORD INTEGER

FF	81	
1	0	BYTE

SHORT INTEGER

FF	FF	FF	81	
3	2	1	0	BYTE

LONG INTEGER

FF	FF	FF	FF	FF	FF	FF	81	
7	6	5	4	3	2	1	0	BYTE

PACKED DECIMAL

80	00	00	00	00	00	00	00	01	27	
9	8	7	6	5	4	3	2	1	0	BYTE

SHORT REAL

C2	FE	00	00	
3	2	1	0	BYTE

LONG REAL

C0	5F	C0	00	00	00	00	00	
7	6	5	4	3	2	1	0	BYTE

TEMPORARY REAL

C0	05	FE	00	00	00	00	00	00	00	
9	8	7	6	5	4	3	2	1	0	BYTE

Figure 5.5. 8087 hexadecimal representation of −127.

Special Data Types

On most computers, every bit pattern represents a valid numerical value. In contrast, the 8087 reserves a large class of bit patterns to represent special non-numerical values. For almost all applications programs, these special data types can be safely ignored. Here is a brief description of these types:

Denormal: Real numbers are usually stored in the normalized format described above. An underflow occurs when the result of an operation would require a negative biased exponent. Rather than merely set the result to zero, the 8087 "stretches" the precision of the result by setting the exponent field equal to zero and shifting the significand right the appropriate number of places. Thus, denormal numbers can be recognized, when stored in memory, by the zero exponent field together with a non-zero significand field. A denormal is converted to an unnormal when loaded into the 8087 from memory or used in an arithmetic operation. Denormals are perfectly acceptable as operands for arithmetic instructions. (With the critical exception of transcendental operations which assume without checking that operands are normals.)

Unnormal: When a denormal is used in an arithmetic operation, the result is an unnormal. Unnormals exist only in temporary real format and can be recognized by a zero in bit 63 (as opposed to one for a normal). Unnormals are also perfectly acceptable in arithmetic operations. (Except that transcendental operations and unnormals don't mix.) The result of an operation on an unnormal is a normal when possible and an unnormal otherwise. The existence of denormals and unnormals provide a major convenience to the applications programmer. Frequently, numerical algorithms create very small intermediate results. Most computers either halt with an underflow signal or set the intermediate result equal to 0.0. In contrast, 8087 routines continue to execute while maintaining maximum possible accuracy.

Zero: Zero hardly seems like a special data type. However, it is very useful to know how the processor treats operations involving zeros. Real zeros may be signed either positive or negative, but the sign is always ignored. The 8087 is extraordinarily well behaved when using zero in arithmetic operations. Where most processors would come to an unpleasant halt, the 8087 produces a sensible answer; for example, the result of 7/0 is infinity and the result of 0/0 is indefinite.

Pseudo-zero: Under certain rare circumstances, temporary reals may end up containing a type known as a pseudo-zero. The pseudo- zero behaves mostly like a zero. For most purposes, this type may be safely ignored.

Infinity: The real formats include the values plus and minus infinity. These are represented by a biased exponent of all ones and a significand with a leading one and trailing zeros. Infinity can be used as an argument for most 8087 arithmetic operations. Infinity in a register is tagged special (in the tag word).

Real indefinite: The 8087 produces the value indefinite as the masked response to an invalid operation. A real indefinite is indicated by a negative sign bit, all ones in the biased exponent, and a significand with two leading ones followed by trailing zeros. Indefinite in a register is tagged special.

Integer and packed decimal indefinite: For each integer type, the largest negative number (for example, -2^{15}) also represents indefinite. Packed decimal indefinite is represented by 16 leading ones with the trailing bits undefined. Use of integer and packed decimal indefinite should be avoided, as the 8087 treats integer indefinite as the largest negative number and gives undefined results after loading a packed decimal indefinite from memory.

NAN (Not-A-Number): Any value, except infinity, with a string of ones for the biased exponent is a member of the class NAN (Not-A-Number). NANs propagate through arithmetic operations. Thus you can design software that treats members of this class as being "special" in any way you'd like (except for real indefinite which is reserved for the use described above). For example, particular NANs might be used to indicate unassigned memory locations while debugging a program or missing data in a statistical or accounting problem.

In the next chapter, we turn away from architectural detail and begin writing our first useful programs.

6

Simple Instruction Set

We write our first program in this chapter: a simple routine to calculate the sum of an array of numbers. Before preparing our program, we discuss the 8087's basic instructions.

The 8087 has six instruction groups: *data transfer, arithmetic, transcendental, constants, comparison,* and *processor control*. We discuss data transfer, a few of the comparison instructions, and the basic arithmetic operations in this chapter. We defer discussion of the less frequently used instructions until Chapter 12. This chapter is divided into five sections. In the first section, we take a close look at the 8087 register stack. The next three sections look at the 8087 data transfer instructions, the 8087 basic arithmetic instructions, and the basic comparison instructions. In the last section we build our first program.

The Stack Mechanism

The 8087 has eight 80-bit registers for holding data internally. On most computers, these registers would be numbered 0, 1, 2, 3, 4, 5, 6, and 7; and a typical instruction would be something like "add register 3 to register 4 and leave the sum in register 3." The 8087 uses a more elegant system for accessing registers—the *stack*.

The stack method is invariably described by analogy to the plate holders found in cafeterias. A stack of plates is loaded on a spring with only the top plate visible. If you put a plate on the stack, all the other plates move down and only the new plate is accessible. Remove the top plate and all the ones below move up one place. On a computer, the action of adding an item to a stack is called a *push* (all the data is pushed down one position), and removing the top item is called a *pop* (all the data pops up one position). For the sake of efficiency, a computer doesn't actually move data up and down. Instead the computer changes a pointer which indicates which register is at the top of the stack.

The register on top of the 8087 stack is called *ST* or *ST(0)*. The 8087 also allows you to reference registers below the stack top. The piece of data immediately below the stack top is called *ST(1)*; one further down is ST(2); and so on through *ST(7)*. As we push and pop data from the stack, these names become attached to different registers.

Figure 6.1 illustrates the stack in action. Initially, the stack is empty. Next, we push the number 3.14 onto the stack. Now, ST(0) has the value 3.14 and ST(1) through ST(7) are undefined. Suppose we push 2.18 onto the stack. ST(0) holds 2.18 and ST(1) holds 3.14. If we pop the stack, then ST(0) will again point to the value 3.14.

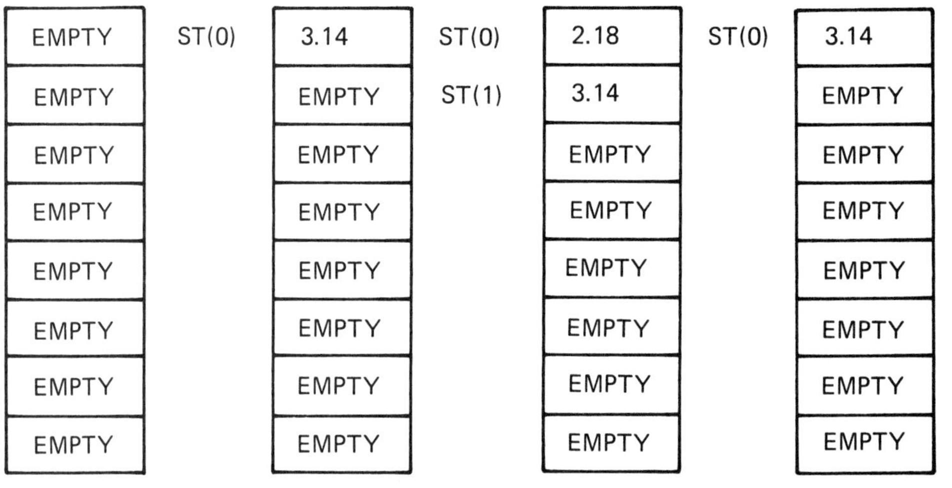

Figure 6.1. 8087 stack mechanism.

Notice that the stack mustn't grow to be more than eight deep, since the 8087 has only eight internal registers. The 8087 leaves responsibility for watching the depth of the stack in your hands. If a program does nine pushes in a row, you'll get incorrect answers—but no error messages. (Technically, the 8087 registers are organized as a chain rather than a stack. On the ninth push, ST(7) becomes ST(0) and the previous contents of ST(7) are lost.)

Data Transfer Instructions

Data transfer instructions move data from memory into the 8087 (load), from the 8087 into memory (store), and between 8087 registers (exchange). Inside the 8087 all data is held in temporary real format. In memory, operands fall into one of the seven data types discussed in Chapters 2 and 5. As data moves into or out of the 8087, it is automatically converted between temporary real and other formats. Three rules summarize the way the 8087 distinguishes among the different types of data.

- Data stored internally in an 8087 register is always temporary real.
- Different instructions reference real, integer, and packed decimal types.
- Within a given type, the 8087 distinguishes between arguments of different precision according to the amount of memory space the argument occupies. For example, an instruction which operates on reals treats an operand referencing a four-byte memory location as a single precision number and an operand referencing an eight-byte memory location as a double precision number.

The data transfer instructions are summarized in Table 6-1.

Table 6-1. 8087 data transfer instructions.

	Real Transfers
FLD	Load real
FST	Store real
FSTP	Store real and pop
FXCH	Exchange registers
	Integer Transfers
FILD	Integer load
FIST	Integer store
FISTP	Integer store and pop
	Packed Decimal Transfers
FBLD	Packed decimal (BCD) load
FBSTP	Packed decimal (BCD) store and pop

(Used with permission of Intel Corporation.)

The typical execution time, on an IBM PC, XT, or compatible, appears to the right of the instruction name in the discussion below. (Throughout the book, execution times are given for an IBM PC unless specified otherwise.) Execution time for an instruction depends on the clock speed of the computer and on the width of the data bus. The times below are calculated for an 8088 running at approximately 5 megahertz. Faster clock speeds will execute proportionately faster. Thus the FLD instruction takes about 13 microseconds on an IBM PC, but only about eight microseconds on an 8 megahertz computer.

Sixteen-bit bus computers (8086, 186, and 286) save roughly two "clock ticks" for each byte transferred to or from memory, when compared to eight-bit bus computers (8088, 188). For example, an instruction which transfers a double precision number between memory and the 8087 will run about 3 microseconds faster on an 8086/8087 than on an 8088/8087.

Except for differences in clock speed and bus width, instruction execution uses equal amounts of time on an 8087 and a 287.

As initially released, the IBM AT runs the 80287 at about 4 megahertz, as compared to the 5 megahertz performance of the 8087 on a PC. Therefore, execution times on an IBM AT are about 25 percent greater than the times indicated below. It is widely anticipated that faster versions of the AT and the 80287 will be released eventually. As an example, execution times on an 8 megahertz AT would be 40 percent less than the times indicated below.

Real Transfer Instructions

FLD source — 13 microseconds

FLD (load real) *pushes* the source data onto the stack by changing the top of stack pointer to point to the next available register and then copying the source data into this register. The source may be either a *real-memory* location or an 8087 register. FLD is the basic instruction for moving data into the 8087.

FST destination — 23 microseconds

FST (store real) copies the contents of the top element of the stack into the indicated destination, either an 8087 register or a single or double precision memory location. Data moved into memory is automatically converted to single or double precision format. FST does not affect the depth of the stack or its contents. FST cannot be used to store a temporary real in memory.

FSTP destination — 23 microseconds

FSTP (store real and pop) stores the top element of the stack and then *pops* the top of the stack. Unlike FST, FSTP will move a temporary real into memory.

The "pop" is accomplished in two steps. First, the register currently at the top of the stack is marked "empty" (in the tag word). Second, the top of stack pointer is changed to point to the register logically "below" the current top of stack. Thus the instruction FSTP ST(0) pops the stack with no effective transfer.

FXCH — 3 microseconds

FXCH destination

FXCH (exchange registers) exchanges the stack top with the designated destination register. If the destination is not specified, ST(1) is assumed. Thus, FXCH with no destination swaps the contents of the two registers at the top of the stack.

Integer and Packed Decimal Data Transfer Instructions

FILD source 12 microseconds

FILD (load integer) *pushes* the integer memory operand onto the stack (converting it to a temporary real).

FIST destination 21 microseconds

FIST (store integer) rounds the value held in ST(0) and stores the resulting integer in the destination memory location. (A copy of the value is made before rounding so that the contents of ST(0) remain unchanged.) The destination may be either a word or short integer. You cannot store a long integer with FIST.

FISTP destination 21 microseconds

FISTP (store integer and pop) rounds the top of stack element and stores it in the destination memory location. The top of stack is then *popped*. Unlike FIST, FISTP will store into a long integer memory location.

FBLD source 69 microseconds

FBLD (load packed decimal) *pushes* the memory source location onto the top of the stack, converting the operand from packed decimal to temporary real. No check is made to see that the data is a valid packed decimal number. The result of loading invalid data is undefined and should be carefully avoided. (The "B" in FBLD comes from an alternative name for packed decimal representation, "BCD or Binary Coded Decimal.")

FBSTP destination 117 microseconds

FBSTP (store packed decimal and pop) converts the contents of the top of stack register into packed decimal representation and transfers the converted number to the destination memory location. The top of stack is then *popped*. If the top of stack element is not already an integer, it is converted to one by adding 0.5 and truncating. This rounding operation sometimes differs from FIST, which operates under 8087 rounding control. Rounding control can be effectively invoked by preceding FBSTP with FRNDINT, which rounds the stack top to an integer. (FRNDINT is described in Chapter 12.)

Basic Arithmetic Instructions

The 8087 has 21 basic arithmetic instructions, summarized in Table 6-2. Of these, 18 provide varieties of addition, subtraction, multiplication, and division. In addition to the standard use of these four basic operations, the 8087 also allows "reversed" subtraction and "reversed" division.

Table 6-2. 8087 arithmetic instructions.

	Addition
FADD	Add real
FADDP	Add real and pop
FIADD	Integer add
	Subtraction
FSUB	Subtract real
FSUBP	Subtract real and pop
FISUB	Integer subtract
FSUBR	Subtract real reversed
FSUBRP	Subtract real reversed and pop
FISUBR	Integer subtract reversed
	Multiplication
FMUL	Multiply real
FMULP	Multiply real and pop
FIMUL	Integer multiply
	Division
FDIV	Divide real
FDIVP	Divide real and pop
FIDIV	Integer divide
FDIVR	Divide real reversed
FDIVRP	Divide real reversed and pop
FIDIVR	Integer divide reversed
	Other Operations
FSQRT	Square root
FSCALE	Scale
FPREM	Partial remainder
FRNDINT	Round to integer
FXTRACT	Extract exponent and significand
FABS	Absolute value
FCHS	Change sign

(Used with permission of Intel Corporation.)

In normal subtraction, the destination is replaced by the destination minus the source. In reversed subtraction, the destination is replaced by the source minus the destination. Reversed division operates analagously. (No reversed operations are needed for addition and multiplication, since both operations are commutative.)

Including the reversed operations, there are six basic arithmetic instructions. Each instruction comes in three formats: *real*, *real-and-pop*, and *integer*. Thus, there are 18 total instructions.

Arguments in the *real* format may take the *stack form*, the *register form*, or the *real-memory* form. In the stack form, the destination is always ST(1) and the source is always ST(0). In the register form, one argument is the stack top, ST(0), and the other is any 8087 register. In real-memory form, the destination is ST(0) and the source is a location in memory. Only *single precision* and *double precision* types may be used in the real-memory form.

The *real-and-pop* format uses the *register form*. After the operation, the stack is popped. For example, FADDP ST(1),ST adds the top two stack elements, stores the sum one element below the top of stack, and pops the stack. After execution, the original contents of the stack top have been discarded, the contents of ST(1) are replaced by the sum, and the register that was formerly ST(1) pops up to the top of the stack.

The *integer* format references a *word integer* or *short integer* location in memory as the source. ST(0) is the destination.

Implicit Operands

Stack operands may be either *implicit* or *explicit*. For example, in the stack form ST is always assumed to be the source and ST(1) is assumed to be the destination. For purposes of illustration, implicit arguments are shown below in curly brackets, as in {ST}, even though these operands are not coded in actual programs.

Use of implicit arguments can lead the unwary programmer into great confusion. Unfortunately, an instruction with two implicit arguments has a different meaning from the same instruction followed by (the implied) explicit arguments. By convention, use of two implicit arguments tells the assembler that you wish to pop the register stack after executing the instruction. For example, the instruction "FADD" implies the source is ST and the destination is ST(1). But the assembler translates the instruction as "FADDP ST(1),ST", which is quite different from "FADD ST(1),ST". You can avoid a lot of trouble by *not* taking "advantage" of this convention. Instead, make both arguments explicit.

The various combinations of instruction formats are summarized in Table 6-3.

Table 6-3. 8087 arithmetic instruction formats.

Instruction Form	*Mnemonic Form*	*Operand Forms destination, source*	*ASM-86 Example*
Classical stack	F*op*	{ST(1),ST}	**FADD**
Register	F*op*	ST(i),ST or ST,ST(i)	**FSUB ST,ST(3)**
Register pop	F*op*P	ST(i),ST	**FMULP ST(2),ST**
Real memory	F*op*	{ST, short-real/long-real}	**FDIV AZIMUTH**
Integer memory	FI*op*	{ST, word-integer/ short-integer}	**FIDIV N_PULSES**

NOTES: Braces {} surround *implicit* operands; these are not coded and are shown here for information only.

op = ADD destination←destination + source
SUB destination←destination − source
SUBR destination←source − destination
MUL destination←destination * source
DIV destination←destination ÷ source
DIVR destination←source ÷ destination

(Used with permission of Intel Corporation.)

Addition Instructions

FADD {ST(1),ST} 18 microseconds
FADD {ST,}real-memory 25 microseconds
FADD ST(i),ST or ST,ST(i) 17 microseconds
FADDP ST(i),ST 18 microseconds
FIADD {ST,}integer-memory 27 microseconds

FADD (add real), FADDP (add real and pop), and FIADD (add integer) add the source operand to the destination operand and leave the sum in the destination. In addition, FADDP pops the stack.

Subtraction Instructions

FSUB {ST(1),ST} 18 microseconds
FSUB {ST,}real-memory 25 microseconds
FSUB ST(i),ST or ST,ST(i) 17 microseconds
FSUBP ST(i),ST 18 microseconds
FISUB {ST,}integer-memory 27 microseconds

FSUB (subtract real), FSUBP (subtract real and pop), and FISUB (subtract integer) subtract the source operand from the destination operand and leave the difference in the destination. In addition, FSUBP pops the stack.

FSUBR {ST(1),ST} 18 microseconds
FSUBR {ST,}real-memory 25 microseconds
FSUBR ST(i),ST or ST,ST(i) 17 microseconds
FSUBRP ST(i),ST 18 microseconds
FISUBR {ST,}integer-memory 27 microseconds

FSUBR (reversed subtract real), FSUBRP (reversed subtract real and pop), and FISUBR (reversed subtract integer) subtract the destination operand from the source operand and leave the difference in the destination. In addition, FSUBRP pops the stack.

Multiplication Instructions

FMUL {ST(1),ST} 28 microseconds
FMUL {ST,}real-memory 34 microseconds
FMUL ST(i),ST or ST,ST(i) 28 microseconds
FMULP ST(i),ST 28 microseconds
FIMUL {ST,}integer-memory 28 microseconds

FMUL (multiply real), FMULP (multiply real and pop), and FIMUL (multiply integer) multiply the source and destination operands and leave the product in the destination. In addition, FMULP pops the stack.

Division Instructions

FDIV {ST(1),ST} 41 microseconds
FDIV {ST,}real-memory 48 microseconds
FDIV ST(i),ST or ST,ST(i) 40 microseconds
FDIVP ST(i),ST 41 microseconds
FIDIV {ST,}integer-memory 49 microseconds

FDIV (divide real), FDIVP (divide real and pop), and FIDIV (divide integer) divide the destination operand by the source operand and leave the quotient in the destination. In addition, FDIVP pops the stack. Note that FIDIV yields a temporary-real quotient.

FDIVR {ST(1),ST} 41 microseconds
FDIVR {ST,}real-memory 48 microseconds
FDIVR ST(i),ST or ST,ST(i) 40 microseconds
FDIVRP ST(i),ST 41 microseconds
FIDIVR {ST,}integer-memory 49 microseconds

FDIVR (divide real reversed), FDIVRP (divide real reversed and pop), and FIDIVR (divide reversed integer) divide the source operand by the destination operand and leave the quotient in the destination. In addition, FDIVRP pops the stack. Note that FIDIVR yields a temporary-real quotient.

Miscellaneous Arithmetic Instructions

FSQRT {ST} 37 microseconds

FSQRT (square root) replaces the top of stack with its square root.

FABS {ST} 3 microseconds

FABS (absolute value) sets the sign of the top of stack element to positive.

FCHS {ST} 3 microseconds

FCHS (change sign) changes the sign of the top of stack element.

One more instruction really belongs in this chapter, even though it is a constant instruction and constant instructions are covered in Chapter 12. However, this instruction is simple and extremely useful. It is:

FLDZ {ST} 3 microseconds

FLDZ (load zero) *pushes* a zero onto the top of the stack.

Comparison Instructions

The 8087 includes a number of instructions for making size comparisons between numbers on the register stack. These instructions are used for tasks such as identifying the largest number in an array or for determining whether a number is less than, equal to, or greater than zero. We describe the instructions here. Illustrative programming examples appear in Chapter 7.

The 8087 instruction set includes six comparison and one examine instruction. All the instructions operate on the stack top. Most compare the stack top to a specified source operand. There are four possible outcomes of a comparison operation: ST > source, ST < source, ST = source, or ST and source are non-comparable. The comparisons are reported by setting the condition code bits C3 and C0 in the status word, as indicated in Table 6-4. The condition code can be examined by using the processor control instruction, FSTSW, discussed below.

Table 6-4. Condition code setting following comparison.

C3	*C0*	*Order*
0	0	ST > source
0	1	ST < source
1	0	ST = source
1	1	non-comparable

(Used with permission of Intel Corporation.)

Note that *non-comparable* results from using NANs or projective infinity. Non-comparable usually indicates a previous overflow or illegal operation.

FCOM {ST,ST(1)} 9 microseconds
FCOM {ST,}ST(i) 9 microseconds
FCOM {ST,}real-memory 17 microseconds

FCOM (compare real) compares the stack top to the source and sets the condition code bits. Temporary real format may not be used in the real-memory form.

FCOMP {ST,ST(1)} 10 microseconds
FCOMP {ST,}ST(i) 10 microseconds
FCOMP {ST,}real-memory 17 microseconds

FCOMP (compare real and pop) executes a FCOM and then pops the stack, discarding the contents of the stack top.

FCOMPP {ST,ST(1)} 10 microseconds

FCOMPP (compare real and pop twice) executes a FCOM and then pops the stack twice. Thus, to compare two numbers in memory, push both onto the stack and then use a FCOMPP.

FICOM {ST,}integer-memory 19 microseconds

FICOM (compare integer) compares the stack top to a word integer or short integer in memory.

FICOMP {ST,}integer-memory 19 microseconds

FICOMP (compare integer and pop) executes a FICOM and then pops the stack.

FTST {ST} 9 microseconds

FTST (test) compares the stack top to zero.

FXAM {ST} 4 microseconds

FXAM (examine) examines the top of stack and sets the condition code bits C0, C1, C2, and C3 to indicate what sort of value is being held. (The various "sorts" were discussed in Chapter 5.) Table 6-5 shows the possible combinations.

Table 6-5. Condition code settings following FXAM.

Condition Code				*Interpretation*
C3	*C2*	*C1*	*C0*	
0	0	0	0	+ Unnormal
0	0	0	1	+ NAN
0	0	1	0	Unnormal
0	0	1	1	− NAN
0	1	0	0	+ Normal
0	1	0	1	+ ∞
0	1	1	0	− Normal
0	1	1	1	− ∞
1	0	0	0	+ 0
1	0	0	1	Empty
1	0	1	0	− 0
1	0	1	1	Empty
1	1	0	0	+ Denormal
1	1	0	1	Empty
1	1	1	0	− Denormal
1	1	1	1	Empty

(Used with permission of Intel Corporation.)

In order to make use of comparison instructions, we need to retrieve the condition code bits. The condition codes are retrieved with the processor control instruction, FSTSW.

FSTSW word-integer 5 microseconds

FSTSW (store status word) stores the 8087 status word at the two-byte destination location. All the comparison instructions set bits in the status word; FSTSW is used to move the status word into memory so that the appropriate bits can be examined and appropriate action taken. Generally, FSTSW should be followed by an FWAIT, to ensure that the condition codes are actually stored in memory before the program proceeds.

There is an extra form of store status word available on the 287. FSTSW AX stores the status word directly into the 286 AX register. This saves a step in executing program branches (see "8087 Branching" in Chapter 7), but use of FSTSW AX prevents a program from running on 8087-based machines.

This completes our coverage of the basic 8087 instruction set. For most programs, these instructions are sufficient. More advanced 8087 instructions are discussed in Chapter 12.

Our First Program—Adding Up An Array of Numbers

Our first program is picked to show off the speed and ease in using the 8087. This program runs about 200 times faster than an equivalent BASIC program without the 8087!

To write a complete 8087 program, we need a number of details that we haven't covered. For example, we really ought to specify how the routine gets its arguments from BASIC. In the interest of preserving everyone's sanity, we are going to cheat just this once by leaving out some details. Therefore, the program below won't run as it stands. (The program appears in full in Chapter 9.)

We assume that, elsewhere in the program, someone has already defined a single precision array named ARRAY. Our task is to add up the numbers stored in ARRAY and place a single precision result in a variable named DSUM. The integer variable N has the number of elements in ARRAY. (ARRAY goes from ARRAY(0) to ARRAY(N-1)). A fragment of a BASIC program to do the job follows:

```
10 DEFDBL D
20 DEFINT I
30 DSUM=0
40   FOR I=0 TO N-1
50   DSUM=DSUM+ARRAY(I)
60   NEXT I
```

Notice that we collected the sum in a double precision variable to ensure getting at least single precision accuracy for the final answer.

Our 8087 code appears below. The program assumes that ARRAY is an array of single precision memory locations, that N holds a non-negative integer, and that DSUM is a double precision memory location. Everything on a line after a semicolon is a comment. We have used comments to number the lines and mark each instruction as either an 8088 or an 8087 instruction.

```
                MOV     CX,N            ;1      {8088}
                FLDZ                    ;2      {8087}
                JCXZ    DONE_ADDING     ;3      {8088}
                MOV     BX,0            ;4      {8088}

LOOP_TOP:       FADD    ARRAY[BX]       ;5      {8087}
                ADD     BX,4            ;6      {8088}
                LOOP    LOOP_TOP        ;7      {8088}

DONE_ADDING:    FSTP    DSUM            ;8      {8087}
```

The program uses the following strategy: place the number of array elements in the 8088 register CX. Subtract one from this register each time through the adding-up loop and quit when the register hits zero. Use 8088 register BX to keep track of where we are in ARRAY. (8088 instructions are covered in detail in the next chapter.) A line-by-line explanation of the program follows:

1. `MOV CX,N`. Load N into the CX register. (The 8088 instruction "LOOP", in line 7, subtracts 1 from the CX register. When CX hits zero, the program has gone all the way through the array, so we will jump out of the loop.)
2. `FLDZ`. Push a zero onto the 8087 stack. We accumulate the running total in the top of stack element.
3. `JCXZ DONE_ADDING`. If CX (that is, N) is zero, jump to DONE_ADDING before entering the loop.
4. `MOV BX,0`. Set the BX register equal to zero. BX is used as an index for ARRAY. When BX equals zero, we get the first element of array.
5. `LOOP_TOP: FADD ARRAY[BX]`. Add the current element of ARRAY into the running sum we are accumulating in the top of the stack.
6. `ADD BX,4`. Add 4 to the count in BX. Why? Single precision numbers occupy four bytes, so we have to move along ARRAY four bytes at a hop. (Some things are just naturally more clumsy in assembly language than in a higher level programming language.)
7. `LOOP LOOP_TOP`. The LOOP instruction subtracts one from CX. If CX is still positive, the program "loops" to LOOP_TOP, otherwise we proceed to the next instruction, falling out of the bottom of the loop since we must have already added up all N numbers.
8. `DONE_ADDING: FSTP DSUM`. Store the answer in DSUM.

Besides the fact that it was a lot easier to write the BASIC program, what's the difference between BASIC and our 8087 code? One, the 8087 program is a little more accurate, though on most problems we'd probably never notice the difference. Two, the 8087 is a bit faster. Adding 10,000 numbers takes approximately 46 seconds in BASIC. The 8087 needs about one-fourth of one second.

7

Introduction to 8088 Assembly Language Programming

Before the era of the 8087, all personal computer thinking was done with a general purpose microprocessor such as the Intel 8088. A number crunching personal computercombines the mathematical power of the 8087 with the general programming capabilities of the 8088. The 8087 needs the 8088 to talk to the outside world. In this chapter, we discuss 8088 programming.

This brings us to a dilemma. The 8087 is a simple, elegant machine. The 8088 is a complex, elegant machine. Chapters 6 and 12 of this book present a complete, detailed description of the 8087 instruction set. A similar description of the 8088 instruction set would require a book, and wouldn't be very interesting to readers who just want to crunch numbers. On the other hand, you can't get to the 8087 except through the 8088.

As a compromise, we discuss just those 8088 features needed to get through to the 8087. We don't attempt to cover all features of the 8088 or to talk about assembly language programming in general. This chapter is oriented toward the BASIC programmer; the experienced assembly language programmer is asked to forgive the occasional simplification. (If you are already comfortable with 8088 assembly language, you can skip this chapter entirely.) For full details on the 8088 (and 8086 family) we recommend:

iAPX 88 Book by Intel;
iAPX 86,88 User's Manual, by Intel;
iAPX 286 Programmer's Reference Manual, by Intel;
The 8086 Primer, by Stephen P. Morse, Hayden Book Company;
IBM PC Assembly Language, by Leo J. Scanlon, Robert J. Brady Co.

The 8088 and 8086 use the same machine language instructions. 8088 instructions also work on machines based on the 188 or 186 cpus. The 286 adds a few new wrinkles, discussed at the end of this chapter. As a practical matter, if an application program works on an 8088, it will work on a 286 as well.

Overview of the 8088

Machine language instructions are much less powerful than BASIC commands. (A typical line of BASIC might be equivalent to 10 to 100 lines of machine language instructions.) Consequently, it's easy to understand what a single line of 8088 code does, but it can be very tedious to put together enough lines to do anything useful. For example, suppose we want to copy the data in integer variable A into integer variable B. In BASIC we write:

```
B=A
```

8088 code might be:

```
MOV  AX,A   ;MOVE CONTENTS OF LOCATION A INTO REGISTER AX
MOV  B,AX   ;MOVE CONTENTS OF REGISTER AX INTO LOCATION B
```

A and B are integer variables in both sets of code, but there the similarity ends. We see the following differences:

- BASIC uses mathematical notation. 8088 notation takes the form of a command to the CPU.
- BASIC deals directly with the variables of interest. The 8088 uses internal registers as intermediaries. In this example, the data in A is transferred into a register named "AX" and then transferred from the AX register into B.
- Anything following a semicolon is a comment in assembly language. BASIC uses the apostrophe and REM statement for this purpose.

Suppose we wanted to deal with single precision numbers instead of integers. In BASIC, we declare the variables A and B to be of the appropriate type. Thereafter, B=A works equally well for any type of variable. 8088 code would have to be modified, leading us to some further differences.

```
MOV  AX,A     ;MOVE THE FIRST HALF OF A INTO AX
MOV  B,AX     ;MOVE AX INTO THE FIRST HALF OF B
MOV  AX,A+2   ;MOVE THE SECOND HALF OF A INTO AX
MOV  B+2,AX   ;MOVE AX INTO THE SECOND HALF OF B
```

- BASIC deals with data a number at a time. The 8088 works either on a word (two bytes) or a byte at a time. Since a single precision number occupies two words, two sets of MOV operations are required to move a single precision number.
- Unlike BASIC, which thinks in terms of variables, *the 8088 fundamentally thinks in terms of memory locations*. In the instruction "MOV

AX,A", "A" represents a memory location to be assigned by the assembler. "A+2" means the memory location 2 bytes after "A". "A+2" does not mean add 2 to the value stored in A.

8088 Program Structure

An 8088 assembly language program is structured into procedures, code segments, and data segments.

Each separate program module is identified to the assembler as a *procedure* by the PROC and ENDP directives (discussed below). The assembler remembers the location of each block of code identified so that the module can be called as a subroutine from another 8088 assembly language program or by use of the BASIC CALL statement. Normally, each procedure is a self-contained unit intended to perform one task in a larger program.

Programs written for the 8088 segregate code and data into different areas of memory called segments. While any number of segments may reside in memory simultaneously, only one *code segment* and one *data segment* (plus a stack and an extra segment described below) may be active at any one time. Segments are identified to the assembler with the SEGMENT and ENDS directives (discussed below). Segments are limited in length to 64K bytes.

One way to think of an assembly language program is that we write out an exact picture of how memory looks before execution begins. Some areas of memory hold program constants or are set aside to hold results produced by the computer. These areas are placed in data segments. Other areas of memory hold the executable code, as translated from assembly language into machine language, by the assembler. The code is logically organized into procedures. One or more procedures is then placed in each code segment. When we run the program, the computer places each segment, as a block, in memory and then begins execution.

To master the 8088, one must understand:

1. General registers
2. Memory addressing
3. Labels and data definition
4. Some basic 8088 instructions
5. Comparisons
6. Branching
7. Segments
8. Memory stack
9. Subroutine branching and returns
10. Assembler directives

General Registers

The 8088 has eight general registers, each of which holds one 16-bit word. The registers are named AX, BX, CX, DX, SI, DI, BP, and SP. In the MOV examples above, any of these registers could have been used in place of AX. However, each register has various special purposes in addition to its general role. The special uses of interest to us are:

AX and DX—Register AX is sometimes called the accumulator. A few 8088 instructions will only work with AX. Instructions that produce a double length result, such as multiplication, place the result in AX and DX.

BX, SI, and DI—base and index registers (see Memory Addressing below).

CX—count register (see Branching below).

BP and SP—stack pointers (see Memory Stack below).

In addition, registers AX, BX, CX, and DX can each be treated as a pair of 8-bit registers. The high-order bytes are addressed as AH, BH, CH, and DH and the low-order bytes are addressed as AL, BL, CL, and DL. Most 8088 operations can operate on either a word at a time or a byte at a time. Moving a byte into AH, for example, changes the high-order half of AX without affecting the low-order half.

The AH half of AX also has a special use in moving "flags" around (see Branching below).

Memory Addressing

In the "MOV AX,A" instruction above, "A" represents a particular memory location called the *displacement*. The first byte of memory is numbered 0, the second 1, and so forth. The assembler figures out the number of the memory location for A and sticks the number into the instruction. Note that the 8088 addresses bytes, not words, so the first word begins at 0, the second at 2, the third at 4. (It is perfectly acceptable to store a byte at 0, a word at 1 and 2, and so forth. Words don't have to fall on even-numbered locations. However, the 8086 side of the 8088/8086 family will run a tiny bit faster when words do fall on even locations.)

If we want to use the byte after location A we code "A+1". Analogously, the word after location A is "A+2", and the byte before location A is addressed as "A−1".

Just as BASIC allows indexed arrays, the 8088 allows us to index memory. In BASIC the first element of an array A is A(0), the second A(1), and so forth. To pick different elements at different points in the program we code A(I), and set the variable I appropriately. In 8088 code we index memory by indicating that the value held in one of the registers is to be added to the displacement in calculating the address. We tell the 8088 which register to use by placing its name in square brackets, as in A[BX]. Further, we can "double index" memory by placing a second register in square brackets, as in A[BX][SI]. Thus, if A is location 75, the BX register holds 150, and the SI register holds 1000, A[BX][SI] is location 1225.

Unfortunately, we are somewhat restricted in which registers can be used as indexes. If we use one register, it can be BX, SI, or DI. If we use two registers, one must be BX and the other can be either SI or DI. (Actually, BP can be used rather than BX as an index, but this is generally not done for reasons that become clear when we discuss the memory stack.)

Thus, a memory address consists of a displacement and zero, one, or two index registers. The displacement may be omitted, in which case a displacement of zero is assumed. This usage is quite common, because when we call a subroutine from BASIC, BASIC passes the subroutine the address of each argument. If we call a subroutine with an argument A(0), the subroutine might place the address of A(0) into the BX register, use the SI register to hold an index, and address the array by [BX][SI] with no displacement.

Note some critical differences between indexing in BASIC and indexing in assembly language. In BASIC if the index is 17, we get the 18th (started at zero, remember) element of the array, regardless of whether the array is of type integer, single precision, or double precision. In machine language if the index is 17, we get the 18th byte, not the 18th element of the array. Depending on the type of data being used, consecutive elements have indexes 0, 2, 4. . ., 0, 4, 8. . ., or 0, 8, 16. . . .Also, in BASIC we can specify multi-dimensional arrays. 8088 indexing is all one-dimensional.

When the displacement is added to the value of the index registers the result is a 16-bit logical address. Therefore, the address must be between 0 and $(2^{16})-1$, or 64K. (It is no coincidence that BASIC is limited to a 64K area.)

Most operations specify a register and a memory location. Instructions can also specify two registers, as in

```
MOV   AX,BX   ;MOVE THE CONTENTS OF THE BX REGISTER INTO AX
```

Some instructions allow one argument to be an *immediate operand*. An immediate operand is a constant built right into the instruction—the value is used "immediately," in contrast to being fetched from memory. For example, to set the register AX to zero and the value of memory location A to minus one:

```
MOV AX,0
MOV A,-1
```

8088 instructions such as MOV can operate either a byte at a time or a word at a time. In truth, MOV is really two separate instructions, "move word" and "move byte." The assembler looks at the specified operands to decide which instruction we mean. Most of the time the assembler can figure out whether we want a byte or a word by examining the specifications used to define the memory location (see Labels and Data Definition below). Sometimes there aren't any such specifications, such as when we use an index register without a displacement, and sometimes we want to override the original specifications. To order the assembler to think in terms of a byte or a word, use the "PTR" (pointer) directive. We indicate that location A is a byte or a word by saying "BYTE PTR A" or "WORD PTR A." So to move an integer whose location is held in BX into a location held in SI we might code:

```
MOV   AX,WORD PTR [BX]
MOV   WORD PTR [SI],AX
```

Labels and Data Definition

An assembly language program consists of a series of one-line commands. Commands are actually of two sorts: instructions and assembler directives. A command may be preceded by an optional identifying label. To label an instruction, begin the line with the desired label and a colon. The program can jump to a labeled instruction in much the same way as a program can GOTO a line number in BASIC. To label a line containing a directive, begin the line with the desired label, but omit the colon.

```
THIS_IS_A_LABEL: MOV AX,A
```

Assembler directives do not generate any machine language code. Instead they give the assembler information or ask it to perform a task, such as setting aside a memory location to be used as data storage. For example, the assembler directive "DW" sets aside two bytes of storage. It can be followed by an initial value and the storage area can be labeled.

```
A DW 37
```

Setting aside and labeling memory is somewhat analogous to the BASIC statement DIM. "DW" stands for "define word." To define a word with no initial value, tell the assembler "DW ?". We can also define a series of words with a directive like "DW 3,5,?, −2". Or we could set aside 10 uninitialized words with "DW 10 DUP(?)". Since an address is actually represented by a 16-bit integer, we can also initialize a memory location to contain the address of some other instruction, as in

```
POINT_TO_A_LABEL DW THIS_IS_A_LABEL
```

The 8088 deals with bytes and words. To set aside one or more bytes, we use the "define byte" instruction, DB. The 8087 deals with many more data types. Table 7-1 shows all the storage allocation directives.

Table 7-1. Storage allocation directives.

Directive	*Interpretation*	*Bytes*	*Pointer type*	*Data types*
DB	Define Byte	1	BYTE PTR	byte
DW	Define Word	2	WORD PTR	word integer
DD	Define Doubleword	4	DWORD PTR	short integer, short real
DQ	Define Quadword	8	QWORD PTR	Long integer, long real
DT	Define Tenbyte	10	TBYTE PTR	Packed decimal, temporary real

(Used with permission of Intel Corporation.)

The assembler knows how much memory is supposed to be associated with a particular storage allocation directive. This knowledge is used in two ways. First, if you set aside storage using Define Byte, as in "A DB 5" and then try to use a word instruction, as in "MOV AX,A", the assembler will warn you of a type mismatch. If you intend to move the two bytes at A and A+1, you can override this mechanism by using the instruction "MOV AX, WORD PTR A".

Second, the assembler uses the storage allocation directives to decide whether 8087 instructions should operate on single or double precision data. For example:

```
FLD   DWORD PTR A
```

loads a single precision number located at bytes A, A+1, A+2, and A+3 onto the 8087 stack. The instruction

```
FLD   QWORD PTR A
```

loads a double precision number located at bytes A through A+7.

We can also label a memory location without setting aside storage by using the directives *EQU* and *THIS WORD*. "THIS WORD" takes on the value of the next memory location and "EQU" assigns a value to a name. For example:

```
A       DW      10 DUP (?)
B       EQU     THIS WORD
        DW      30 DUP (?)
```

These instructions set aside 40 words of storage. If A ends up being located at byte 100 of memory, then B will reference location 120.

Some Basic 8088 Instructions

In this section, we cover a few of the most common 8088 instructions, concentrating on those instructions we need later for programs.

ADD destination,source

ADD (Add) adds the destination and the source and places the sum in the destination.

AND destination,source

AND (Logical and) does a bit by bit "and" operation. Bit "i" in the destination is set to one if bit "i" is one in both source and destination, otherwise it is set to zero.

DEC destination

DEC (Decrement) subtracts one from the destination.

INC destination

INC (Increment) adds one to the destination.

MOV destination,source

MOV (Move) copies the value of the source into the destination.

MUL source

MUL (Multiply) multiplies the source by AL or AX. If the source is a byte, it is multiplied by AL, and the result is placed in AH and AL (that is, the 16-bit answer that occupies AX). If the source is a word, the 32-bit answer is placed (upper 16 bits) in DX and (lower 16 bits) in AX. Both operands are treated as unsigned binary numbers. The source cannot be an immediate operand.

OR destination,source

OR (Logical inclusive or) does a bit by bit "or" operation. Bit "i" in the destination is set to one if bit "i" is one in either the source or the destination, otherwise it is set to zero.

SHL destination,source

SHL (Shift logical left) shifts the bits in the destination to the left. Bits that move out on the left "fall off the end" and zeros are moved in on the right. The source can either be "1," in which case the destination is shifted left one bit, or it can be CL, the lower half of the CX register, in which case the destination is shifted left the number of places indicated by the value held in CL.

Notice that shifting a number left one place is the same as multiplying the number by two. It turns out that we frequently have need to multiply by two or by a power of two. The SHL instruction takes only six microseconds, while the MUL instruction takes about 30.

SHR destination,source

SHR (Shift logical right) shifts the bits in the destination to the right. Bits that move out on the right "fall off the end" and zeros are moved in on the left. The source can either be "1," in which case the destination is shifted right one bit, or it can be CL, in which case the destination is shifted right the number of places indicated by the value held in CL.

- Don't shift left or right by more than 31 bits. One, the 8088 and the 286 treat shifts of more than 31 bits differently. Two, there are only 16 bits in a word anyhow.

SUB destination,source

SUB (Subtract) subtracts the source from the destination and places the difference in the destination.

Comparisons

Controlling the flow of a program is easier in BASIC than in assembly language. In BASIC, we would jump to line 100 when A is greater than B with a statement combining a comparison and a conditional jump, such as

```
IF A>B THEN GOTO 100
```

In assembly language, the comparison and branching are two logically separate steps. First, we use a comparison (or other) operation to set "flags" inside the 8088. Then, we execute a branching instruction which examines the flags and jumps if it sees the right ones "flying." The 8088 has six internal "flags." These flags can be thought of as occupying six out of the 16 bits of a "flag register." The flags, their position, and meaning are:

CF—bit 0—carry flag
PF—bit 2—parity flag
AF—bit 4—auxiliary carry flag
ZF—bit 6—zero flag
SF—bit 7—sign flag
OF—bit 11—overflow flag

The flag names are suggestive of their general use. We care about the flags for two reasons. First, 8088 comparison instructions set some of the flags to zero or one. Second, 8087 comparison instructions indirectly set some of the flags.

The 8088 compares two numbers by using the CMP instruction.

CMP destination,source

CMP (Compare) compares the destination to the source, setting the flags to indicate the result of the comparison. The flags are read by the jump instructions outlined in Table 7-2.

The 8087 does its own comparisons, but relies on the 8088 for program branching. To set up an 8088 branch following an 8087 comparison, we need to set the 8088 flags. SAHF is used for this purpose.

SAHF

SAHF (Store register AH into flags) sets SF, ZF, AF, PF, and CF from bits 7, 6 ,4, 2, and 0 of AH.

Branching

JMP address

The 8088 jump instruction is analogous to GO TO in BASIC. The program jumps from its current position to the address specified by the jump.

The 8088 also has 18 conditional jump instructions. These instructions cause a jump to the specified address only if the flags have a certain pattern, otherwise execution continues with the next instruction. For example, if we execute a "JG SOME_LABEL" following a CMP, the program goes to SOME_LABEL if the destination was greater than the source, and continues on to the next instruction otherwise. Table 7-2 describes the conditional jump instructions.

One warning: an 8087 comparison sets different bits than an 8088 comparison. See below.

A simple program illustrates 8088 branching technique. Suppose we want to add up an array of 100 integers in memory and put the answer in a location called SUM.

```
           MOV   AX,0            ;CLEAR OUT AX TO HOLD THE
                                  RUNNING SUM
           MOV   CX,100          ;PUT A COUNT INTO CX
           MOV   BX,0            ;USE BX AS AN INDEX REGISTER
NEXT_ADD:  ADD   AX,ARRAY[BX]
           ADD   BX,2            ;POINT BX AT THE NEXT ELEMENT
           DEC   CX              ;SUBTRACT ONE FROM THE COUNTER
           CMP   CX,0            ;IS THE COUNTER ZERO YET?
           JG    NEXT_ADD        ;IF NOT, ADD ANOTHER ELEMENT
           MOV   SUM,AX

ARRAY      DW    100 DUP(?)
SUM        DW    ?
```

Because looping is so important, the 8088 has specialized instructions for this sort of routine.

Table 7-2. 8088 conditional jump instructions.

Mnemonic	*Condition tested*	*"Jump if . . ."*
JA/JNBE	(CF OR ZF)=0	above/not below or equal
JAE/JNB	CF=0	above or equal/not below
JB/JNAE	CF=1	below/not above nor equal
JBE/JNA	(CF OR ZF)=1	below or equal/not above
JC	CF=1	carry
JE/JZ	ZF=1	equal/zero
JG/JNLE	((SF XOR OF) OR ZF)=0	greater/not less nor equal
JGE/JNL	(SF XOR OF)=0	greater or equal/not less
JL/JNGE	(SF XOR OF)=1	less/not greater nor equal
JLE/JNG	((SF XOR OF) OR ZF)=1	less or equal/not greater
JNC	CF=0	not carry
JNE/JNZ	ZF=0	not equal/not zero
JNO	OF=0	not overflow
JNP/JPO	PF=0	not parity/parity odd
JNS	SF=0	not sign
JO	OF=1	overflow
JP/JPE	PF=1	parity/parity equal
JS	SF=1	sign

NOTE: "above" and "below" refer to the relationship of two unsigned values: "greater" and "less" refer to the relationship of two signed values.
(Used with permission of Intel Corporation.)

JCXZ address

JCXZ (Jump if CX equals zero) takes a conditional branch if the CX register equals zero. In the program above, "CMP CX,0" and "JG NEXT_ADD" test the CX register at the bottom of the loop. We could instead use JCXZ to test the CX register at the top of the loop, as we illustrate below. The choice between testing at the bottom versus the top of a loop is largely a matter of style. We use both styles in this book to provide you with a variety of examples. However, as a matter of good programming practice, you may want to choose one style or the other and stick with it.

```
          MOV   AX,0          ;CLEAR OUT AX TO HOLD THE
                               RUNNING SUM
          MOV   CX,100        ;PUT A COUNT INTO CX
          MOV   BX,0          ;USE BX AS AN INDEX REGISTER
NEXT_ADD: JCXZ  DONE          ;GO TO DONE IF CX EQUALS 0
          ADD   AX,ARRAY[BX]
          ADD   BX,2          ;POINT BX AT THE NEXT ELEMENT
          DEC   CX            ;SUBTRACT ONE FROM THE COUNTER
          JMP   NEXT_ADD      ;GO TO NEXT_ADD
DONE:     MOV   SUM,AX

ARRAY     DW    100 DUP(?)
SUM       DW    ?
```

LOOP address

LOOP (Loop on CX) subtracts one from CX and then jumps to the address if CX is not equal to zero. Thus LOOP is like a BASIC FOR-NEXT loop with a FOR statement "FOR initial-value TO 1 STEP—1". We could further modify the original program by replacing "DEC CX", "CMP CX,0", and "JG NEXT_ADD" with "LOOP NEXT_ADD".

You should be warned that the conditional jumps in Table 7-2, JCXZ, and LOOP all have one limitation. They only work when the target is within plus or minus 127 bytes. Usually, the target is close enough that the limitation isn't binding. (The assembler will warn you if the target is too far away.) Unconditional jumps (JMP) don't have this limitation, so, if you do get stuck, the solution is to write in an extra, close-by, unconditional JMP as the target of the conditional jump instruction.

8087 Branching

An 8087 comparison sets the internal 8087 condition codes. These condition codes must be transferred into the 8088 flags prior to executing a conditional jump instruction. Because the 8087 condition codes do not exactly parallel the 8088 flags, a little more programming is required following an 8087 comparison than following an 8088 comparison.

Making an 8087-comparison based decision involves three steps.

- Execute an 8087 instruction to set the 8087 condition codes.
- Transfer the 8087 condition codes through memory and into the 8088 flags, using FSTSW and SAHF.
- Execute an 8088 branching instruction.

The 8087 processor control instruction FSTSW, store status word, stores the 8087 condition codes, among other things, into a two-byte area of memory. (FSTSW must be followed in this usage by the processor control instruction FWAIT.) After the FSTSW, the second byte of the memory area holds the condition code bits in just the right position to be loaded into an 8088 register and then dropped into the 8088 flags. The 8088 does not have four separate branching instructions corresponding to the four combinations of C3 and C0, the two condition code bits set by the 8087 comparison instructions. The 8088 instruction JB jumps if C0 is on and JE jumps if C3 is on. Thus a fragment of code to consider all possible outcomes of the condition codes might look like this:

```
;ASSUME STATUS_WORD IS A 2-BYTE AREA OF SCRATCH MEMORY
                        DEFINED ELSEWHERE

; DO A COMPARISON TO SET CONDITION CODES
      FSTSW      STATUS_WORD
      FWAIT
;NOW GET CONDITION CODES INTO FLAGS
      MOV        AH, BYTE PTR STATUS_WORD+1
```

```
        SAHF
;NOW BRANCH AND TAKE ANY APPROPRIATE ACTIONS
        JB          LESS_OR_NON_COMP
        JE          EQUAL
;COME HERE FOR GREATER THAN
;EQUAL: ; COME HERE FOR EQUAL
;
;LESS_OR_NON_COMP:
            JE      NON_COMP
;COME HERE FOR LESS THAN
;NON_COMP:
;COME HERE FOR NON-COMPARABLE
```

On a 287, the three instructions "FSTSW, FWAIT, and MOV" could all be replaced by "FSTSW AX". Doing so will save a few bytes and a few microseconds. However, as FSTSW AX is only available on the 287 and not the 8087, the savings from the substitution is probably not worth the loss of compatibility.

Segments

The ability of the 8088 to address over a million bytes of memory provides PC owners with far greater power than was available on old 8-bit machines. The designers of the 8088 had to solve a difficult problem in order to access such a large address space. 8088 registers are 16 bits wide. 2^{16} is 64K. Addressing a megabyte requires 20 bits. The solution is found in the 8088 *segment registers*.

The 8088 has four internal 16-bit registers called segment registers. When calculating an address, the 8088 picks the value from one of the segment registers, shifts it left four places, and then adds the logical address made up from displacement and index registers. The resulting 20-bit address is called the *effective address*. For the most part, we ignore the segment registers. However, we sometimes need to manipulate them when dealing with subroutines. For example, the BASIC statement DEF SEG= defines the beginning of a segment.

An address is completely specified by giving both a *segment* location and an *offset* location. For example, location 100 in the data segment can be written DS:100. The assembler directives SEG and OFFSET separate a complete address back into its component parts. For example, if the complete address of A is 8000:100, then SEG A equals 8000 and OFFSET A equals 100.

The four segment registers are *CS*—code segment, *DS*—data segment, *SS*—stack segment, and *ES*—extra segment.

Since the 8088 uses an area in memory for the stack, we can choose its size. (You will remember that the 8087 stack was limited to eight items.) We need to know about the stack for two reasons. First, BASIC passes arguments to subroutines by placing each argument's address on the stack. Second, we can temporarily save small amounts of information on the stack without having to allocate extra storage.

On the 8088, the *stack segment* register, SS, gives the location of the stack segment. The *stack pointer* register, SP, points to the top of the stack. The stack grows (upside) down in memory, progressing toward location zero as it grows. Since the stack is just an area in memory, we can access data on it with any of the usual 8088 instructions. For example, "MOV BX,SP" and "MOV WORD PTR SS:[BX],0" will move the offset of the stack top into register BX and then replace the element on top of the stack with a zero.

Usually, however, we use the stack manipulation instructions PUSH and POP.

PUSH source

PUSH (Push) subtracts two from the stack pointer, SP, and then transfers two bytes from the source into the word at SS:SP.

- In one particular instance, PUSH SP, the 8088 and 286 give different results. The 286 pushes the value the stack pointer held before the subtraction—the 8088 pushes the value after the subtraction. To preserve compatibility, do not use the instruction PUSH SP!

POP destination

POP (Pop) transfers two bytes from SS:SP to the destination and then adds two to SP. POP effectively undoes the previous PUSH.

- As an aid to manipulating data on the stack, whenever you code BP as a base register, as in "[BP] + 10", the 8088 assumes you want the stack segment rather than the data segment.

Subroutine Branching and Returns

BASIC has the GOSUB and RETURN. The 8088 has CALL and RET. We describe the 8088 calling and returning mechanism here. The next chapter treats the BASIC-to-8088/8087 routine-calling mechanism in depth.

CALL far-procedure-name

CALL near-procedure-name

CALL (Call a subroutine) is actually two instructions: one for calling subroutines in another segment, CALL far; and one for calling subroutines within the current code segment, CALL near. BASIC always uses a far CALL. Near CALLs are used in writing relocatable subroutines.

CALL far pushes CS and IP (the *instruction pointer*, which holds the address of the next instruction) onto the stack. The address of the code segment of the subroutine and the location of the subroutine within the segment are taken from the procedure-name argument. (The assembler fills these in automatically.) CS is set to the address of the new code segment and execution begins at the beginning of the new subroutine.

These conventions should sound a bit familiar to anyone who has called a machine language routine from BASIC. The DEF SEG= statement tells BASIC what value to load into CS. The command CALL SUB() tells BASIC to do an 8088 CALL to location SUB in the new code segment.

CALL near pushes IP onto the stack and jumps to the location given as the procedure name.

RET immediate-operand

RET (Return) effectively undoes a CALL. The assembler codes a RET to undo either a far CALL or a near CALL, depending on whether the current procedure is marked FAR or NEAR. (See Assembler Directives below.) In a FAR return, the top two words are popped off the stack. The first gives the address of the next instruction and the second a new value for CS. In a NEAR return, one word is popped off the stack and then used as the address of the next instruction. In either case, "immediate-operand" additional bytes are popped off the stack. (The stack operates on words, not bytes. However, addresses are always specified in bytes. So, to pop one extra word, code "RET 2".) The immediate-operand is optional.

Note that PUSH/POP and CALL/RET are matched pairs, much like FOR/NEXT or WHILE/WEND in BASIC or parentheses in mathematics. If the pairing is mismatched, things go very wrong.

Assembler Directives

Assembler directives aren't actually 8088 instructions. Rather, they supply the assembler program with necessary information. We've already met some of the most important assembler instructions above under "Labels and Data Definition." The other important directives follow:

```
label  SEGMENT  'class'
         .
         .
         .
label  ENDS
```

SEGMENT and ENDS (END Segment) define the enclosed series of code or data definitions to be a segment named "label". The segment may optionally be given a "class" in single quotes. Because some software looks for the class of a segment, it is a good idea to give a code segment the class 'CODE' and a data segment the class 'DATA'.

```
ASSUME CS:segment-label1,DS:segment-label2,
       SS:segment-label3,ES:segment-label4
```

ASSUME promises the assembler that the segment registers will contain the indicated segment addresses. (It's the programmer's responsibility to see to it that the promise is kept at execution time.) Since a section of code always has a code segment, "CS:. . ." must always be present, the three remaining ASSUME specifications appear as needed.

```
label  PROC FAR
        .
        .
        .
label  ENDP
```

PROC (PROCedure) and ENDP (END Procedure) mark the boundaries of a procedure just as SEGMENT and ENDS mark the boundaries of a segment. FAR signals the assembler that the procedure will be called with a CALL FAR instruction. When the assembler sees a RETurn instruction, it generates a RET FAR. (For a NEAR procedure, which you can't call from BASIC, code NEAR in place of FAR).

```
PUBLIC  symbol
EXTRN  name:type
```

PUBLIC and EXTRN (EXTeRNal) are used to supply information necessary for linking together separately assembled or compiled programs. Information about a symbol defined to be PUBLIC is made available to other programs. EXTRN tells the assembler to treat "name," which has been defined in another program, as being of type "type." The following example shows the most common use of PUBLIC and EXTRN.

```
        program1
         PUBLIC  LABEL1
LABEL1   PROC      FAR
         .
         .
         .
LABEL1   ENDP

program2

    EXTRN LABEL1:FAR
    CALL LABEL1
```

Any label declared PUBLIC can be accessed by any program declaring the same name to be EXTRN. A label which is to be used by separately assembled programs should be declared PUBLIC. The declaration should be made exactly once, in the program where the label is defined. Any number of other programs may declare the label EXTRN. In particular, the name of an assembly language procedure should be declared PUBLIC if the procedure is to be called as a BASIC subroutine.

SEGMENT/ENDS and PROC/ENDP are also matched pairs. Since these directives carry labels, the assembler will probably catch the error if you omit a half of either pair.

END

END marks the end of the entire assembly language program.

286 Instruction Extensions

While the 286 has extraordinarily more power than the 8088 family, there are very few differences relevant to 8087 or 287 programming. Essentially, any program written for the 8088/8087 will run unchanged on the 286/287, but not vice versa. Several of the noteworthy features of the 286 are:

1. There are quite a few new instructions on the 286. See the *iAPX 286 Programmer's Reference Manual.*
2. The 286 runs much faster than the 8088. For example, use of the MOV instruction to transfer a word from memory to a register requires 3 clock ticks on the 286 versus 17 to 25 clock ticks on the 8088. The speed advanatage of the 286 is somewhat less on other instructions, so the actual advantage of a 286 over an 8088 will vary from program to program. As a ballpark estimate, figure that a 286 is two-and-a-half to three times as fast as an 8088.
3. The 286 is really two computers on one chip. When running in *Real Address Mode*, the 286 differs little from the 8088 family, except for its greater speed. When running in *Protected Virtual Address Mode*, the 286 is more like a minicomputer than a micro. The 286 can run several simultaneous tasks for several users. It can address 16 megabytes of real memory and over a gigabyte of virtual memory.

Use of Virtual Address Mode involves a fundamental change in the way memory is addressed. As discussed earlier under *Segments*, on the 8088 (or in Real Address Mode on the 286) an address is calculated by taking a 16-bit offset, taking a 16-bit segment address, shifting the segment address to the left four bits, adding the offset and segment, to produce, finally, a twenty bit effective address. Virtual Address Mode uses the same offset. However, the 16-bit segment is used to locate the beginning of the segment, which may be anywhere in memory. (The 286 maintains a special table of segment addresses for this purpose.)

Many 8088 programs rely on the physical layout of segments within memory. For example, adding one to a segment address or 16 to an offset are equivalent operations on the 8088. They are unrelated operations in 286 Virtual Address Mode. Programs which manipulate segment registers on the 8088 will almost certainly not work in 286 Virtual Address Mode.

While 286 Virtual Address Mode programs are generally incompatible with the 8088, this has nothing to do with the 287 *per se*. Operation of the 287 is essentially the same in Virtual Address Mode and in Real Address Mode. If you can arrange for the 286 part of your program to work in either mode, then the 287 will follow along.

Note that the IBM AT running PC-DOS operates exclusively in Real Address Mode (at least as initially released). Note also that version 2.0 of the IBM Macro Assembler supports only Real Address Mode.

This chapter has been heavy on required detail. In Chapter 8, we put this detail to work writing real 8087 programs.

8

BASIC and the 8087

Assembly language subroutines, in combination with BASIC programs, join the convenience of a high-level language with the speed of the 8087. In this chapter, we discuss the software conventions that must be observed in writing the 8087 routines. (If you want to use the 8087 procedures in this book for languages other than Microsoft BASIC, you may have to observe different conventions. See the brief discussion at the end of this chapter.)

Calling a Subroutine

Calling a subroutine requires three tasks. First, we have to set up a list of arguments that can be retrieved by the subroutine. Second, we have to store away a return address in a place the subroutine can find. Third, we jump to the subroutrine. The CALL instruction takes care of the latter two tasks. The first is accomplished by pushing the addresses of the arguments onto the 8088 stack.

Calling a subroutine is most easily explained with an illustration. Suppose we wanted to imitate the following BASIC code:

```
DEF SEG=&H1800
SUB=0
CALL SUB(A(0),SUM,N)
```

We could use the following 8088 program:

```
      ASSUME CS:CSEG,DS:DATA_SEGMENT,SS:STACK_SEGMENT
CSEG  SEGMENT'CODE'
      MOV    AX,DATA_SEGMENT        ;MOVE ADDRESS OF DATA
                                     SEGMENT
      MOV    DS,AX                  ;THROUGH AX INTO DS
      MOV    AX,STACK_SEGMENT       ;MOVE ADDRESS OF STACK
                                     SEGMENT
      MOV    SS,AX                  ;THROUGH AX INTO SS
      MOV    SP,OFFSET STACK_TOP    ;SET SP TO STACK TOP
      MOV    AX,OFFSET A            ;PUSH ADDRESS OF A
      PUSH   AX                     ;ONTO STACK
```

```
      MOV    AX,OFFSET SUM          ;PUSH ADDRESS OF SUM    ;10
      PUSH   AX                     ;ONTO STACK             ;11
      MOV    AX,OFFSET N            ;PUSH ADDRESS OF N      ;12
      PUSH   AX                     ;ONTO STACK             ;13
      CALL   FAR PTR 1800H:0        ;CALL SUBROUTINE        ;14
NEXT_LOCATION:            ;RETURN HERE WHEN SUBROUTINE ENDS
CSEG ENDS                                                   ;15

DATA_SEGMENT SEGMENT   'DATA'                               ;16
A     DW     1000 DUP (?)                                   ;17
SUM   DW     ?                                              ;18
N     DW     1000                                           ;19
DATA_SEGMENT ENDS                                           ;20

STACK_SEGMENT  SEGMENT   'STACK'                            ;21
STACK_AREA     DW     100 DUP (?)                           ;22
STACK_TOP      EQU    THIS WORD                             ;23
STACK_SEGMENT  ENDS                                         ;24
               END                                          ;25
```

1. `ASSUME CS . . . .` ASSUME promises the assembler we will set up the segment registers appropriately.
2. `CSEG SEGMENT 'CODE'`. Tell the assembler we are beginning the code segment.

3-4. `MOV AX,DATA_SEGMENT` and `MOV DS,AX`. Put the address of the data segment into the data segment register, by transferring it through the AX register. We require two steps because the MOV instruction allows immediate operands, like an address, to be moved into memory or a general register, but not into a segment register.

5-6. `MOV AX,STACK_SEGMENT` and `MOV SS,AX`. Put the address of the stack segment into the stack segment register.

Note that we do not have to load the code segment register. Someone else must have already done this for us since we can't execute code to load the code segment register, or to do anything else, until the code segment register is loaded. The program that calls our subroutine is responsible for loading CSEG into CS. (And how does that program get CS loaded? And the one that calls it? The operating system initially loads the CS register when it first calls BASIC (or whatever). The CS value for the operating system is wired into the hardware.)

7. `MOV SP,OFFSET STACK_TOP`. Set the stack pointer register to point to the memory location after the end of the stack area. We could have written "MOV SP,STACK_AREA+200" with identical results. But by doing it this way, the assembler will load the correct address for the stack top even if we decide to change the size of the stack in line 22.

8-9. `MOV AX,OFFSET A` and `PUSH AX`. We now push the addresses of the arguments onto the stack, in the order of appearance in the CALL statement. Since PUSH does not allow an immediate operand, we have to go again though a general register. The assembler directive "OFFSET" tells the assembler to load the address of A rather than the value of the number stored in A. ("OFFSET" means use the address relative to the beginning of the segment.) The convention of passing the address of an argument, instead of its value or its name, is sometimes called a "call by address."

10-13. `MOV AX,OFFSET SUM` and `PUSH AX` and `MOV AX,OFFSET N` and `PUSH AX`. The addresses of SUM and N are pushed in a similar manner. Notice that no distinction is made between a scalar variable and the first word of an array.

14. `CALL FAR PTR 1800H:0`. CALL a FAR procedure. The current contents of the CS register and the Instruction Pointer (the address NEXT_LOCATION) are pushed onto the stack. Then CS is set to 1800H. ("H" indicates hexadecimal to the assembler just as "&H" does to BASIC. Hex addresses start with a digit, not a letter; for example, 0AH, not AH, so that the assembler can distinguish a number from a name.) The program then jumps to location 0 in a code segment beginning at 18000H. (Remember that segment registers always have four zero bits added at the right.)

15. `CSEG ENDS`. Tell the assembler we are ending the code segment.

16. `DATA_SEGMENT SEGMENT 'DATA'`. Tell the assembler we are beginning the data segment. The compiler is smart enough to know that "OFFSET A" is an address in the data segment and that OFFSET STACK_TOP is an address in the stack segment.

17. `A DW 1000 DUP (?)`. Set aside 1000 uninitialized words for A.

18. `SUM DW ?`. Set aside one uninitialized word for SUM.

19. `N DW 1000`. Set aside one word for N, initialized to 1000.

20. `DATA_SEGMENT ENDS`. End the data segment.

21. `STACK_SEGMENT SEGMENT 'STACK'`. Begin the stack segment.

22. `STACK_AREA DW 100 DUP (?)`. Set aside 100 words for the stack.

23. `STACK_TOP EQU THIS WORD`. STACK_TOP is equivalent to the address appearing after the 100 words allocated for the STACK_AREA.

24. `STACK_SEGMENT ENDS`. End the stack segment.

25. `END`. End the program.

The receiving subroutine finds the DS and SS registers pointing to the data and stack segments defined above. The CS register points to 1800 hex. Most of the important information appears on the stack, which is shown in Figure 8.1. Remember that the 8088 stack actually grows upside down in memory, so that as we push addresses onto the stack, SP moves toward zero. Since we have pushed five words onto the stack (three argument addresses, CS, and NEXT_LOCATION), SP equals (STACK_AREA + 200) − 10.

Acting Like a Called Subroutine

Machine language subroutines called from BASIC must obey a number of rules. The important ones are:

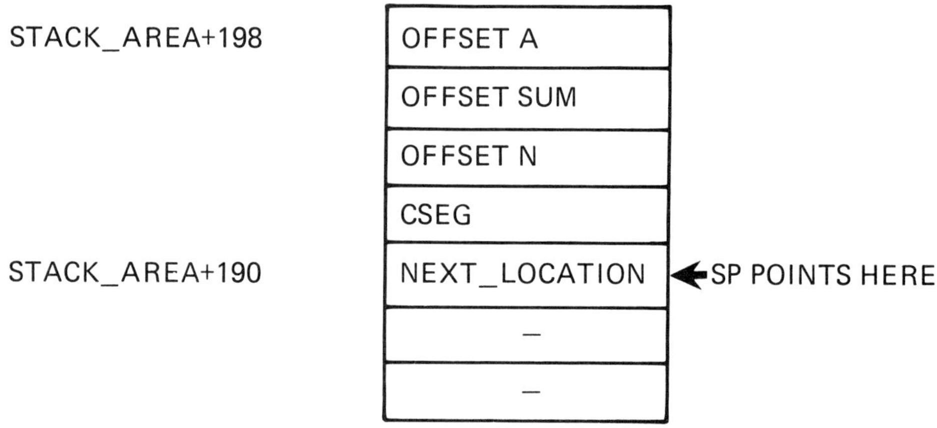

Figure 8.1. Memory stack after subroutine call.

- At entry, CS is set according to the last DEF SEG. The other segment registers point to the beginning of BASIC's data area.
- At exit, all segment registers and registers SP and BP should hold their original values. The other registers, and the flags, may be changed.
- BASIC promises that the stack pointed to by SP will have eight free words. If the subroutine needs a larger stack, it must set up its own.
- The subroutine must pop the argument addresses off the stack before returning.

Let's write a subroutine, to add up an array of integers, in a form that could be called by the code sequence appearing in the preceding section.

```
            PUBLIC SUB
            ASSUME CS:CSEG
CSEG        SEGMENT 'CODE'
SUB         PROC   FAR
            PUSH   BP              ;SAVE BP
            MOV    BP,SP           ;FIND ARGUMENT LIST
            MOV    BX,[BP]+10      ;ADDRESS A
            MOV    SI,[BP]+6       ;ADDRESS N
            MOV    CX,[SI]         ;CX GETS N
            MOV    AX,0            ;CLEAR AX
ADD_LOOP:
            ADD    AX,WORD PTR [BX]        ;ADD A[BX]
            ADD    BX,2                    ;NEXT ELEMENT
            LOOP   ADD_LOOP                ;DO IT AGAIN

            MOV    DI,[BP]+8               ;ADDRESS SUM
            MOV    [DI],AX                 ;STORE SUM
            POP    BP                      ;RESTORE BP
            RET    6                       ;RETURN
```

```
SUB         ENDP                                    ;19
CSEG        ENDS                                    ;20
            END                                     ;21
```

1-3. The `PUBLIC`, `ASSUME`, and `SEGMENT` statements supply the usual information to the assembler.

4. `PROC FAR` tells the assembler that this routine will be called with a FAR CALL; information needed to generate the proper type of return instruction in line 18.

5. `PUSH BP`. Save the value of the BP register by pushing it onto the stack for later retrieval. Note this instruction subtracts two from SP, so SP now equals STACK_AREA + 188.

6. `MOV BP,SP`. Copy the stack pointer, SP, into BP. The instructions that follow retrieve information from the stack. BP can serve as a base register, as in [BP], while SP cannot.

7. `MOV BX,[BP]+10`. Copy the contents of [BP] + 10 into BX. Since BP equals STACK_AREA + 188, [BP] + 10 is STACK_AREA + 198. STACK_AREA + 198 holds OFFSET A, so after this instruction BX holds the address of the first word of A.

8. `MOV SI,[BP]+6`. By the same logic, move the address of N into SI.

9. `MOV CX,[SI]`. Now move the value of N into the count register, CX.

10. `MOV AX,0`. Clear out the accumulator, AX.

11. `ADD_LOOP:`. Label the top of the loop. Notice that this loop does not worry about errors such as negative or zero N nor about the accumulator overflowing. (Not very good programming practice!)

12. `ADD AX,[BX]`. Adds the element of A currently pointed to it by BX into AX. The first time through, this is A(0); the second time, A(1); and so forth.

13. `ADD BX,2`. Increment BX by 2 so it points to the next word.

14. `LOOP ADD_LOOP`. Decrements the count register and jump back up to the top of ADD_LOOP if we haven't run the count down to zero.

15. `MOV DI,[BP]+8`. Move the address of SUM into DI.

16. `MOV [DI],AX`. Move the contents of AX into the address pointed at by the DI register, that is, into SUM.

17. `POP BP`. Now restore the original value of BP. Also, add two to SP.

18. `RET 6`. Set the Instruction Pointer to point to NEXT_LOCATION and set CS equal to CSEG, in the process add four to SP. Add the optional pop value to SP. Now SP equals STACK_AREA + 200, as it did before the subroutine was called.

19-21. `SUB ENDP` and `CSEG ENDS` and `END`. Tell the assembler to close up the procedure, segment, and program.

In coding the subroutine, a pattern appears.

- If the subroutine is called with "n" arguments, then the address of argument "i" is stored in [BP]+6+2*(n−i). In other words, the right-most argument has its address stored at [BP]+6; the right-most-but-one is at [BP]+8; one further to the left is at [BP]+10; and so forth. (These addresses are valid *after* we set BP, as in lines 5 and 6, with a PUSH and a MOV.)

- It takes one instruction to retrieve the address of the argument; two to retrieve the argument's value.
- The last instruction should be RET 2*n, where n is the number of arguments.

Subroutine Relocation and Segment Addressing

The BASIC command BLOAD allows us to load a subroutine at any memory location. It is therefore highly desirable that our 8087 routines be *dynamically relocatable*. We can run into difficulty if the segment addresses at which a routine is initially loaded (see "Loading A Subroutine into Interpreted BASIC") differ from those at which we later BLOAD the routine. Dynamic relocation is automatic for programs which do not explicitly reference segment locations, but is somewhat more complicated otherwise.

For the purposes of this discussion, suppose we had initially loaded SUB with DEF SEG=&H1800 and then BSAVED it from this location with an offset of zero.

Suppose we now load SUB back in at DEF SEG=&H1900. When BASIC calls SUB, it sets the code segment register to &H1900 and the instruction pointer to zero. Execution procedes correctly.

Suppose instead that we load SUB at DEF SEG=&H1900 and offset 125. SUB "thinks" it will find the first instruction at offset zero in the code segment. Actually, the first instruction is at offset 125. However, when we call SUB we specify the offset. BASIC sets the instruction pointer to 125. All the instructions we have used, though not every instruction the 8088 knows, operates relative to the instruction pointer. SUB still executes correctly.

SUB is fully relocatable. What sort of subroutine isn't? Unfortunately, any subroutine that explicitly contains a value for a segment register is not relocatable, since the segment may end up at some other memory location than the one originally specified. This is particularly a problem when we define a data, extra, or stack segment inside a routine.

Consider the following, not very useful routine.

```
EXTRA_SEG SEGMENT 'DATA'                                        ;1
FOOLISH   DW  ?                                                 ;2
EXTRA_SEG ENDS                                                  ;3
```

```
;SUBROUTINE SILLY(JUNK%)
        PUBLIC SILLY                                            ;4
        ASSUME CS:CSEG,ES:EXTRA_SEG                             ;5
CSEG    SEGMENT 'CODE'                                          ;6
SILLY   PROC   FAR                                              ;7
        PUSH   BP                                               ;8
        MOVE   BP,SP                                            ;9

        PUSH   ES              ;POINT ES                        ;10
        MOVE   AX,EXTRA_SEG    ;AT                              ;11
        MOVE   ES,AX           ;EXTRA SEGMENT                   ;12

        MOVE   AX,FOOLISH      ;RETURN WHATEVER                 ;13
        MOVE   DI,[BP]+6       ;NUMBER WAS                      ;14
        MOVE   [DI],AX         ;LYING AROUND                    ;15
        POP    ES                                               ;16
        POP    BP                                               ;17
        RET    2                                                ;18
SILLY   ENDP                                                    ;19
CSEG    ENDS                                                    ;20

        END                                                     ;21
```

This subroutine references the extra segment (if not to any good purpose). Instructions 1-9 and 14-21 are standard. Lines 10, 11, and 12 save ES on the stack and then load the address of EXTRA_SEG into ES. Line 13 copies FOOLISH. (Note that the assembler should be smart enough to use ES to reference FOOLISH.) Subroutine SILLY will work if loaded and used at one location, since the loader will figure out the value for EXTRA_SEG. However, if we relocate SILLY, EXTRA_SEG will no longer be at its original location, and unpredictable consequences may ensue.

We can make SILLY relocatable by having the subroutine figure out for itself how far it's been moved from its original location. The subroutine "thinks" it begins at location 16*CSEG. In truth, when BLOADed by interpreted BASIC, SILLY begins at 16*DEF SEG + offset. Similarly, the subroutine thinks the extra segment begins at 16*EXTRA_SEG, while it actually begins at 16*EXTRA_SEG + (16*DEF SEG + offset − 16*CSEG). We can use this relation to correctly load segment registers. Life is complicated a slight bit more because the only way to find "offset" is by examining the value of the instruction pointer at entry.

The following subroutine, SMART, will work correctly, *as long as the code segment and extra segment are loaded together at a memory location that is an even multiple of 16.*

```
EXTRA_SEG  SEGMENT 'DATA'                                       ;1
FOOLISH    DW   ?                                               ;2
EXTRA_SEG  ENDS                                                 ;3

;SUBROUTINE SMART(JUNK%)
           PUBLIC SMART                                         ;4
           ASSUME CS:CSEG,ES:EXTRA_SEG                          ;5
CSEG  SEGMENT      'CODE'                                       ;6
```

```
FIRST_INST EQU      THIS WORD                                  ;7
SMART      PROC     FAR                                        ;8
           PUSH     BP                                         ;9
           MOV      BP,SP                                      ;10

           PUSH     ES                                         ;11
           CALL     NEXT                                       ;12
NEXT:      POP      AX                                         ;13
           SUB      AX,(OFFSET NEXT)-(OFFSET FIRST_INST)       ;14
           MOV      CL,4                                       ;15
           SHR      AX,CL                                      ;16
           MOV      BX,CS                                      ;17
           ADD      BX,EXTRA_SEG                               ;18
           SUB      BX,CSEG                                    ;19
           ADD      AX,BX                                      ;20
           MOV      ES,AX                                      ;21

           MOV      AX,FOOLISH                                 ;22
           MOV      DI,[BP]+6                                  ;23
           MOV      [DI],AX                                    ;24
           POP      ES                                         ;25
           POP      BP                                         ;26
           RET      2                                          ;27
SMART      ENDP                                                ;28
CSEG       ENDS                                                ;29
           END                                                 ;30
```

Lines 1-6, 8-10, 22-24, and 27-30 are standard.

7. `FIRST_INST EQU THIS WORD`. Define the location of the first instruction in the code segment to be FIRST_INST. (FIRST_INST equals zero here.)

11. `PUSH ES`. Save ES on the stack. Note we don't change BP so argument references don't change.

12-13. `CALL NEXT` and `NEXT: POP AX`. This is a devious way to retrieve the instruction pointer. CALL pushes IP onto the stack. (The instruction pointer will point to the true offset of NEXT, no matter where the routine is located.) POP pops the stack into AX. Now AX holds the true offset of NEXT.

14. `SUB AX,(OFFSET NEXT)-(OFFSET FIRST_INST)`. Now we subtract the expected offset of NEXT from the true offset. AX now holds the number of bytes by which the offset of SMART has changed as compared to the position at which it was originally loaded.

15-16. `MOV CL,4` and `SHR AX,CL`. Divide AX by 16 since we are going to set a segment register. *Notice that if the program was relocated by any number other than an even multiple of 16, the program will bomb in an unpredictable manner.* Nor will any other method work, since the 8088 requires segments to be placed at addresses that are even multiples of 16.

17-19. `MOV BX,CS` and `ADD BX,EXTRA_SEG` and `SUB BX,CSEG`. Figure out how far the code segment has been displaced from its original location and how far the extra segment is from the code segment.

20-21. `ADD AX,BX` and `MOV ES,AX`. Combine the offset and segment correction and set ES.

25. `POP ES`. Restore ES before leaving the routine.

While all this manipulation is a bit of a nuisance, it is worth the extra trouble to be able to more easily load subroutines into BASIC.

- *If you only use a compiler, then relocation is handled by the LINK program and this extra code is unnecessary.*

Loading Assembly Language Programs

At the end of the chapter, we show two complete interactive sessions in which SMART is used in a BASIC program: one session for the interpreted BASIC built into the IBM Personal Computer and one session for IBM's BASIC compiler. Most of the remainder of this chapter describes the general steps involved. These procedures focus more specifically than most of the material in the book on the IBM Personal Computer running PC-DOS. If you have a different machine or different software (especially if you are not using Microsoft software), you may have to adjust these procedures somewhat.

Loading a Routine Into Interpreted BASIC

The assembler transforms an 8087/8088 source program into an *object module*. Several further steps are required to get the routine into a form suitable for BLOADing into BASIC. These steps involve running the program through the LINKer, through DEBUG, and finally through BASIC. Suppose we begin with a program held in file FOO.ASM.

The ASSEMBLER replaces the instructions and (most) addresses with their binary representation and creates a file FOO.OBJ.

LINK is able to combine several different object files. It creates FOO.EXE.

We use DEBUG to load FOO.EXE. DEBUG figures out the actual memory address at which each segment begins. We can also ask DEBUG to tell us where the program begins.

Finally, we use BASIC to BSAVE the routine. Once the routine is BSAVED, we can BLOAD it whenever desired.

The exact procedure for getting from FOO.ASM to the BSAVEd version is described in Appendix C of the IBM PC BASIC manual. (The descriptions of LINK and DEBUG in the DOS manual supply some additional information.) The exact procedure may vary according to which version of DOS and BASIC you use. The steps described below usually work for the author.

1. Assemble FOO.ASM. (Be warned that the assembler occasionally produces erroneous error messages.)
2. Link FOO.OBJ. Tell the linker to load HIGH (LOW is the default). Get a MAP file from LINK so that you can find the total length of the output file, FOO.EXE. If FOO doesn't have a stack segment, LINK will report its absence as an error. Ignore this message.
3. Enter the DEBUGer with DEBUG BASIC.COM.
4. Type "r" to examine the registers. Copy down the values of CS, SS, IP, and SP.
5. Enter "N FOO.EXE". Type "L". This tells DEBUG to load your routine.
6. Type "r" again. Copy down the new values of CS and IP.
7. Restore SS and SP by using the "r" command. Enter "RSS". The computer will tell you the current value of SS. Respond by entering the value of SS you copied down in step 4. Now enter "RSP" and respond to the computer with the value of SP from step 4.
8. Enter "g=CS:IP" where CS and IP are replaced by the values copied down in step 4.
9. BASIC should start up now, possibly with an irrelevant warning about a DIRECT STATEMENT IN FILE. Execute DEF SEG=cs, where cs is the value of CS copied down in step 6. Execute a BSAVE filespec,offset,length command; where filespec gives the name of the file in which you wish to save the routine, offset is the value of IP from step 6, and length is the length in bytes of FOO.

From now on, to use FOO from BASIC just do a "DEF SEG=" and "BLOAD filespec".

By the way, all that this confusing detail accomplishes is to stick seven bytes at the beginning of the final file. You can avoid use of Debug entirely by coding these bytes directly into your program. Unfortunately, doing so makes the object files incompatible with compiled BASIC. For this reason, we won't pursue this method here. However, if you use only the BASIC interpreter, take a look at IBM's *BASIC Reference Manual*, appendix B (version 3.0).

Loading a Routine Into Compiled BASIC

Combining an assembled program with the output of the PC-BASIC compiler is considerably easier than loading the program into interpreted BASIC.

1. Assemble FOO.ASM. Include subroutine names in a PUBLIC statement.
2. Compile the BASIC program. Omit DEF SEG and BLOAD statements. You need not worry about the location of the subroutine in memory.

3. LINK the output of the BASIC compiler together with FOO.
4. Execute the ".EXE" module.

Interactive Session for Interpreted BASIC

Assume that the routine SMART is in file FOO.ASM on disk B:. The following BASIC program is in a file USEFOO.BAS, also on disk B:.

```
10 DEF SEG=&H1800
20 BLOAD "B:FOO.SAV",0
30 SMART%=0
40 FOOLISH%=9999
50 PRINT FOOLISH%
60 CALL SMART%(FOOLISH%)
70 PRINT FOOLISH%
80 END
```

A sample interactive session for loading FOO into interpreted BASIC follows. Your responses have been underlined.

```
B>A:MASM FOO;
THE IBM PERSONAL COMPUTER MACRO ASSEMBLER
VERSION 1.00 (C)COPYRIGHT IBM CORP 1981

0004 E8 0007 R                       CALL NEXT
     ;12
E R R O R   ---          64:NEAR JMP/CALL TO DIFFERENT CS

WARNING  SEVERE
ERRORS   ERRORS
0        1
B>A:LINK FOO

IBM PERSONAL COMPUTER LINKER
VERSION 1.10 (C)COPYRIGHT IBM CORP 1982

OBJECT MODULES [.OBJ]:FOO/HIGH/MAP
RUN RILE [FOO.EXE]:
LIST FILE [NUL.MAP]: FOO;
WARNING: NO STACK SEGMENT

THERE WAS 1 ERROR DETECTED.
```

The assembler produces the correct code despite this message

Ignore these messages

```
B>TYPE FOO.MAP
LOADING HIGH
WARNING: NO STACK SEGMENT
START     STOP      LENGTH    NAME                   CLASS
00000H    0002AH    002BH     CSEG                   CODE
00030H    00031H    0002H     EXTRA_SEG              DATA

 ADDRESS        PUBLICS BY NAME

0000:0000       SMART
```

NOTE: Total length is 31H

offset of Smart is Ø into CSEG

```
  ADDRESS      PUBLICS BY VALUE

 0000:0000     SMART

 B>A:DEBUG A:BASIC.COM
 -R
AX=0000  BX=0000  CX=3F80  DX=0000  SP=FFFE  BP=0000  SI=0000  DI=0000
DS=0905  ES=0905  SS=0905  CS=0905  IP=0100  NV UP DI PL NZ NA PO NC
0905:0100 E9E338        JMP     39E6
 -N FOO.EXE
 -L
 -R
AX=FF47  BX=0000  CX=0080  DX=0000  SP=0000  BP=0000  SI=0000  DI=0000
DS=0905  ES=0905  SS=4F94  CS=4F94  IP=0000  NV UP DI PL NZ NA PO NC
4F94:0000 55            PUSH    BP
 -RSS
 SS 4F94
 :905
 -RSP
 SP 0000
 :FFFE
 -G=905:100                      The screen clears here

 DIRECT STATEMENT IN FILE  ---- Ignore this message
 OK
 DEF SEG=&H4F94
 OK
 BSAVE "FOO.SAV",0,&H31
 OK
 SYSTEM
 PROGRAM TERMINATED NORMALLY
 -Q                              The screen clears here

 B>A:BASIC
 THE IBM PERSONAL COMPUTER BASIC
 VERSION D1.10 COPYRIGHT IBM CORP. 1981, 1982
 61371 BYTES FREE
 OK
 LOAD "USEFOO"
 OK
 RUN
  9999
  0
 OK
```

Interactive Session For Compiled BASIC

Assume that the routine SMART is in file FOO.ASM on disk B:. The following BASIC program is in a file USEFOO.BAS, also on disk B:.

```
10 FOOLISH%=9999
20 PRINT FOOLISH%
30 CALL SMART(FOOLISH%)
```

```
30 CALL SMART(FOOLISH%)
40 PRINT FOOLISH%
50 END
```

A sample interactive session for loading FOO into compiled BASIC follows. Your responses have been underlined.

```
B>A:MASM FOO;
THE IBM PERSONAL COMPUTER MACRO ASSEMBLER
VERSION 1.00 (C)COPYRIGHT IBM CORP 1981

 0004 E8 0007 R            CALL NEXT                      The assembler
      ;12                                                 produces the
 E R R O R    ---     64:NEAR JMP/CALL TO DIFFERENT CS    correct code despite
                                                          this message
WARNING SEVERE
ERRORS  ERRORS
0       1

B>A:BASCOM USEFOO;  <----------------  The screen clears here

IBM PERSONAL COMPUTER BASIC COMPILER

(C)COPYRIGHT IBM CORP 1982 VERSION 1.00
(C)COPYRIGHT MICROSOFT, INC. 1982

22151 BYTES AVAILABLE
22032 BYTES FREE
0 WARNING  ERROR(S)
0 SEVERE   ERROR(S)

B>A:LINK USEFOO+FOO;

IBM PERSONAL COMPUTER LINKER
VERSION 1.10 (C)COPYRIGHT IBM CORP 1982
B>USEFOO
9999
0
```

Linking with Other Languages

What about linking assembly language routines with FORTRAN or Pascal or some other language? The principles are no different from those used in linking to BASIC, but the details may be quite different. Each language passes argument to subroutines and stores data a little differently. BASIC stores all data in the data segment. Turbo Pascal, for example, stores data in both the data segment and the stack segment. When calling a subroutine, Turbo Pascal passes both the segment address and the offset of each argument. BASIC passed only the offset. Microsoft FORTRAN also passes both the segment address and the offset. However, in FORTRAN, it is possible that each argument will be in a segment of its very own.

The lesson is that an assembly language routine which works in one language won't necessarily work in another. All the routines in our *Cook-*

book work with Microsoft interpreted and compiled BASIC. If you want to use them with another language, you will have to fiddle with them a little bit.

9

Simple 8087 Routines

Several fairly simple 8087 routines are presented in this chapter. The purpose of the presentation is twofold. First, the routines themselves are quite useful. For example, our first program can be called from BASIC to add up a series of numbers. Second, we illustrate a number of principles of 8087 subroutine programming including:

- Indexing through a single array.
- Using single precision and double precision arithmetic.
- Indexing through multiple arrays.

The Cookbook—Chapter 9

Program:	**SUM**
Purpose:	Sums up a single precision array.
Call:	CALL SUM(ARRAY(0),N,DSUM).
Input:	ARRAY—single precision array.
	N—integer number of elements of ARRAY.
Output:	DSUM—double precision sum of ARRAY.
Language:	8087/8088 assembly language.
Program:	**PRODUCT**
Purpose:	Product of elements of a single precision array.
Call:	CALL PRODUCT(ARRAY(0),N,DPRODUCT).
Input:	ARRAY—single precision array.
	N—integer number of elements of ARRAY.
Output:	DPRODUCT—double precision product of ARRAY.
Language:	8087/8088 assembly language.
Program:	**GSUM**
Purpose:	Sums up an integer, single, or double precision array.
Call:	CALL GSUM(ARRAY(0),TYPE,N,SUM).
Input:	ARRAY—array to be summed.
	TYPE—integer variable giving the length of one element of ARRAY

	N—integer number of elements of ARRAY.
Output:	SUM—double precision sum of ARRAY.
Language:	8087/8088 assembly language.
Program:	**VADD**
Purpose:	Adds two single precision vectors.
Call:	CALL VADD(A(0),B(0),C(0),N).
Input:	A—input array.
	B—input array.
	N—integer number of elements of A,B,C.
Output:	C—output array, C = A + B.
Language:	8087/8088 assembly language.
Program:	**VADD3**
Purpose:	Adds three single precision vectors.
Call:	CALL VADD3(A(0),B(0),C(0),D(0),N).
Input:	A—input array.
	B—input array.
	C—input array.
	N—integer number of elements of A,B,C,D.
Output:	D—output array, C = A + B + D.
Language:	8087/8088 assembly language.
Program:	**VSET**
Purpose:	Sets array to a constant.
Call:	CALL VSET(A(0),SCALAR,N).
Input:	SCALAR—single precision constant.
	N—integer number of elements of A.
Output:	A—output array, A = SCALAR.
Language:	8087/8088 assembly language.
Program:	**ADDSC**
Purpose:	Adds scalar to single precision array.
Call:	CALL ADDSC(A(0),SCALAR,B(0),N).
Input:	A—input array.
	SCALAR—single precision constant.
	N—integer number of elements of A.
Output:	B—output array, B = A + SCALAR.
Language:	8087/8088 assembly language.
Program:	**SQRT**
Purpose:	Takes square root of vector.
Call:	CALL SQRT(A(0),B(0),N).
Input:	A—input array.
	N—integer number of elements of A,B.
Output:	B—output array, B = SQR(A).
Language:	8087/8088 assembly language.
Program:	**GCOPY**
Purpose:	Copies integer, single, or double precision array.
Call:	CALL GCOPY(A(0),B(0),TYPE,N).

Input: A—input array.
TYPE—integer giving length of element of A.
N—integer number of elements of A,B.
Output: B—output array, B=A.
Language: 8087/8088 assembly language.

Program: **GBCOPY**
Purpose: Copies integer, single, or double precision array, backwards.
Call: CALL GBCOPY(A(0),B(0),TYPE,N).
Input: A—input array.
TYPE—integer giving length of element of A.
N—integer number of elements of A,B.
Output: B—output array, B=A.
Language: 8088 assembly language.

Program: **GADDSAFR**
Purpose: Adds two vectors, with error checking.
Call: CALL GADDSAFR(A(0),B(0),C(0),TYPEA,TYPEB, TYPEC,N,IER).
Input: A—input array.
B—input array.
TYPEA—integer giving length of element of A.
TYPEB—integer giving length of element of B.
TYPEC—integer giving length of element of C.
N—integer number of elements of A,B,C.
Output: C—output array, C=A+B.
IER—integer error indicator.
Language: 8087/8088 assembly language.

Program: **REALERR**
Purpose: Check array for invalid data.
Call: CALL REALERR(ARRAY(0),TYPE,N,IFDEN,IFINF, IFNAN,ELEMENT).
Input: ARRAY—input array (single or double precision).
TYPE—integer giving length of element of ARRAY.
N—integer number of elements of ARRAY.
Output: IFDEN—integer (−1 if denormal found).
IFINF—integer (−1 if infinity found).
IFNAN—integer (−1 if Not-A-Normal found).
ELEMENT—integer, index of last invalid data.
Language: 8087/8088 assembly language.

Program: **DENTO0**
Purpose: Replace denormal values with zero.
Call: CALL DENTO0(ARRAY(0),TYPE,N).
Input: ARRAY—input array (single or double precision).
TYPE—integer giving length of element of ARRAY.
N—integer number of elements of ARRAY.

Output:	ARRAY—denormals replaced with 0.
Language:	8087/8088 assembly language.

Array Indexing

Our first 8087 subroutine sums a series of numbers and returns their total. Assuming that a single precision array named ARRAY, dimensioned ARRAY(N − 1), has been defined elsewhere, that N has been set equal to the number of elements of ARRAY, and that DSUM is a double precision variable, a BASIC instruction sequence might look like this:

```
10 DSUM=0
20   FOR I=0 TO N-1
30   DSUM=DSUM+ARRAY(I)
40   NEXT I
```

An equivalent 8087 routine appears below. Assuming the routine has been loaded into memory at the location SUM, we could call it from BASIC with the instruction

```
10 CALL SUM(ARRAY(0),N,DSUM)
```

The 8087 routine has three logical sections. First, it must accept the information passed to it from BASIC. Secondly, the routine calculates the sum of the array elements. Third, the answer is passed back into the BASIC variable DSUM. Notice that we execute an FWAIT before returning from the subroutine. The FWAIT guarantees that the sum will have reached memory before the calling program attempts to access it.

```
;SUBROUTINE SUM(ARRAY,N,DSUM)
; ASSUMPTIONS: ARRAY IS A SINGLE PRECISION ARRAY OF LENGTH N
;              N IS AN INTEGER
;              DSUM IS DOUBLE PRECISION
;

          PUBLIC   SUM
CSEG      SEGMENT  'CODE'
          ASSUME   CS:CSEG
SUM       PROC     FAR
          PUSH     BP
          MOV      BP,SP
          MOV      BX,[BP]+10          ;BX=ADDR(ARRAY)
          MOV      SI,[BP]+8           ;SI=ADDR(N)
          MOV      CX,[SI]             ;CX=N
;
;NOW ALL SET UP TO GO
          FLDZ                         ;INITIALIZE ST=0
          CMP      CX,0H               ;HOPE N > 0
          JLE      DONE
;THE NEXT 3 INSTRUCTIONS DO ALL THE HARD WORK
```

```
ADD_LOOP:  FADD     DWORD PTR [BX]   ;DWORD=> SINGLE
                                     PRECISION
           ADD      BX,4             ;READY FOR NEXT
                                     ELEMENT
           LOOP     ADD_LOOP

DONE:
;
;NOW FILE ANSWER BACK IN DSUM
           MOV      DI,[BP]+6        ;DI=ADDR(DSUM)
           FSTP     QWORD PTR [DI]   ;QWORD=> DOUBLE
                                     PRECISION
                                     ;DSUM IS NOW PUT AWAY
           POP      BP
           FWAIT                     ;BE SURE 8087 IS DONE
           RET      6
SUM        ENDP
CSEG       ENDS
           END
```

How long does the addition routine take? Essentially, all the execution time is in the three-instruction "ADD_LOOP." (Calling the subroutine from BASIC, and the beginning and end of the routine obviously takes a little time. But this overhead time is inconsequential for large N.)

The FADD instruction takes approximately 25 microseconds. The ADD instruction uses approximately 1 microsecond. The LOOP instruction requires about 4 microseconds. Thus the routine should take about 30 microseconds per array element. Right?

Wrong, actually. The 8087 and 8088 run in parallel. So, while the 8087 is adding one number, the 8088 is adding to the BX register, decrementing the count in register CX, testing CX, and looping back up. Hence, the routine takes about 25 microseconds per element. Adding 10,000 single precision numbers takes just under one-fourth of a second. How long would a comparable BASIC routine take? Without the 8087, about 46 seconds.

In addition to the speed advantage, the 8087 produces a more accurate answer because it accumulates in 80-bit temporary real format rather than 64-bit double precision.

SUM is quite a useful subroutine. Of more general importance, SUM illustrates how to write a routine that indexes through a single array. We use a three-part trick. First we load the address of the array into a convenient base or index register (we could have used SI or DI instead of BX) and the count into the CX register. Second, we add four to BX (and so forth) at each step. Third, we use the LOOP instruction to count off the steps.

Operations other than addition are easily written using the same procedure. For example, to take the product of an array of numbers we could do:

```
10 DPRODUCT=1
20 FOR I=0 TO N-1
30 DPRODUCT=DPRODUCT*ARRAY(I)
40 NEXT I
```

or:

```
;SUBROUTINE PRODUCT(ARRAY,N,DPRODUCT)
; ASSUMPTIONS: ARRAY IS A SINGLE PRECISION ARRAY OF LENGTH N
;              N IS AN INTEGER
;              DPRODUCT IS DOUBLE PRECISION
;
            PUBLIC     PRODUCT
CSEG        SEGMENT    'CODE'
            ASSUME     CS:CSEG
PRODUCT     PROC       FAR
            PUSH       BP
            MOV        BP,SP
            MOV        BX,[BP]+10        ;BX=ADDR(ARRAY)
            MOV        SI,[BP]+8         ;SI=ADDR(N)
            MOV        CX,[SI]           ;CX=N
;
;NOW ALL SET UP TO GO
            FLD1                         ;INITIALIZE ST=1
                                         ;FLD1 PUSHES A 1, JUST AS
                                         ;FLDZ PUSHES A 0

            CMP        CX,0H             ;HOPE N > 0
            JLE        DONE              ;IF NOT, RETURN 1
MULT_LOOP:  FMUL       DWORD PTR [BX]
            ADD        BX,4              ;READY FOR NEXT ELEMENT
            LOOP       MULT_LOOP
DONE:
;
;NOW FILE ANSWER BACK IN PRODUCT

            MOV        DI,[BP]+6         ;DI=ADDR(DPRODUCT)
            FSTP       QWORD PTR [DI]    ;PRODUCT IS NOW PUT AWAY
            POP        BP
            FWAIT                        ;BE SURE 8087 IS DONE
            RET        6
PRODUCT     ENDP
CSEG        ENDS
            END
```

The FMUL instruction takes approximately 29 microseconds. Multiplying 10,000 single precision numbers takes just over one-fourth of a second. A comparable BASIC routine takes about 56 seconds. Accuracy of the 8087 PRODUCT subroutine will, under some circumstances, considerably exceed the accuracy of the equivalent BASIC code. The 8087 temporary real exponent allows a much greater range than the double precision exponent, so intermediate overflows or underflows are much less likely to occur with the 8087 routine.

Double Precision Arguments

The choice between single precision and double precision arithmetic requires a tradeoff between accuracy and memory space. Double precision numbers take up twice as much space as single precision numbers, but are somewhat more than twice as accurate. Good numerical programming practice dictates using double precision throughout. Unfortunately, because of storage limitations this is rarely practical. In fact, there is a "folk theorem" to the effect that problem size expands to use up all available space. The following stages of compromise are recommended:

1. If the problem can be done entirely in double precision, do it that way.
2. Hold raw input and final results in single precision—everything else in double precision. There is little loss to storing original input in single precision—real data can rarely be measured with the seven significant digits provided for by single precision storage. The problem with single precision is the loss of accuracy from cumulative errors. Doing all the calculations in double precision is almost as good as holding everything in double precision.
3. Retain critical intermediate steps in double precision. Delay conversion into single precision as long as possible.

Of course, the 8087's 80-bit temporary real format is even more accurate than double precision. The most accurate answers are found by doing as many intermediate calculations as possible within the 8087, storing only final results in memory.

In practice, programs use both single and double precision. One advantage of BASIC is that programs "know" whether variables are single or double precision. Our 8087 routines need to be told. There are two ways, both valuable, to "tell" our routines what precision to use. First, we can write separate routines, one for single and one for double precision. Second, we can write routines which handle both cases and include an extra argument to tell the routine which type of data is being used. The first is easier to write, but the flexibility of the second is sometimes worth the extra effort.

Changing a single precision routine to double precision requires only two simple steps: change the 8087 instructions to reference double precision memory, and change the step size to eight rather than four bytes. Thus, we can change subroutine SUM into a double precision subroutine DSUM with the following amendments:

`FADD QWORD PTR [BX]` instead of `FADD DWORD PTR [BX]`
and

`ADD BX,8` instead of `ADD BX,4`

The second approach to the problem of variable precision is to pass the needed information on to the subroutine. As long as we're solving this problem, we may as well make things a bit more general. Subroutine GSUM accepts a single precision, double precision, or integer vector.

```
;SUBROUTINE GSUM(ARRAY,TYPE,N,SUM)
; ASSUMPTIONS: ARRAY IS AN ARRAY OF LENGTH N
;              TYPE IS AN INTEGER: 2-INTEGER 4-SINGLE 8-
                DOUBLE
;              N IS AN INTEGER
;              SUM IS DOUBLE PRECISION
;
          PUBLIC  GSUM
CSEG      SEGMENT 'CODE'
          ASSUME  CS:CSEG
GSUM      PROC    FAR
          PUSH    BP
          MOV     BP,SP
          MOV     BX,[BP]+12        ;BX=ADDR(ARRAY)
          MOV     SI,[BP]+10        ;SI=ADDR(TYPE)
          MOV     AX,[SI]           ;AX=TYPE
          MOV     SI,[BP]+8         ;SI=ADDR(N)
          MOV     CX,[SI]           ;CX=N
;
;NOW ALL SET UP TO GO
          FLDZ                      ;INITIALIZE ST=0
          CMP     CX,0H             ;HOPE N > 0
          JLE     DONE
;
ADD_LOOP:
          CMP     AX,2              ;IS IT INTEGER?
          JNE     NOT_INTEGER
          FIADD   WORD PTR [BX]
          JMP     NEXT_ELEMENT
NOT_INTEGER:
          CMP     AX,4              ;IS IT SINGLE?
          JNE     NOT_SINGLE
          FADD    DWORD PTR [BX]
          JMP     NEXT_ELEMENT
NOT_SINGLE:                         ;BETTER BE DOUBLE
          FADD    QWORD PTR [BX]
;
NEXT_ELEMENT:
          ADD     BX,AX             ;READY FOR NEXT ELEMENT
          LOOP    ADD_LOOP
DONE:
;NOW FILE ANSWER BACK IN SUM
          MOV     DI,[BP]+6         ;DI GET ADDRESS OF SUM
          FSTP    QWORD PTR [DI]    ;SUM IS NOW PUT AWAY
          POP     BP
          FWAIT                     ;BE SURE 8087 IS DONE
          RET     8
GSUM      ENDP
CSEG      ENDS
          END
```

Subroutine GSUM will accept any of the three BASIC numeric variable types. GSUM is slightly more complex than SUM and we have to pass it one extra argument. It may look like GSUM will also be slower, since it has to check TYPE each time through and also jump around extra instructions. However, the comparison and jump only take about five microseconds, so the 8088 executes these instructions while the 8087 is working on the addition.

If you have a recent version of BASIC, you can "automate" passing the TYPE to GSUM by using the VARPTR$ function. For example:

```
DESCRIPTOR$=VARPTR$(ARRAY(0))  'INTERNAL DESCRIPTION OF ARRAY
TYPE$=LEFT$(VARPTR$,1)         'FIRST CHARACTER IS TYPE
TYPE%=ASC(TYPE$)               'NEED INTEGER 2, 4, OR 8
CALL GSUM%(ARRAY(0),TYPE%,N%,SUM)
```

Indexing Through Multiple Arrays

In the routines above, we used the BX register to index ARRAY. This procedure works with a single array, but more complicated problems may require us to keep track of several indexes. Up to three indexes may be kept in the registers BX, SI, and DI. In addition, registers AX, DX, and CX are convenient for holding temporary values.

Our next subroutine adds two single precision vectors, returning a single precision vector result.

```
;SUBROUTINE VADD(A,B,C,N)
; ASSUMPTIONS: A,B,C ARE SINGLE PRECISION ARRAYS OF LENGTH N
;              N IS AN INTEGER
;
;
          PUBLIC    VADD
CSEG      SEGMENT   'CODE'
          ASSUME    CS:CSEG
VADD      PROC      FAR
          PUSH      BP
          MOV       BP,SP
          MOV       SI,[BP]+6         ;SI=ADDR(N)
          MOV       CX,[SI]           ;CX=N
          MOV       BX,[BP]+12        ;BX=ADDR(A)
          MOV       SI,[BP]+10        ;SI=ADDR(B)
          MOV       DI,[BP]+8         ;DI=ADDR(C)
;
;NOW ALL SET UP TO GO
          CMP       CX,0H             ;HOPE N > 0
          JLE       DONE
ADD_LOOP:
          FLD       DWORD PTR [BX]    ;LOAD A(I)
          ADD       BX,4              ;READY FOR NEXT A
          FADD      DWORD PTR [SI]    ;ADD B(I)
          ADD       SI,4              ;READY FOR NEXT ELEMENT
```

```
                FSTP      DWORD PTR [DI]   ;C(I)=A(I)+B(I)
                ADD       DI,4             ;READY FOR NEXT C
                LOOP      ADD_LOOP
    DONE:
    ;
                POP       BP
                FWAIT                      ;BE SURE 8087 IS DONE
                RET       8
    VADD        ENDP
    CSEG        ENDS
                END
```

Subroutine VADD requires just over half a second to add two 10,000 long vectors. Note that while we have specified three vectors, nothing prevents A and B or A and C, or even all three from being the same vector. Thus the command CALL VADD(A(0),A(0),A(0),N) doubles each element of A.

Creating routines to perform subtraction, multiplication, and division requires us only to change the 8087 addition instruction to an 8087 subtraction, or other type of instruction. Thus we can change one line in VADD:

```
C=A+B    :    "FADD DWORD PTR [SI]"
```

to make VSUB:

```
C=A-B    :    "FSUB DWORD PTR [SI]"
```

or to make VMULT:

```
C=A*B    :    "FMUL DWORD PTR [SI]"
```

or to make VDIV:

```
C=A/B    :    "FDIV DWORD PTR [SI]"
```

(Note VMULT and VDIV perform element-by-element operations, not "matrix operations.")

The same technique we used for changing SUM into GSUM can be used to change VADD into a routine for single precision or double precision or integer vector addition.

After we have more than three vectors, we run out of index registers. We can program around this limit through use of the 8088's ability to double index. In the next program, the address of each array is loaded into BX just before we need to reference the array. The array element is indexed in SI. Routine VADD3 adds three single precision vectors and returns the result in a fourth.

```
;SUBROUTINE VADD3(A,B,C,D,N)
;  ASSUMPTIONS:  A,B,C,D ARE SINGLE PRECISION ARRAYS OF
                    LENGTH N
;                N IS AN INTEGER
;
```

```
            VADD3       PUBLIC
CSEG        SEGMENT     'CODE'
            ASSUME      CS:CSEG
VADD3       PROC        FAR
            PUSH        BP
            MOV         BP,SP
            MOV         SI,[BP]+6               ;SI=ADDR(N)
            MOV         CX,[SI]                 ;CX=N
            MOV         SI,0                    ;SI=0
;
;NOW ALL SET UP TO GO
            CMP         CX,0H                   ;HOPE N > 0
            JLE         DONE
ADD_LOOP:
            MOV         BX,[BP]+14              ;BX=ADDR(A)
            FLD         DWORD PTR [BX][SI]      ;LOAD A(I)
            MOV         BX,[BP]+12              ;BX=ADDR(B)
            FADD        DWORD PTR [BX][SI]      ;ADD B(I)
            MOV         BX,[BP]+10              ;BX=ADDR(C)
            FADD        DWORD PTR [BX][SI]      ;ADD C(I)
            MOV         BX,[BP]+8               ;BX=ADDR(D)
            FSTP        DWORD PTR [BX][SI]      ;D(I)=C(I)+A(I)+B(I)
            ADD         SI,4                    ;READY NEXT ELEMENT
            LOOP        ADD_LOOP
DONE:
;
            POP         BP
            FWAIT                               ;BE SURE 8087 IS DONE
            RET         10
VADD3       ENDP
CSEG        ENDS
            END
```

Scalar Routines

Mathematical operations frequently involve a scalar and a vector. ("Scalar" is the word mathematicians use for a single number, as opposed to an entire vector of numbers.) The simplest example would be setting an entire vector to a constant, as in A=5. Subroutine VSET performs this service. VSET first loads the value SCALAR onto the 8087 stack and then copies the 8087 register ST into each element of A.

```
;SUBROUTINE VSET(A,SCALAR,N)
; ASSUMPTIONS: A IS A SINGLE PRECISION ARRAY OF LENGTH N
;              SCALAR IS SINGLE PRECISION
;              N IS AN INTEGER
;
            PUBLIC      VSET
CSEG        SEGMENT     'CODE'
            ASSUME      CS:CSEG
```

```
VSET        PROC        FAR
            PUSH        BP
            MOV         BP,SP
            MOV         SI,[BP]+6        ;SI=ADDR(N)
            MOV         CX,[SI]          ;CX=N
            MOV         BX,[BP]+10       ;BX=ADDR(A)
            MOV         SI,[BP]+8        ;SI=ADDR(SCALAR)
            FLD         DWORD PTR [SI]   ;PUSH SCALAR ONTO STACK
;NOW ALL SET UP TO GO
            CMP         CX,0H            ;HOPE N > 0
            JLE         DONE
VSET_LOOP:
            FST         DWORD PTR [BX]   ;STORE A(I)
            ADD         BX,4             ;READY FOR NEXT A
            LOOP        VSET_LOOP
DONE:
;
            FSTP        ST(0)            ;GET RID OF SCALAR
            POP         BP
            FWAIT                        ;BE SURE 8087 IS DONE
            RET         6
VSET        ENDP
CSEG        ENDS
            END
```

A typical mathematical operation is to add a scalar to every element of a vector. Routine ADDSC performs this function.

```
;SUBROUTINE ADDSC(A,SCALAR,B,N)
; ASSUMPTIONS: A,B ARE SINGLE PRECISION ARRAYS OF LENGTH N
;
                SCALAR IS SINGLE PRECISION
;               N IS AN INTEGER
;
            PUBLIC      ADDSC
CSEG        SEGMENT     'CODE'
            ASSUME      CS:CSEG
ADDSC       PROC        FAR
            PUSH        BP
            MOV         BP,SP
            MOV         SI,[BP]+6        ;SI=ADDR(N)
            MOV         CX,[SI]          ;CX=N
            MOV         BX,[BP]+12       ;BX=ADDR(A)
            MOV         SI,[BP]+10       ;SI=ADDR(SCALAR)
            FLD         DWORD PTR [SI]   ;PUSH SCALAR ONTO STACK
            MOV         SI,[BP]+8        ;SI=ADDR(B)
;NOW ALL SET UP TO GO
            CMP         CX,0H            ;HOPE N > 0
            JLE         DONE
ADD_LOOP:
            FLD         DWORD PTR [BX]   ;LOAD A(I)
            ADD         BX,4             ;READY FOR NEXT A
```

```
            FADD        ST,ST(1)          ;ADD SCALAR
            FSTP        DWORD PTR [SI]    ;B(I)=A(I)+SCALAR
            ADD         SI,4              ;READY FOR NEXT B
            LOOP        ADD_LOOP
DONE:
;
            FSTP        ST(0)             ;GET RID OF SCALAR
            POP         BP
            FWAIT                         ;BE SURE 8087 IS DONE
            RET         8
ADDSC       ENDP
CSEG        ENDS
            END
```

Adapting ADDSC for subtraction, multiplication, and division is straightforward. (Remember, of course, that "A−SCALAR" is quite different from "SCALAR−A!")

Unary Operations

Operations requiring only one argument are said to be "unary" (as opposed to two-argument "binary" operations such as "A+B"). For example we might want to find the square root, absolute value, or negative of the elements of an array. Routine SQRT, which we used for timing examples in Part I (Chapters 1–4), computes B=SQR(A).

```
;SUBROUTINE SQRT(A,B,N)
; ASSUMPTIONS: A,B ARE SINGLE PRECISION ARRAYS OF LENGTH N
;              N IS AN INTEGER
;
            PUBLIC      SQRT
CSEG        SEGMENT     'CODE'
            ASSUME      CS:CSEG
SQRT        PROC        FAR
            PUSH        BP
            MOV         BP,SP
            MOV         SI,[BP]+6         ;SI=ADDR(N)
            MOV         CX,[SI]           ;CX=N
            MOV         BX,[BP]+10        ;BX=ADDR(A)
            MOV         SI,[BP]+8         ;SI=ADDR(B)
;NOW ALL SET UP TO GO
            CMP         CX,0H             ;HOPE N > 0
            JLE         DONE
SQRT_LOOP:
            FLD         DWORD PTR [BX]    ;LOAD A(I)
            ADD         BX,4
                                          ;READY FOR NEXT A
            FSQRT                         ;FIND SQRT(A(I))
            FSTP        DWORD PTR [SI]    ;B(I)=SQRT(A(I))
            ADD         SI,4              ;READY FOR NEXT B
            LOOP        SQRT_LOOP
```

```
DONE:
;
            POP       BP
            FWAIT                         ;BE SURE 8087 IS DONE
            RET       6
SQRT        ENDP
CSEG        ENDS
            END
```

Routine SQRT is easily changed to compute absolute value or to yield the negative of the input vector by changing FSQRT to FABS or FCHS.

Utility Routines

The speed of the routines above reflects both the 8087's prodigious mathematical ability and the vast speed advantage of 8088 assembly language code over BASIC. It can be very useful to use assembly language routines even for such "non-computational" tasks as copying one array of numbers into another. We can use the 8087's automatic precision conversion to allow the transfer between single precision, double precision, and integer arrays as a bonus.

The BASIC code

```
10 DIM A(4999),B(4999)
20 N%=5000
30    FOR I=0 TO N%-1
40    B(I)=A(I)
50    NEXT I
```

takes about 18 seconds or more to execute, even if we rewrite the code all on one line, for maximum efficiency (and minimum clarity). We would actually be better off with the code

```
10 DIM A(4999),B(4999)
20 N%=5000:SCALAR=0
30 CALL ADDSC(A(0),SCALAR,B(0),N%)
```

which would only take about a quarter of a second, despite its 5,000 useless addition operations! For greater convenience, we create a routine GCOPY that not only copies one array into another, but also handles type conversions for us.

```
;SUBROUTINE GCOPY(A,B,TYPEA,TYPEB,N)
; ASSUMPTIONS: A,B ARE ARRAYS OF LENGTH N
;              TYPEA IS AN INTEGER: 2-INTEGER 4-SINGLE 8-
;               DOUBLE
;              TYPEB "
;              N IS AN INTEGER
;
           PUBLIC    GCOPY
```

```
CSEG        SEGMENT     'CODE'
            ASSUME      CS:CSEG
GCOPY       PROC        FAR
            PUSH        BP
            MOV         BP,SP
            MOV         SI,[BP]+10          ;SI=ADDR(TYPEA)
            MOV         AX,[SI]             ;AX=TYPEA
            MOV         SI,[BP]+8           ;SI=ADDR(TYPEB)
            MOV         DX,[SI]             ;DX=TYPEB
            MOV         SI,[BP]+6           ;SI=ADDR(N)
            MOV         CX,[SI]             ;CX=N
            MOV         BX,[BP]+14          ;BX=ADDR(A)
            MOV         SI,[BP]+12          ;SI=ADDR(B)
;
;NOW ALL SET UP TO GO
            CMP         CX,0H               ;HOPE N > 0
            JLE         DONE
;
COPY_LOOP:
            CMP         AX,2                ;IS A INTEGER?
            JNE         A_NOT_INTEGER
            FILD        WORD PTR [BX]
            JMP         STORE_IT
A_NOT_INTEGER:
            CMP         AX,4                ;IS A SINGLE?
            JNE         A_NOT_SINGLE
            FLD         DWORD PTR [BX]
            JMP         STORE_IT
A_NOT_SINGLE:                               ;BETTER BE DOUBLE
            FLD         QWORD PTR [BX]
;
STORE_IT:
            ADD         BX,AX               ;READY FOR NEXT ELEMENT
            CMP         DX,2                ;IS B INTEGER?
            JNE         B_NOT_INTEGER
            FISTP       WORD PTR [SI]
            JMP         LOOP_END
B_NOT_INTEGER:
            CMP         DX,4                ;IS B SINGLE?
            JNE         B_NOT_SINGLE
            FSTP        DWORD PTR [SI]
            JMP         LOOP_END
B_NOT_SINGLE:                               ;BETTER BE DOUBLE
            FSTP        QWORD PTR [SI]
;
LOOP_END:
            ADD         SI,DX               ;READY FOR NEXT ELEMENT
            LOOP        COPY_LOOP
DONE:
            POP         BP
            FWAIT                           ;BE SURE 8087 IS DONE
            RET         10
```

```
GCOPY       ENDP
CSEG        ENDS
            END
```

GCOPY is about 100 times faster than the equivalent BASIC code.

Our second utility routine is GBCOPY. GBCOPY is like GCOPY, except that it begins copying at A(N−1) and works down to A(0), rather than vice versa, and that GBCOPY does not perform type conversions.

```
;SUBROUTINE GBCOPY(A,B,TYPE,N)
; ASSUMPTIONS: A,B ARE ARRAYS OF LENGTH N
;             TYPE IS AN INTEGER: 2-INTEGER 4-SINGLE 8-
;              DOUBLE
;             N IS AN INTEGER
;
          PUBLIC      GBCOPY
CSEG      SEGMENT     'CODE'
          ASSUME      CS:CSEG
GBCOPY    PROC        FAR
          PUSH        BP
          MOV         BP,SP
          MOV         BX,[BP]+6        ;BX=ADDR[N]
          MOV         CX,[BX]          ;CX=N
          CMP         CX,0
          JLE         DONE
          MOV         BX,[BP]+8        ;BX=ADDR(TYPE)
          MOV         AX,[BX]          ;AX=TYPE
          MUL         CX               ;AX=N*TYPE
          MOV         BX,AX            ;BX=N*TYPE
          MOV         CX,AX            ;CX=N*TYPE
          SHR         CX,1             ;CX=N*TYPE/2
                                       ;(WORDS TO BE MOVED)
          MOV         SI,[BP]+12       ;SI=ADDR(A)
          MOV         DI,[BP]+10       ;DI=ADDR(B)
BCOPY_LOOP:
          SUB         BX,2             ;NEXT INDEX
          MOV         AX,[SI][BX]      ;GET A
          MOV         [DI][BX],AX      ;STORE B
          LOOP        BCOPY_LOOP
DONE:     POP         BP
          RET         8
GBCOPY    ENDP
CSEG      ENDS
          END
```

GBCOPY illustrates backwards operations on an array. Our first task was to locate the last element of each array. If an array element takes TYPE bytes to store and the first element begins at location ADDR, then the second element begins at location ADDR+TYPE, the third at ADDR+2*TYPE . . . and the Nth at ADDR+(N−1)*TYPE. Once these locations are found, GBCOPY is like GCOPY except that GBCOPY subtracts to move the elements down to where GCOPY adds to move the elements up.

Why move an array backwards anyhow? Consider the following two problems. First, copy A(I+1) into A(I) for an entire array. This can be done either in BASIC:

```
10   FOR I=0 TO N-2
20   A(I)=A(I+1)
30   NEXT I
```

or with GCOPY:

```
10   N1%=N-1:TYPEA%=4
20   CALL GCOPY(A(1),A(0),TYPEA%,TYPEA%,N1%)
```

Second, copy A(I) into A(I+1) for an entire array. One might be tempted do this in BASIC with

```
10   FOR I=0 TO N-2
20   A(I+1)=A(I)
30   NEXT I
```

but this won't work. On the first step, this puts A(0) into A(1). On the next step, when BASIC tries to move A(1), it picks up the value originally in A(0). The original value of A(1) has been wiped out. Correct BASIC code would be

```
10   FOR I=N-2 TO 0 STEP -1
20   A(I+1)=A(I)
30   NEXT I
```

GCOPY(A(0),A(1),TYPEA%,TYPEA%,N1%) would generate the same incorrect results as the first BASIC program. GBCOPY(A(0),A(1), TYPEA%,N1%) works correctly. Since GBCOPY's primary use is copying data from one part of an array to another part of the same array, nothing was lost by omitting the type conversion.

On Errors

Errors that might result from using number crunching subroutines can be loosely grouped into four classes:

- Programming errors in the subroutines.
- Errors in using the subroutines.
- Recoverable precision errors.
- Non-recoverable precision errors.

Programming Errors

Computer hardware does not make mistakes. (Not often, anyway.) People who program computers *do* make mistakes. As you develop your own number crunching routines for the 8087, you'll naturally hit an occasional bug. Be warned that a personal computer is not quite so forgiving when programmed at the machine language level as it is when programmed in BASIC.

About the worst that can happen in a BASIC program, aside from getting the wrong answer, is that BASIC halts the program and prints a somewhat cryptic error message. Usually, BASIC at least tells you what line caused the error.

What's the worst that can happen with an undebugged machine language program? Frequently, you CALL a machine language program and nothing happens . . . nothing *at all* happens. The only thing to do is to hit the reset key (Ctrl-Alt-Del on an IBM PC) and restart the system from scratch.

Unfortunately, things can be even a bit worse. Sometimes the reset key doesn't do anything either. A machine language program can, after all, write into any location in memory—including writing garbage into areas that only DOS is supposed to use. When this happens, the only solution is to power down, leave the machine off for a few seconds, and then turn the power back on. *It pays to be careful in debugging 8087/8088 programs.*

Errors in Using the Subroutines

Even bug-free routines can go wrong if fed invalid input. As a simple example, suppose we feed the wrong value for N to one of the vector routines prepared above. It would be nice if the routines would check for valid input and return an error indication when given garbage.

Consider what our routines do instead. If N gives the correct length of the data arrays, the routines return the correct answer. Notice that special consideration is given to the case of zero length arrays and these are handled properly. Suppose we set N to a negative value. The routines act as if N were zero, but do not report the error. Suppose instead that the arrays are really 100 long, but we mistakenly set N to 50. The routines give the wrong answer, but return to BASIC without other errors. Suppose we commit the reverse error, setting N to 100 when the arrays are only of length 50. The routines will merrily write into an area of memory assigned to something other than the arrays we are supposed to be using. If we are lucky, the routine will overwrite something vital and the machine will stop cold. In this way we will come to suspect there is an error. If we are unlucky, the routine will change totally unrelated variables, causing our final answers to be wrong without giving any indication of a possible problem.

It is an unfortunate fact of life that there is no sure-fire way to catch these kinds of errors in a machine language program, or, for that matter, in many other computer languages. For the routines in this book, we have decided to place all error checking responsibility on the BASIC programmer. However, it is certainly possible to rewrite the routines to catch a few errors. Routine GADDSAFR (General precision ADDition, but SAFeR) illustrates one such approach.

```
;SUBROUTINE GADDSAFR(A,B,C,TYPEA,TYPEB,TYPEC,N,IER)
; ASSUMPTIONS: A,B,C ARE ARRAYS OF LENGTH N
;              TYPEA IS AN INTEGER: 2-INTEGER 4-SINGLE 8-
                DOUBLE
;              TYPEB "    "
;              TYPEC "    "
;              N IS AN INTEGER
;              IER IS AN INTEGER RETURNING 0 IF NO ERROR
;                 1 IF N IS NEGATIVE
;                 2 IF TYPEA,TYPEB,OR TYPEC IS ILLEGAL
;
;
          PUBLIC    GADDSAFR
CSEG      SEGMENT   'CODE'
          ASSUME    CS:CSEG
GADDSAFR  PROC      FAR
          PUSH      BP
          MOV       BP,SP
;CHECK TYPES
          MOV       SI,[BP]+14        ;SI=ADDR(TYPEA)
          MOV       AX,[SI]           ;AX=TYPEA
          CMP       AX,2
          JE        TYPEA_OK
          CMP       AX,4
          JE        TYPEA_OK
          CMP       AX,8
          JE        TYPEA_OK
          JMP       TYPE_ERROR
TYPEA_OK:
          MOV       SI,[BP]+12        ;SI=ADDR(TYPEB)
          MOV       AX,[SI]           ;AX=TYPEB
          CMP       AX,2
          JE        TYPEB_OK
          CMP       AX,4
          JE        TYPEB_OK
          CMP       AX,8
          JE        TYPEB_OK
          JMP       TYPE_ERROR
TYPEB_OK:
          MOV       SI,[BP]+10        ;SI=ADDR(TYPEC)
          MOV       AX,[SI]           ;AX=TYPEC
          CMP       AX,2
          JE        TYPEC_OK
          CMP       AX,4
          JE        TYPEC_OK
          CMP       AX,8
```

```
            JE          TYPEC_OK
            JMP         TYPE_ERROR
TYPEC_OK:   JMP         CHECK_N
TYPE_ERROR:
            MOV         AX,2
            JMP         DONE
;
CHECK_N:
            MOV         SI,[BP]+8          ;SI=ADDR(N)
            MOV         CX,[SI]            ;CX=N
            CMP         CX,0H
            JNE         L11                ;DONE TOO FAR FOR
            JMP         DONE               ;DIREGT JE
L11:        JG          START_ADD
;                                          ;OOPS, N>0
            MOV         AX,1
            JMP         DONE
;
START_ADD:
            MOV         AX,[BP]+20         ;AX=ADDR(A)
            MOV         DI,[BP]+18         ;DI=ADDR(B)
            MOV         DX,[BP]+16         ;DX=ADDR(C)
ADD_LOOP:
            MOV         BX,AX              ;BX=ADDR(A)
            MOV         SI,[BP]+14         ;SI=ADDR(TYPEA)
            MOV         SI,[SI]            ;SI=TYPEA
            CMP         SI,2               ;IS IT INTEGER?
            JNE         A_NOT_INTEGER
            FILD        WORD PTR [BX]
            JMP         ADD_B
A_NOT_INTEGER:
            CMP         SI,4               ;IS IT SINGLE?
            JNE         A_NOT_SINGLE
            FLD         DWORD PTR [BX]
            JMP         ADD_B
A_NOT_SINGLE:
            FLD         QWORD PTR [BX]
;
ADD_B:      ADD         AX,SI              ;READY FOR A NEXT TIME
            MOV         SI,[BP]+12         ;SI=ADDR(TYPEB)
            MOV         SI,[SI]            ;SI=TYPEB
            CMP         SI,2               ;IS IT INTEGER?
            JNE         B_NOT_INTEGER11
            FIADD       WORD PTR [DI]
            JMP         NEXT_C
B_NOT_INTEGER:
            CMP         SI,4               ;IS IT SINGLE?
            JNE         B_NOT_SINGLE
            FADD        DWORD PTR [DI]
            JMP         NEXT_C
```

```
B_NOT_SINGLE:
          FADD        QWORD PTR [DI]
;
NEXT_C:   ADD         DI,SI              ;READY FOR NEXT B

          MOV         BX,DX              ;BX=ADDR(C)
          MOV         SI,[BP]+10         ;SI=ADDR(TYPEC)
          MOV         SI,[SI]            ;SI=TYPEC
          CMP         SI,2               ;IS IT INTEGER?
          JNE         C_NOT_INTEGER
          FISTP       WORD PTR [BX]
          JMP         NEXT_ELEMENT
C_NOT_INTEGER:
          CMP         SI,4               ;IS IT SINGLE?
          JNE         C_NOT_SINGLE
          FSTP        DWORD PTR [BX]
          JMP         NEXT_ELEMENT
C_NOT_SINGLE:
          FSTP        QWORD PTR [BX]
;
NEXT_ELEMENT:
          ADD         DX,SI              ;READY FOR NEXT C
          LOOP        ADD_LOOPER         ;LOOP ONLY JUMPS
                                          127 . . .
          MOV         AX,0               ; -NO ERROR-
          JMP         DONE
ADD_LOOPER:JMP        ADD_LOOP           ;. . . BYTES
DONE:
          MOV         SI,[BP]+6          ;SI=ADDR(IER)
          MOV         [SI],AX            ;IER=ERROR CODE
          POP         BP
          FWAIT                          ;BE SURE 8087 IS DONE
          RET         16
GADDSAFR  ENDP
CSEG      ENDS
          END
```

Error checking adds only about 20 lines of code and a negligible increase in execution time. Unfortunately, many illegal input errors still won't be caught. Besides N simply having the incorrect value, any of the arrays might actually be of a different type than that stated; the type, N, or IER arguments might not be integers; or we might call GADDSAFR with the wrong number or order of arguments.

Precision Errors

A fact of life that programmers find most difficult to accept is that *perfectly "correct" programs sometimes give the wrong answer*. Computer arithmetic has only limited accuracy. The 8087 is more accurate than most mainframes. Nonetheless, for any finite degree of precision, there exists some problem for which the degree of precision is insufficient. The problem is somewhat aggravated by the fact that a program will work perfectly with one set of data and not at all with another. With some work, one can even construct a series of numbers which add correctly when added from first to last but give a nonsensical result when added backwards. There are several programming approaches to handling precision errors:

- Ignore the problem and hope no errors ever occur.
- Handle each error as soon as it occurs.
- Set up a general scheme to allow computation to proceed as far as possible.

Ignoring the problem is not quite as silly as it sounds. The 8087 is extremely accurate. Furthermore, the 8087 designers have built in automatic error handling capabilities which operate very sensibly. For most problems, precision errors will not occur. For most precision errors that do occur, the 8087 error handling will apply the correct solution.

As an extreme alternative, the 8087 can be set to stop every time an error occurs. *Exception handling* software can be written to take care of every error on a problem-specific basis. This approach requires you to hand-tailor every subroutine, so it isn't practical for this book. Exception handling routines are discussed in the *Intel iAPX 86,88 User's Manual.*

In considering a general scheme for error handling, it is constructive to review what BASIC does about the problem. Among BASIC's rules are the following:

- Integer overflow generates an error message and halts the program.
- Real overflow generates an error message. The result is set to machine infinity. Execution continues.
- Real underflow causes the result to be set to zero. Execution continues without a warning message.
- Passing an invalid argument to a function results in an error message. Execution halts.

The error handling routines in the 8087 hardware always allow execution to continue, while generally indicating errors by producing an answer that is not a "normal" number. All our routines allow the 8087 automatic error handling procedures to maintain control. As a result, the final answers may include an error indication. We need a routine to check whether data is valid or invalid. We would also like to fix those errors for which some obvious fix-up exists. Single and double precision output of the 8087 take one of the following forms, which were discussed at length in Chapter 5:

- Normal—a valid number.
- Denormal—indicates a previous underflow.
- Infinity—may indicate a previous overflow.
- Not-A-Number (NAN)—invalid datum.

Routine REALERR accepts an input array of single or double precision numbers. It returns three integer variables, each of which is set to -1

(true) if any denormal, infinity, or NAN, respectively, is stored in the array, or to 0 (false) otherwise. ELEMENT is an integer variable giving the element number of the last other than normal number found.

Routines REALERR and DENTO0 use some processor control instructions defined in Chapter 12. We include these routines here because of their usefulness for even simple numerical programs.

```
;SUBROUTINE REALERR(ARRAY,TYPE,N,IFDEN,IFINF,IFNAN,ELEMENT)
; ASSUMPTIONS: ARRAY IS OF LENGTH N
;              TYPE IS AN INTEGER: 4-SINGLE, 8-DOUBLE
;              N IS AN INTEGER
;              IFDEN,IFINF,IFNAN ARE INTEGER
;                  RETURNING 0 (FALSE) OR -1 (TRUE)
;              ELEMENT IS AN INTEGER
;
           PUBLIC     REALERR
CSEG       SEGMENT    'CODE'
           ASSUME     CS:CSEG,ES:EXTRA_SEG
FIRST_INST EQU        THIS WORD
REALERR    PROC       FAR
           PUSH       BP
           MOV        BP,SP
;
;SET UP EXTRA SEGMENT TAKING CARE OF RELOCATION
           PUSH       ES
           CALL       NEXT
NEXT:      POP        AX
           SUB        AX,(OFFSET NEXT)-(OFFSET FIRST_INST)
           MOV        CL,4
           SHR        AX,CL
           MOV        BX,CS
           ADD        BX,EXTRA_SEG
           SUB        BX,CSEG
           ADD        AX,BX
           MOV        ES,AX
;
;SET TENTATIVE RETURN VALUES TO ZERO
           MOV        SI,[BP]+12         ;CLEAR IFDEN
           MOV        WORD PTR [SI],0
           MOV        SI,[BP]+10         ;CLEAR IFINF
           MOV        WORD PTR [SI],0
           MOV        SI,[BP]+8          ;CLEAR IFNAN
           MOV        WORD PTR [SI],0
           MOV        SI,[BP]+6          ;CLEAR ELEMENT
           MOV        WORD PTR [SI],0
           MOV        SI,[BP]+14
           MOV        CX,[SI]            ;CX=N
           MOV        BX,[BP]+18         ;BX=ADDR(ARRAY)
           MOV        SI,[BP]+16         ;SI=ADDR(TYPE)
           MOV        AX,[SI]            ;AX=TYPE
;
```

```
;NOW ALL SET UP TO GO
          CMP       CX,0H               ;HOPE N > 0
          JL        DONE
;
CHECK_LOOP:
          CMP       AX,4                ;IS A SINGLE?
          JNE       NOT_SINGLE
          FLD       DWORD PTR [BX]
          JMP       CHECK_IT
NOT_SINGLE:                             ;BETTER BE DOUBLE
          FLD       QWORD PTR [BX]
;
CHECK_IT:
          ADD       BX,AX               ;READY FOR NEXT
                                         ELEMENT
          FXAM                          ;WHAT DID WE LOAD?
          FSTSW     STATUS_WORD
          FSTP      ST(0)
          FWAIT
          MOV       DH,BYTE PTR STATUS_WORD+1
          AND       DH,01000101B        ;BLANK OTHER BITS
          CMP       DH,00000100B        ;NORMAL?
          JE        OK
          CMP       DH,01000000B        ;ZERO?
          JE        OK
          CMP       DH,00000101B        ;INFINITY?
          JE        INF
          CMP       DH,0                ;UNNORMAL?
          JE        DEN
          CMP       DH,01000100B        ;DENORMAL?
          JE        DEN
;MUST BE NAN
          MOV       SI,[BP]+8
          JMP       SET_ERROR
DEN:      MOV       SI,[BP]+12          ;SET IFDEN
          JMP       SET_ERROR
INF:      MOV       SI,[BP]+10          ;SET IFINF
SET_ERROR:
          MOV       WORD PTR [SI],-1    ;ERROR IS TRUE
          MOV       SI,[BP]+14          ;GET N BACK
          MOV       SI,[SI]
          SUB       SI,CX
          MOV       DI,[BP]+6
          MOV       [DI],SI             ;SET ELEMENT
OK:       LOOP      LOOPER
          JMP       DONE
LOOPER:   JMP       CHECK_LOOP

DONE:
          POP       ES
          POP       BP
```

```
            FWAIT                              ;BE SURE 8087 IS DONE
            RET        14
REALERR     ENDP
CSEG
ENDS

EXTRA_SEG  SEGMENT    'DATA'
STATUS_WORD   DW ?
EXTRA_SEG  ENDS
           END
```

REALERR is a little complicated, but is nonetheless quite fast, checking an array of 10,000 numbers in about a quarter of a second.

After execution of REALERR, IFDEN, IFINF, and IFNAN are easily tested with BASIC IF statements. The question remains as to what action should follow as a result of the test. The following general rules can serve as a guide:

- NAN—halt execution with an error message.
- Infinity—Halting execution or allowing it to continue depends somewhat on circumstances. Infinity usually indicates a meaningless value, resulting from either an overflow or from some sort of invalid operation. However, there are occasionally functions for which infinity is a sensible number. Consider evaluating the following function:

  $$1/(1+1/x)$$

  As x goes to zero, the function goes to zero. Since the 8087 is designed to report 1 divided by zero as infinity, 1 plus infinity as infinity, and 1 divided by infinity as zero, this function will be correctly evaluated, if we ignore intermediate infinite results. If X equals -1, then the final result will be infinity, as it should be.
- Denormals are a somewhat different case. A denormal indicates that an underflow has occurred. The datum therefore represents a number very close to zero. We can either leave the number as a denormal, in which case the 8087 will continue to treat it as a number very close to zero, or we can set the number to true zero.

Routine DENTO0 replaces all the denormals in an array with true zeros.

```
;SUBROUTINE DENTO0(ARRAY,TYPE,N)
; ASSUMPTIONS: ARRAY IS OF LENGTH N
;              TYPE IS AN INTEGER: 4-SINGLE, 8-DOUBLE
;              N IS AN INTEGER
;
            PUBLIC     DENTO0
CSEG        SEGMENT    'CODE'
            ASSUME     CS:CSEG,ES:EXTRA_SEG
FIRST_INST  EQU        THIS WORD
DENTO0      PROC       FAR
            PUSH       BP
            MOV        BP,SP
;
```

```
;SET UP EXTRA SEGMENT TAKING CARE OF RELOCATION
            PUSH      ES
            CALL      NEXT
NEXT:       POP       AX
            SUB       AX,(OFFSET NEXT)-(OFFSET FIRST_INST)
            MOV       CL,4
            SHR       AX,CL
            MOV       BX,CS
            ADD       BX,EXTRA_SEG
            SUB       BX,CSEG
            ADD       AX,BX
            MOV       ES,AX
;
            MOV       SI,[BP]+6
            MOV       CX,[SI]           ;CX=N
            MOV       BX,[BP]+10        ;BX=ADDR(A)
            MOV       SI,[BP]+8         ;SI=ADDR(TYPE)
            MOV       AX,[SI]           ;AX=TYPE
;
;NOW ALL SET UP TO GO
            CMP       CX,0H             ;HOPE N > 0
            JL        DONE
;
CHECK_LOOP:
            CMP       AX,4              ;IS A SINGLE?
            JNE       NOT_SINGLE
            FLD       DWORD PTR [BX]
            JMP       CHECK_IT
NOT_SINGLE:                             ;BETTER BE DOUBLE
            FLD       QWORD PTR [BX]
;
CHECK_IT:
            FXAM                        ;WHAT DID WE LOAD?
            FSTSW     STATUS_WORD
            FSTP      ST(0)
            FWAIT
            MOV       DH,BYTE PTR STATUS_WORD+1
            AND       DH,01000101B      ;BLANK OTHER BITS
            CMP       DH,0              ;UNNORMAL?
            JE        DEN
            CMP       DH,01000100B      ;DENORMAL?
            JE        DEN
            JMP       LOOP_BOTTOM
DEN:
            FLDZ                        ;MAKE A ZERO
            CMP       AX,4              ;IS A SINGLE?
            JNE       STILL_NOT_SINGLE
            FSTP      DWORD PTR [BX]
            JMP       LOOP_BOTTOM
STILL_NOT_SINGLE:                       ;BETTER BE DOUBLE
            FSTP      QWORD PTR [BX]
```

```
LOOP_BOTTOM:
            ADD         BX,AX
            LOOP        LOOPER
            JMP         DONE
LOOPER:     JMP         CHECK_LOOP

DONE:
            POP         ES
            POP         BP
            FWAIT                             ;BE SURE 8087 IS DONE
            RET         6
DENTOO      ENDP
CSEG        ENDS

EXTRA_SEG   SEGMENT     'DATA'
STATUS_WORD    DW ?
EXTRA_SEG   ENDS
            END
```

One last warning about ignoring the presence of denormals, infinities, and NANs. A few 8087 instructions insist on valid data as input. In particular, *the transcendental instructions discussed in Chapter 12 will produce an undefined result if fed invalid data and will do so without signaling any error condition*!

Our error handling has been limited to single and double precision reals to the exclusion of integers. There are two reasons for this exclusion.

First, if you use 16-bit integers, the only kind available in BASIC, for holding numerical results, you are asking for trouble. Merely multiplying two random integers may result in integer overflow! Floating point arithmetic is every bit as fast as integer arithmetic on the 8087. Use integer variables for subscripts, flags, and subroutine addresses. Otherwise stay away.

Second, the integer data type cannot be set to indicate invalid data in the way real variables can be set. If a number cannot be converted to a valid integer, the 8087 reports the most negative value, −32,768. Both BASIC and the 8087 treat −32,768 as they do any other integer, so invalid data will not be flagged. If integer variables must be used, all results should be checked and execution should be stopped if −32,768 appears.

10

Basic Matrix Operations

Matrix operations occupy the center of the number crunching world. Large scale supercomputers, costing tens of millions of dollars, have special built-in hardware devoted entirely to fast matrix operations. There are even computer languages, such as APL, where the matrix replaces the scalar as the fundamental variable type. Matrices are so important that some versions of BASIC (mostly on large computers) have a special set of "MAT" functions devoted to efficient matrix computation. While the 8087 does not have matrix hardware, its stack design allows for easily written, efficient, matrix subroutines.

We cover matrix operations in two chapters. In this chapter, we prepare routines for the most common matrix operations. Chapter 11 concentrates on advanced methods for solving systems of linear equations and on the related problem of matrix inversion.

The Cookbook—Chapter 10

Program:	**COLCOPY**
Purpose:	Copy one column of a matrix into a vector.
Call:	CALL COLCOPY(A(0,0),B(0),COL,N,M).
Input:	A—N by M single precision matrix.
	COL—integer column number to be copied.
	N—integer number of rows of A.
	M—integer number of columns of A.
Output:	B—array N long; B(I) = A(I,COL).
Language:	8088 assembly language.
Program:	**ROWCOPY**
Purpose:	Copy one row of a matrix into a vector.
Call:	CALL ROWCOPY(A(0,0),B(0),ROW,N,M).
Input:	A—N by M single precision matrix.
	ROW—integer row number to be copied.
	N—integer number of rows of A.
	M—integer number of columns of A.

Output:	B—array M long; B(I) = A(ROW,I).
Language:	8088 assembly language.
Program:	**DIAGCOPY**
Purpose:	Copy the diagonal of a square matrix into a vector.
Call:	CALL DIAGCOPY(A(0,0),B(0),N).
Input:	A—N by N single precision matrix.
	N—integer number of rows of A.
Output:	B—array N long; B(I) = A(I,I).
Language:	8088 assembly language.
Program:	**TRANS**
Purpose:	Transpose a matrix.
Call:	CALL TRANS(A(0,0),B(0,0),N,M).
Input:	A—N by M single precision matrix.
	N—integer number of rows of A.
	M—integer number of columns of A.
Output:	B—M by N matrix; B(I,J) = A(J,I).
Language:	8088 assembly language.
Program:	**SQTRANS**
Purpose:	Transpose a square matrix in place.
Call:	CALL SQTRANS(A(0,0),N).
Input:	A—N by N single precision matrix.
	N—integer number of rows of A.
Output:	A—new A(I,J) = old A(J,I).
Language:	8088 assembly language.
Program:	**INPROD**
Purpose:	Inner product of two single precision vectors.
Call:	CALL INPROD(A(0),B(0),C,N).
Input:	A—N long single precision vector.
	B—N long single precision vector.
	N—integer number of rows of A.
Output:	C—double precision scalar; C = inner product of A,B.
Language:	8087/8088 assembly language.
Program:	**GINP**
Purpose:	Inner product of two generalized vectors.
Input:	A—N element vector.
	B—N element vector.
	TYPEA—integer giving length of element of A.
	TYPEB—integer giving length of element of B.
	SKIPA—integer "skip factor" (see text) for A.
	SKIPB—integer "skip factor" (see text) for B.
	N—integer number of rows of A.
Output:	8087 register ST; ST = inner product of A,B.
Language:	8087/8088 assembly language.
Note:	NEAR procedure; see GINPROD.

Program:	**GINPROD**
Purpose:	Inner product of two generalized vectors.
Call:	CALL GINPROD(A(0),B(0),C,TYPEA,TYPEB, SKIPA,SKIPB,N).
Input:	A—N element vector. B—N element vector. TYPEA—integer giving length of element of A. TYPEB—integer giving length of element of B. SKIPA—integer "skip factor" (see text) for A. SKIPB—integer "skip factor" (see text) for B. N—integer number of rows of A.
Output:	C—double precision scalar; C=inner product of A,B.
Language:	8087/8088 assembly language.
Note:	Requires NEAR procedure GINP.

Program:	**MATMULT**
Purpose:	Matrix multiplication.
Call:	CALL MATMULT(A(0,0),B(0,0),C(0,0),L,M,N).
Input:	A—L by M single precision matrix. B—M by N single precision matrix. L—integer number of rows of A. M—integer number of columns of A, rows of B. N—integer number of columns of B.
Output:	C—L by N single precision matrix; C=AB.
Language:	8087/8088 assembly language.
Note:	Requires NEAR procedure GINP.

Program:	**GAUSS**
Purpose:	Solve linear equations by Gaussian elimination.
Input:	A—N by N coefficient matrix. Y—N vector. N—number of rows and columns of A.
Output:	X—N vector; X solves equations Y=AX.
Language:	BASIC.

Program:	**GAUSS-SE**
Purpose:	Solve linear equations by Gaussian elimination, using space efficient method.
Input:	A—N by N coefficient matrix. Y—N vector. YSTAR—N vector, scratch space. N—number of rows and columns of A.
Output:	X—N vector; X solves equations Y=AX. A—A replaced with Gaussian reduction.
Language:	BASIC.

What is a Matrix?

In computer terms, a matrix is a two-dimensional array. The values in the array can be thought of as being laid out in a rectangular grid, where the first array index is the row number and the second array index is the column number. An example of a "2 by 3" matrix is

5	−7	11
0	2	18

Such a matrix might be stored in BASIC by DIMensioning an array with two rows and three columns. The BASIC statement "DIM A(1,2)" produces a matrix laid out like

A(0,0)	A(0,1)	A(0,2)
A(1,0)	A(1,1)	A(2,1)

Since BASIC arrays are numbered starting at zero, an N row by M column matrix is dimensioned A(N − 1,M − 1).

Why Are Matrices Interesting?

Invariably, matrix algebra is motivated as notation for solving systems of simultaneous linear equations. This may seem a bit strange, as most of us don't have any great need for solving such systems. The truth is that most interesting numerical computation problems have the same mathematical structure as a system of linear equations. Computational aspects of statistics, differential equations, and constrained optimization all center around linear equations and matrix operations. We briefly lay out the linear equation interpretation of matrices here.

As a sample, consider the following system of two linear equations in two unknowns.

$$18 = 4x_1 + 2x_2$$
$$9 = 2x_1 - 2x_2$$

There is exactly one pair of values for x_1 and x_2 that will make both equations true. To find these values, we draw the two equations on a piece of graph paper. Label the horizontal axis x_1 and the vertical axis x_2. Pick any two values for x_1. Plug each into the top equation and solve for the corresponding value of x_2. Connect the two (x_1,x_2) points to get a straight line. Do the same for the bottom equation. The top equation is true for any (x_1,x_2) point on the first line and the bottom equation is true for any point on the second line. Where the two lines intersect, both equations are true. The point (4.5,0) is the solution to this system of equations.

Matrices provide a compact notation for discussing such systems. In matrix notation, the two equations appear as:

$$y = Ax$$

where y is a 2 by 1 matrix.

$$y = \begin{bmatrix} 18 \\ 9 \end{bmatrix}$$

A is a 2 by 2 matrix

$$A = \begin{bmatrix} 4 & 2 \\ 2 & -2 \end{bmatrix}$$

and x is a 2 by 1 matrix.

$$x = \begin{bmatrix} x_1 \\ x_2 \end{bmatrix}$$

If we are given values for x, we can solve for y by *matrix multiplication*. If we are given values for y, we can solve for x by *solving a system of linear equations*.

Storage Allocation and Memory Access

In order to manipulate matrices, we need to know how BASIC stores a matrix in memory. If A is a 2 by 3 matrix, we can think of it as being logically laid out as shown in Figure 10.1. Since computer memory is one-dimensional, BASIC arranges to store the six elements in consecutive order with the first dimension varying most rapidly as we move up in memory. The two-dimensional matrix is placed in memory in this order: A(0,0), A(1,0), A(0,1), A(1,1), A(0,2), A(1,2). Each element occupies four bytes for a single precision array and eight bytes for double precision.

Another way to say the same thing is that BASIC stores each column in order, placing one column after the next in memory. Suppose the (single precision) matrix A is stored in memory with A(0,0) located at memory address 100. The first column of A will be at locations 100 and 104; the second column at 108 and 112; the third at 116 and 120. The first row of A will be at locations 100, 108, and 116; the second at 104, 112, and 120. Figure 10.1 illustrates the two-dimensional array to one-dimensional-memory mapping.

A(0,0)-100	A(0,1)-108	A(0,2)-116
A(1,0)-104	A(1,1)-112	A(2,1)-120

Figure 10.1

*In general, for an n by m matrix, element (i,j) is stored in position (i + n*j)*k,* where k equals four for single and eight for double precision.

Notice that a 1 by n matrix, called a *row vector,* and an n by 1 matrix, called a *column vector,* will both be stored in the same locations as an n element one-dimensional array.

It is often convenient to think of a matrix as a set of column vectors or a set of row vectors. The routines COLCOPY and ROWCOPY illustrate column and row access. COLCOPY(A,B,COL,N,M) copies column COL of n by m matrix A into the N long array B. Analogously, ROWCOPY copies row ROW of matrix A into an M long array B. The BASIC code below illustrates COLCOPY. (Note that here, as elsewhere, we have written "DIM A(N − 1,M − 1)" for clarity, where BASIC actually requires "N1 = N − 1:M1 = M − 1:DIM A(N1,M1)".)

```
10 DEFINT I-N
15 REM DEFINE N,M HERE
20 DIM A(N-1,M-1),B(N-1)
25 REM FILL IN VALUES OF A
30      FOR I=0 TO N-1
40      B(I)=A(I,COL)
50      NEXT I
```

```
;SUBROUTINE COLCOPY(A,B,COL,N,M)
; ASSUMPTIONS: A IS A SINGLE PRECISION N BY M MATRIX
;              B IS A SINGLE PRECISION ARRAY N LONG
;              COL,N,M ARE INTEGERS
              PUBLIC       COLCOPY
CSEG          SEGMENT      'CODE'
              ASSUME       CS:CSEG
COLCOPY       PROC         FAR
              PUSH         BP
              MOV          BP,SP
              MOV          BX,[BP]+8        ;BX=ADDR(N)
              MOV          CX,[BX]          ;CX=N
              MOV          BX,[BP]+10       ;BX=ADDR(COL)
              MOV          AX,[BX]          ;AX=COL
              MUL          CX               ;AX=N*COL
              SHL          AX,1             ;AX=4*N*COL
              SHL          AX,1
              MOV          SI,[BP]+14       ;SI=ADDR(A)
              ADD          SI,AX            ;SI=ADDR(A(0,COL)
              MOV          DI,[BP]+12       ;DI=ADDR(B)
              JCXZ         DONE
COL_LOOP:
              MOV          AX,[SI]
              MOV          [DI],AX
              MOV          AX,[SI]+2
              MOV          [DI]+2,AX
              ADD          SI,4             ;NEXT COLUMN
              ADD          DI,4
              LOOP         COL_LOOP
```

```
DONE:
            POP         BP
            RET         10
COLCOPY     ENDP
CSEG        ENDS
END
```

```
;SUBROUTINE ROWCOPY(A,B,ROW,N,M)
; ASSUMPTIONS: A IS A SINGLE PRECISION N BY M MATRIX
;              B IS A SINGLE PRECISION ARRAY N LONG
;              ROW,N,M ARE INTEGERS
            PUBLIC      ROWCOPY
CSEG        SEGMENT     'CODE'
            ASSUME      CS:CSEG
ROWCOPY     PROC        FAR
            PUSH        BP
            MOV         BP,SP
            MOV         BX,[BP]+6        ;BX=ADDR(M)
            MOV         CX,[BX]          ;CX=M
            MOV         BX,[BP]+10       ;BX=ADDR(ROW)
            MOV         AX,[BX]          ;AX=ROW
            SHL         AX,1             ;AX=4*ROW
            SHL         AX,1
            MOV         SI,[BP]+14       ;SI=ADDR(A)
            ADD         SI,AX            ;SI=ADDR(A(ROW,0))
            MOV         DI,[BP]+12       ;DI=ADDR(B)
            MOV         BX,[BP]+8        ;BX=ADDR(N)
            MOV         BX,[BX]          ;BX=N
            SHL         BX,1             ;BX=4*N
            SHL         BX,1
            JCXZ        DONE
ROW_LOOP:
            MOV         AX,[SI]          ;MOVE ELEMENT OF ROW
            MOV         [DI],AX
            MOV         AX,[SI]+2
            MOV         [DI]+2,AX
            ADD         SI,BX            ;NEXT ROW
            ADD         DI,4             ;NEXT B
            LOOP        ROW_LOOP
DONE:       POP         BP
            RET         10
ROWCOPY     ENDP
CSEG        ENDS
            END
```

COLCOPY and ROWCOPY illustrate four useful points about moving through a matrix:

- *Column COL begins at location 4*N*COL.*
- *Sequential elements in a column are located 4 bytes apart.*

- *Row ROW begins at location 4*ROW.*
- *Sequential elements in a row are located 4*N bytes apart.*

Of course, "8" would replace "4" for a double precision matrix.

A matrix with an equal number of rows and columns is called, for obvious reasons, a square matrix. The elements A(0,0), A(1,1),. . ., A(N − 1,N − 1) form the *principal diagonal* of the matrix. To illustrate accessing the principal diagonal, we present DIAGCOPY:

```
;SUBROUTINE DIAGCOPY(A,B,N)
; ASSUMPTIONS: A IS A SINGLE PRECISION N BY N MATRIX
;              B IS A SINGLE PRECISION ARRAY N LONG
;              N IS AN INTEGER
           PUBLIC      DIAGCOPY
CSEG       SEGMENT     'CODE'
           ASSUME      CS:CSEG
DIAGCOPY   PROC        FAR
           PUSH        BP
           MOV         BP,SP
           MOV         BX,[BP]+6       ;BX=ADDR(N)
           MOV         CX,[BX]         ;CX=N
           MOV         BX,CX           ;BX=N
           INC         BX              ;BX=N+1
           SHL         BX,1            ;BX=4*(N+1)
           SHL         BX,1            ;NOTE BX HAS DISTANCE
                                        BETWEEN DIAGONAL
                                        ELEMENTS
           MOV         SI,[BP]+10      ;SI=ADDR(A)
           MOV         DI,[BP]+8       ;DI=ADDR(B)
           JCXZ        DONE
DIAG_LOOP:
           MOV         AX,[SI]         ;MOVE ONE ELEMENT
           MOV         [DI],AX
           MOV         AX,[SI]+2
           MOV         [DI]+2,AX
           ADD         SI,BX           ;NEXT ELEMENT
           ADD         DI,4            ;NEXT B
           LOOP        DIAG_LOOP
DONE:      POP         BP
           RET         6
DIAGCOPY   ENDP
CSEG       ENDS
           END
```

Moving across a diagonal is equivalent to moving down one column and over one row. Note the following two facts about accessing elements of the diagonal of a square matrix:

- Diagonal element i is at location i*4*(N + 1).
- Sequential diagonal elements are 4*(N + 1) bytes apart.

Basic Matrix Operations

Matrix operations fall into six categories:

1. Scalar operations.
2. Element-by-element operations.
3. Matrix transposition.
4. Inner products and matrix multiplication.
5. Solving systems of linear equations.
6. Matrix inversion.

Scalar and Element-by-Element Operations

Operations between scalars and matrices operate by applying the scalar operation to every element of the matrix. For example, if A is an n by m matrix, the mathematical operation B = A + 5 could be done with the BASIC program:

```
10 DEFINT I-N
20 DIM A(N-1,M-1), B(N-1,M-1)
30   FOR I= 0 TO N-1
40      FOR J= 0 TO M-1
50      B(I,J)=A(I,J) + 5
60      NEXT J
70   NEXT I
```

This BASIC program could be replaced with the 8087 subroutine SCALADD.

```
;SUBROUTINE SCALADD(A,SCALAR,B,N,M)
; ASSUMPTIONS: A,B ARE SINGLE PRECISION N BY M MATRICES
;              SCALAR IS SINGLE PRECISION
;              N,M ARE INTEGERS
           PUBLIC     SCALADD
CSEG       SEGMENT    'CODE'
           ASSUME     CS:CSEG
SCALADD    PROC       FAR
           PUSH       BP
           MOV        BP,SP
           MOV        BX,[BP]+12           ;BX=ADDR(SCALAR)
           FLD        DWORD PTR [SI]       ;PUSH SCALAR ONTO
                                            STACK
           MOV        BX,[BP]+6            ;BX=ADDR(M)
           MOV        DX,[BX]              ;DX= # OF COLUMNS
           MOV        SI,[BP]+14           ;SI=ADDR(A)
           MOV        DI,[BP]+10           ;DI=ADDR(B)
           FWAIT
COLUMN_LOOP:
           MOV        BX,[BP]+8            ;BX=ADDR(N)
           MOV        CX,[BX]              ;CX=COLUMN LENGTH
           MOV        BX,0
```

```
ADD_LOOP:
            FLD         DWORD PTR [BX][SI]  ;LOAD A(I,J)
            FADD        ST(0),ST(1)         ;ADD SCALAR
            FSTP        DWORD PTR [BX][DI]  ;B(I,J)=SCALAR+A(I,J)
            ADD         BX,4                ;READY FOR NEXT
                                             ELEMENT
            LOOP        ADD_LOOP
;NOW MOVE TO NEXT COLUMN BY ADDING 4*N TO SI AND DI
            MOV         BX,[BP]+8           ;BX=ADDR(N)
            MOV         AX,[BX]             ;AX=COLUMN LENGTH
            SHL         AX,1                ;MULTIPLY AX
            SHL         AX,1                ;BY 4
            ADD         SI,AX
            ADD         DI,AX
;ARE WE DONE YET?
            DEC         DX
            CMP         DX,0
            JLE         COLUMN_LOOP
;
            FSTP        ST(0)               ;GET RID OF SCALAR
            POP         BP
            FWAIT
            RET         10
SCALADD     ENDP
CSEG        ENDS
            END
```

Routine SCALADD takes about 53 microseconds per element. The time for the same routine in BASIC varies according to the number of rows and columns, but, for a 50 by 50 matrix, BASIC requires about 6400 microseconds per element.

SCALADD illustrates indexing down the columns and across the rows of a matrix. It would be straightforward to write routines for the other scalar operations as well as for element-by-element matrix addition, subtraction, and so forth. However, a slight "trick" of observation suggests an even easier solution. Computer memory doesn't "know" that the n by m storage locations represent a matrix. The locations could equally well represent an n by m element one-dimensional array. *All element-by-element and scalar matrix operations can be done by using vector routines,* as developed in Chapter 9.

For example, the following BASIC code, using ADDSC from Chapter 9, works as well as SCALADD.

```
10   DEFINT I-N
20   DIM A(N-1,M-1), B(N-1,M-1)
30   SCALAR=5.0: ISIZE=N*M
40   CALL ADDSC(A(0),SCALAR,B(0),ISIZE)
```

Matrix Transposition

The matrix operation *transpose* exchanges the rows and columns of a matrix. If A is an n by m matrix, then "A transpose" is an m by n matrix such that (A transpose)(i,j) = A(j,i). A transpose is often written A^T or A′ (pronounced "A transpose" or "A prime"). A BASIC program to transpose a matrix is straightforward. For example:

```
10 DEFINT I-N
20 DIM A(N-1,M-1), AT(M-1,N-1)
30   FOR I=0 TO N-1
40      FOR J-0 TO M-1
50      AT(J,I)=A(I,J)
60      NEXT J
70 NEXT I
```

The 8088 subroutine TRANS accomplishes the same task as the BASIC code above. We take advantage of the fact that we can move down the columns of A by counting off memory locations four at a time and move across the rows of A′ by counting off memory locations 4*M bytes at a time.

Notice that TRANS requires A and B to be different matrices. If A and B were to occupy the same memory locations, the copying operations would write over some A locations before we were able to read them into B. Subroutine TRANS uses about 16 microseconds per element.

```
;SUBROUTINE TRANS(A,B,N,M)
; ASSUMPTIONS: A IS A SINGLE PRECISION N BY M MATRIX
;              B IS A SINGLE PRECISION M BY N MATRIX
;              N,M ARE INTEGERS
          PUBLIC    TRANS
CSEG      SEGMENT   'CODE'
          ASSUME    CS:CSEG
TRANS     PROC      FAR
          PUSH      BP
          MOV       BP,SP
          MOV       BX,[BP]+8        ;BX=ADDR(N)
          MOV       CX,[BX]          ;CX=N
          JCXZ      DONE
          MOV       BX,[BP]+6        ;BX=ADDR(M)
          MOV       DX,[BX]          ;DX=M
          CMP       DX,0
          JLE       DONE
          MOV       SI,[BP]+12       ;SI=ADDR(A)
          MOV       DI,[BP]+10       ;DI=ADDR(B)
ROW_LOOP:
          MOV       BX,[BP]+8        ;BX=ADDR(N)
          MOV       CX,[BX]          ;CX=N (COL LENGTH)
          MOV       BX,0             ;BX=0
COL_LOOP:
          MOV       AX,[SI]          ;MOVE 4 BYTES
```

```
            MOV       [DI][BX],AX
            MOV       AX,[SI]+2
            MOV       [DI][BX]+2,AX
            ADD       SI,4                ;NEXT A ELEMENT
            MOV       AX,BX               ;SAVE B ROW POSITION
            MOV       BX,[BP]+6           ;BX=ADDR(M)
            MOV       BX,[BX]             ;BX=M
            SHL       BX,1                ;BX=4*M
            SHL       BX,1
            ADD       BX,AX               ;NEXT B ELEMENT
            LOOP      COL_LOOP            ;IF NOT DONE

            ADD       DI,4                ;NEXT ROW OF B
            DEC       DX                  ;ONE ROW DONE
            JG        ROW_LOOP

DONE:       POP       BP
            RET       8
TRANS       ENDP
CSEG        ENDS
            END
```

Transposition of a square matrix leads to an important special case. To conserve space, we frequently transpose a square matrix "in place," as in the following BASIC code. Notice that the second FOR loop only runs from the diagonal element to the end of the row. The "lower triangle" of the square gets swapped with the upper triangle.

```
10 DEFINT I-N
20 DIM A(N-1,N-1)
30   FOR I=0 TO N-1
40      FOR J=I TO N-1
50      SWAP A(I,J) , A(J,I)
60      NEXT J
70   NEXT I
```

We can think of this code as moving along the diagonal of a matrix and swapping the row from the diagonal point to the right with the column from the diagonal down. Subroutine SQTRANS performs this task. The BASIC code above takes about $2800n^2$ microseconds to transpose A in place. SQTRANS requires only $8n^2$ microseconds.

```
;SUBROUTINE SQTRANS(A,N)
; ASSUMPTIONS: A IS A SINGLE PRECISION N BY N MATRIX
;              N IS AN INTEGER
            PUBLIC    SQTRANS
CSEG        SEGMENT   'CODE'
            ASSUME    CS:CSEG
SQTRANS     PROC      FAR
            PUSH      BP
            MOV       BP,SP
            MOV       BX,[BP]+6      ;BX=ADDR(N)
            MOV       DX,[BX]        ;DX=N
            MOV       BX,DX          ;BX=N
```

```
          SHL      BX,1          ;BX=4*N
          SHL      BX,1
          MOV      BP,[BP]+8     ;WE'RE SHORT OF REGISTERS
                                 ;SO WE'LL USE BP TO POINT
                                 ;TO DIAGONAL ELEMENT
                                 ;BP=ADDR(A)
          CMP      DX,0
          JLE      DONE
DIAG_LOOP:
          MOV      CX,DX         ;DX # OF ELEMENTS LEFT
          MOV      SI,BP         ;SI POINTS TO ROW
          MOV      DI,BP         ;DI POINTS TO COLUMN
ROW_LOOP:                        ;SWAP ROW AND COLUMN
          MOV      AX,[SI]       ;MOVE 4 BYTES
          XCHG     [DI],AX
          MOV      [SI],AX
          MOV      AX,[SI]+2
          XCHG     [DI]+2,AX
          MOV      [SI]+2,AX
          ADD      SI,BX         ;NEXT ROW ELEMENT
          ADD      DI,4          ;NEXT COLUMN ELEMENT
          LOOP     ROW_LOOP      ;IF NOT DONE

          ADD      BP,BX         ;NEXT DIAGONAL ELEMENT
          ADD      BP,4
          DEC      DX            ;NEXT COLUMN IS SHORTER
          CMP      DX,0
          JG       DIAG_LOOP
DONE:     POP      BP
          RET      4
SQTRANS   ENDP
CSEG      ENDS
          END
```

Inner Products and Matrix Multiplication

More scientific computation time is spent computing *inner products* than on any other single problem. Inner products are at the heart of both matrix multiplication and matrix inversion. If x and y are vectors, then to find the inner product of x and y one multiplies the two vectors element by element and sums the products, as in the following BASIC program.

```
10 DEFINT I-N
20 DEFDBL S
30 DIM X(N-1),Y(N-1)
40 SUM=0
50     FOR I=0 TO N-1
60     SUM=SUM+X(I)*Y(I)
70     NEXT I
```

At first glance, the inner product doesn't appear to be a particularly interesting operation. However, consider the specification of our system of linear equations earlier in the chapter. The first equation was

$$y_1 = A_{0,0}x_1 + A_{0,1}x_2$$

Thus y_1 equals the inner product of the first row of A with the vector x. Similarly, the second equation specifies that y_2 equals the inner product of the second row of A with x. In this manner, an entire system of equations can be specified in terms of inner products. This leads to a natural definition of matrix multiplication in terms of inner products.

If C=AB, then C_{ij} *equals the inner product of row i of A with column j of B.*

Note that this definition implicitly assumes that A and B are *conformable* for multiplication, that is, the number of columns of A equal the number of rows of B. A further natural result of the definition is that if A is a l by m matrix and B is an m by n matrix, then C will be l by m.

BASIC code to multiply two matrices is:

```
10 DEFINT I-N
20 DEFDBL S
25 REM REMEMBER TO DEFINE L,M,N AND USE L1=L-1,ETC IN LINE
 30
30 DIM A(L-1,M-1),B(M-1,N-1),C(L-1,N-1)
35     REM DEFINE MATRICES A AND B HERE
40         FOR IROW=0 TO L-1
50             FOR JCOL=0 TO N-1
60             SUM=0
70                 FOR K=0 TO M-1
80                 SUM=SUM+A(IROW,K)*B(K,JCOL)
90                 NEXT K
100             C(IROW,JCOL)=SUM
110             NEXT JCOL
120         NEXT IROW
```

Lines 70, 80, and 90 are executed l*m*n times. For matrices of order 50, that's 125,000 additions and multiplications. You can see why we want these lines to be as efficient as possible!

Notice that we collected the inner product in a temporary variable "SUM," rather than directly in "C(IROW,JCOL)." We did this for two reasons. First, it is somewhat more efficient, since BASIC need calculate the location of C(IROW,JCOL) only l*n times, rather than l*m*n times. Second, and far more important, accuracy is improved greatly by accumulating the sum in double precision even if it is to be stored later as a single precision variable.

Because of the central role of inner products and matrix multiplications in numerical computation, accuracy and speed are vital. We present several 8087 routines written with these objectives in mind. Our first routine forms the inner product of two one-dimensional arrays.

```
;SUBROUTINE INPROD(A,B,C,N)
; ASSUMPTIONS: A,B ARE SINGLE PRECISION N ARRAYS
;              C IS A DOUBLE PRECISION SCALAR
;              N IS AN INTEGER
           PUBLIC     INPROD
CSEG       SEGMENT    'CODE'
           ASSUME     CS:CSEG
INPROD     PROC       FAR
           PUSH       BP
           MOV        BP,SP
           MOV        BX,[BP]+6              ;BX=ADDR(N)
           MOV        CX,[BX]                ;CX=N
           MOV        SI,[BP]+12             ;SI=ADDR(A)
           MOV        DI,[BP]+10             ;DI=ADDR(B)
           MOV        BX,0
           FLDZ                              ;SET RUNNING SUM=0
           JCXZ       DONE
ADD_LOOP:
           FLD        DWORD PTR [BX][SI]     ;LOAD A(I)
           FMUL       DWORD PTR [BX][DI]     ;MULTIPLY BY B(I)
           FADDP      ST(1),ST               ;SUM=SUM+A(I)*B(I)
           ADD        BX,4                   ;READY FOR NEXT
                                              ELEMENT
           LOOP       ADD_LOOP
DONE:
           MOV        BX,[BP]+8              ;BX=ADDR(C)
           FSTP       QWORD PTR [BX]         ;C=INNER PRODUCT
           POP        BP
           FWAIT
           RET        8
INPROD     ENDP
CSEG       ENDS
           END
```

Routine INPROD takes about 59 microseconds per array element.

You might expect our next step would be an 8087 routine to multiply two matrices. Instead of proceeding directly to a matrix multiplication program, we are going to take a short strategic detour. A matrix multiplication subroutine presents two difficulties. First, writing such a routine is complicated by the need to keep track of too many indices. As you can see from the BASIC program above, the program needs to remember IROW, JCOL, K, L, M, N and the locations of A, B, and C. Using a direct approach, we would run out of registers rather quickly. Second, a straightforward matrix multiplication routine could be used only on one specific argument type; for example, multiplying two single precision matrices and returning a single precision result.

Our strategic approach is to write a very general inner product routine upon which we can build more complicated programs. Subroutine GINP, below, calculates the inner product of two n-element arrays. The result is left on the top of the 8087 stack. In addition to specification of the input vectors, GINP accepts two kinds of options. The first option allows us to specify either single or double precision input arrays. The second option allows us to tell GINP how far apart in memory the elements of each array are spaced. Thus if array A has a "skip" parameter of one, the elements are stored sequentially. If the skip parameter is two, then elements are stored in every other location—with four bytes between elements for a single precision array and eight bytes between elements for a double precision array.

Of what use is the "skip" parameter? Think about accessing a row of a matrix. The elements of an m by n matrix are located 4*n bytes apart. Thus we can move across the row of an m by n matrix by specifying n as the skip parameter.

```
;SUBROUTINE GINP(A,B,TYPEA,TYPEB,SKIPA,SKIPB,N)
; ASSUMPTIONS: A,B ARE ADDRESSES OF N-ARRAYS IN DATA SEGMENT
;              TYPEA,TYPEB,SKIPA,SKIPB,N ARE INTEGERS
;              NOTE THIS PROCEDURE CANNOT BE CALLED FROM
;               BASIC
;              IT FINDS ITS ARGUMENTS ON THE STACK
;              NOT THEIR ADDRESSES
;
;              THERE MUST BE AT LEAST 2 FREE LOCATIONS ON
;              THE 8087 STACK AND AT LEAST 14 FREE BYTES ON
;              THE MEMORY STACK
;
;              GINP RETURNS THE INNER PRODUCT OF A AND B ON
;              THE 8087 STACK
;
;              GINP TAKES EVERY SKIPA ELEMENT OF A AND
;              EVERY SKIPB ELEMENT OF B
;
          ASSUME    CS:CSEG
GINP      PROC      NEAR
          PUSH      BP
          MOV       BP,SP
;SINCE THIS IS A NEAR PROCEDURE, ARGUMENTS BEGIN AT [BP]+4
          PUSH      AX
          PUSH      BX
          PUSH      CX
          PUSH      DX
          PUSH      SI
          PUSH      DI
          FLDZ                          ;SET RUNNING SUM=0
          MOV       CX,[BP]+4           ;CX=N
          MOV       SI,[BP]+16          ;SI=ADDR(A)
          MOV       DI,[BP]+14          ;DI=ADDR(B)
          MOV       AX,[BP]+10          ;AX=TYPEB
          MUL       WORD PTR [BP]+6     ;AX=TYPEB*SKIPB
          MOV       BX,AX               ;BX=B ELEMENT DISTANCE
          MOV       AX,[BP]+12          ;AX=TYPEA
```

```
            MUL         WORD PTR [BP]+8    ;AX=A ELEMENT DISTANCE
            JCXZ        DONE
GIN_PLOOP:
            CMP         WORD PTR [BP]+12,4 ;IS A SINGLE?
            JNE         A_DOUBLE
            FLD         DWORD PTR [SI]     ;LOAD SINGLE A(I)
            JMP         MULT_B
A_DOUBLE:   FLD         QWORD PTR [SI]     ;LOAD DOUBLE A(I)

MULT_B:     CMP         WORD PTR [BP]+10,4 ;IS B SINGLE?
            JNE         B_DOUBLE
            FMUL        DWORD PTR [DI]     ;MULTIPLY SINGLE B(I)
            JMP         NEXT_ELEMENT
B_DOUBLE:   FMUL        QWORD PTR [DI]     ;MULTIPLY DOUBLE B(I)

NEXT_ELEMENT:
            FADDP       ST(1),ST           ;SUM=SUM+A(I)*B(I)
            ADD         SI,AX
            ADD         DI,BX
            LOOP        GINP_LOOP

DONE:
            POP         DI
            POP         SI
            POP         DX
            POP         CX
            POP         BX
            POP         AX
            POP         BP
            RET         14
GINP        ENDP
```

Subroutine GINP is written as a *NEAR procedure*. This means it cannot be called directly from BASIC. However, it also means that GINP is automatically relocatable. Below, we write a FAR procedure, GINPROD, to call GINP from BASIC. Because an 8088 NEAR call jumps to a location relative to the current value in the instruction pointer, GINPROD and GINP can be moved together without changing the CALL instruction in GINPROD.

GINP should be assembled together with GINPROD and any other routines which call GINP. This helps insure that our dynamic relocation scheme will function properly. For this same reason, we have omitted the PUBLIC and SEGMENT/ENDS statements, as we will with all NEAR procedures. In fact, the most convenient way to use our matrix routines is to combine them all into one assembly language package. Combining the routines makes it easy for them to share the same copy of GINP and the scratch space we define in GINPROD. (We'll assume that you combine the routines this way and won't set up separate scratch space areas for each.)

Since GINP won't be called from BASIC, we have used slightly different parameter passing conventions for convenience. The addresses of the two arrays, A and B, are pushed onto the stack, then the values of the "types" (four for single precision or eight for double precision), rather than the addresses of the "types," of A and B, the skip parameters for A and B, and the value of N, are pushed onto the stack. Since GINP is a NEAR procedure, the parameters begin in the stack at [BP]+4 rather than [BP]+6. GINP saves registers on the 8088 stack, and expects that any routine calling it will leave free at least seven words on the stack. The calling routine should set up its own stack area rather than rely on the area provided by BASIC.

Procedure GINP uses about 125 microseconds for overhead (finding addresses and so forth) plus 59 microseconds for each array element.

Routine GINPROD makes GINP accessible from BASIC. GINPROD returns, in C, the double precision value of the inner product.

```
;SUBROUTINE GINPROD(A,B,C,TYPEA,TYPEB,SKIPA,SKIPB,N)
; ASSUMPTIONS: A,B ARE N-ARRAYS
;              C IS A DOUBLE PRECISION SCALAR
;              TYPEA,TYPEB,SKIPA,SKIPB,N ARE INTEGERS
;
;    THIS SUBROUTINE CALLS THE INTERNAL SUBROUTINE GINP
            PUBLIC      GINPROD
CSEG        SEGMENT     'CODE'
            ASSUME      CS:CSEG,ES:ESEG
FIRST_INST    EQU THIS WORD
GINPROD     PROC        FAR
            PUSH        BP
            MOV         BP,SP

;SET UP STACK AREA IN ESEG
            PUSH        ES
            CALL        NEXT
NEXT:       POP         AX
            SUB         AX,(OFFSET NEXT)-(OFFSET FIRST_INST)
            MOV         CL,4
            SHR         AX,CL
            MOV         BX,CS
            ADD         BX,ESEG
            SUB         BX,CSEG
            ADD         AX,BX
            MOV         ES,AX
;
            MOV         LOCAL_SPACE,SS
            MOV         LOCAL_SPACE+2,SP
            MOV         AX,ES
            MOV         SS,AX
            MOV         SP,OFFSET STACK_TOP
;
```

```
;SET UP CALL PARAMETERS
;NOTICE THAT WE HAVE CHANGED THE SS REGISTER
;SO, WE HAVE TO TAKE ADVANTAGE OF THE FACT THAT BASIC SETS
;SS AND DS TO THE SAME LOCATION
            PUSH      DS:[BP]+20          ;ADDR(A)
            PUSH      DS:[BP]+18          ;ADDR(B)
            MOV       BX,DS:[BP]+14       ;TYPEA
            PUSH      [BX]
            MOV       BX,DS:[BP]+12       ;TYPEB
            PUSH      [BX]
            MOV       BX,DS:[BP]+10       ;SKIPA
            PUSH      [BX]
            MOV       BX,DS:[BP]+8        ;SKIPB
            PUSH      [BX]
            MOV       BX,DS:[BP]+6        ;N
            PUSH      [BX]
;
            CALL      GINP
            MOV       SP,LOCAL_SPACE+2
            MOV       SS,LOCAL_SPACE
            MOV       BX,[BP]+16          ;BX=ADDR(C)
            FSTP      QWORD PTR [BX]      ;STORE C
            POP       ES
            POP       BP
            FWAIT
            RET       16
GINPROD     ENDP
CSEG        ENDS

ESEG        SEGMENT   'DATA'
            DW        50 DUP (?)
STACK_TOP   EQU       THIS WORD
LOCAL_SPACE   DW      20 DUP (?)
ESEG        ENDS
```

One programming "trick" bears special attention here. The stack area provided by BASIC when GINPROD is called may have only eight words on it. Since this isn't enough, GINPROD sets up its own stack segment in the ESEG area. GINPROD changes the stack segment register, SS, to point to this area. Once SS has been changed, we need to use some other segment register when retrieving arguments from BASIC. In GINPROD, we use the DS register since BASIC sets SS and DS to the same value. This works quite well when GINPROD is called from BASIC, but some other method might be necessary if GINPROD is used with another language.

GINPROD leads immediately to a fast BASIC routine for matrix multiplication.

```
10 DEFINT I-N
20 DEFDBL S
30 DIM A(L-1,M-1),B(M-1,N-1),C(L-1,N-1)
```

```
35  IONE=1 : ITYPE=4
40      FOR IROW=0 TO L-1
50         FOR JCOL=0 TO N-1
55    CALL GINPROD(A(IROW,0),B(0,JCOL),SUM,ITYPE,ITYPE,M,IONE,M)
56     REM FIND INNER PRODUCT OF ROW IROW OF A WITH
57     REM COLUMN JCOL OF B RETURNING THE ANSWER IN SUM
58     REM NOTE ITYPE=4 INDICATES SINGLE PRECISION
60             REM SUM=0
70             REM FOR K=0 TO M-1
80             REM SUM=SUM+A(IROW,K)*B(K,JCOL)
90             REM NEXT K
100         C(IROW,JCOL)=SUM
110         NEXT JCOL
120      NEXT IROW
```

For convenient comparison, we have adapted the earlier BASIC program for matrix multiplication by adding statements 35 and 55-58 and changing 70, 80, and 90 into REMARKS. This program directly takes the inner product of each row of A with each column of B.

How much time do we save by multiplying matrices using GINPROD instead of straight BASIC code? For large m, both programs are roughly proportional to l*m*n. The constant of proportionality is about 9600 microseconds for BASIC. Using GINPROD, the constant of proportionality falls to 61 microseconds. Thus, multiplying two 50 by 50 matrices takes about 20 minutes in BASIC without the 8087. Using the 8087, the program takes about eight seconds.

Suppose the middle index, m, is small compared to l and n. Lines 70, 80, and 90 use time proportional to l*m*n. Lines 40-60 and 100-120 execute in time proportional to l*n. Ordinarily in timing analysis, if a cubic term, such as l*m*n, is present, we drop quadratic terms, such as l*n. If m is small, the quadratic terms become important. For example, if m = 1, the program spends as much time in lines 40-60 and 100-120 as in 70-90; use of the routine GINPROD doesn't speed up anything at all.

Speed considerations thus suggest a pure 8087 routine for matrix multiplication. Routine MATMULT essentially imitates the BASIC code above.

```
;SUBROUTINE MATMULT(A,B,C,L,M,N)
; ASSUMPTIONS: A,B,C ARE SINGLE PRECISION MATRICES
;              A IS L BY M
;              B IS M BY N
;              C IS L BY N
;              L,M,N ARE INTEGERS
;
; THIS SUBROUTINE PERFORMS THE MATRIX MULTIPLICATION C=AB
; SUCCESSIVE ROWS OF A ARE MULTIPLIED BY THE FIRST COLUMN
  OF B
; THEN REPEAT FOR SECOND COLUMN, ETC.
            PUBLIC     MATMULT
CSEG        SEGMENT    'CODE'
            ASSUME     CS:CSEG,ES:ESEG
```

```
FIRST_INST EQU THIS WORD
MATMULT    PROC      FAR
           PUSH      BP
           MOV       BP,SP

;SET UP STACK AREA IN ESEG
           PUSH      ES
           CALL      NEXT
NEXT:      POP       AX
           SUB       AX,(OFFSET NEXT)-(OFFSET FIRST_INST)
           MOV       CL,4
           SHR       AX,CL
           MOV       BX,CS
           ADD       BX,ESEG
           SUB       BX,CSEG
           ADD       AX,BX
           MOV       ES,AX
;
           MOV       LOCAL_SPACE,SS
           MOV       LOCAL_SPACE+2,SP
           MOV       AX,ES
           MOV       SS,AX
           MOV       SP,OFFSET STACK_TOP
;
; TO CALL GINP WE MUST PUSH ONTO THE STACK:
; A(I,0)
; B(0,J)
; 4
; 4
; L
; 1
; M
;
; ON RETURN THE RESULT GOES IN C(I,J)
; USE SOME LOCAL STORAGE TO SAVE ADDRESSES OF
;          A(I,0)   B(0,J)   C(I,J)
SOME_SPACE EQU LOCAL_SPACE+4
ADDRA_HOLD EQU       SOME_SPACE
ADDRB_HOLD EQU       ADDRA_HOLD+2
L_HOLD     EQU       ADDRB_HOLD+2
M4_HOLD    EQU       L_HOLD+2
M_HOLD     EQU       M4_HOLD+2
N_HOLD     EQU       M_HOLD+2
           MOV       BX,DS:[BP]+16     ;BX=ADDR(A(0,0))
           MOV       ADDRA_HOLD,BX
           MOV       SI,DS:[BP]+14     ;SI=ADDR(B(0,0))
           MOV       ADDRB_HOLD,SI
           MOV       DI,DS:[BP]+12     ;DI=ADDR(C(0,0))
           MOV       BX,DS:[BP]+10     ;BX=ADDR(L)
           MOV       AX,[BX]
           MOV       L_HOLD,AX         ;L_HOLD HAS L
           MOV       BX,DS:[BP]+8      ;BX=ADDR(M)
           MOV       DX,[BX]           ;DX=M
```

```
            MOV         M_HOLD,DX
            MOV         M4_HOLD,DX
            SHL         M4_HOLD,1         ;GET 4*M
            SHL         M4_HOLD,1
            MOV         BX,DS:[BP]+6      ;BX=ADDR(N)
            MOV         CX,[BX]           ;CX=N
            MOV         N_HOLD,CX
            MOV         AX,4              ;SAVE USEFUL 4
            MOV         BX,1              ;SAVE USEFUL 1
;
COL_LOOP:   CMP         N_HOLD,0          ;COL DONE?
            JE          DONE
            MOV         SI,ADDRA_HOLD
            MOV         CX,L_HOLD
ROW_LOOP:
            PUSH        SI                ;A(I,0)
            PUSH        ADDRB_HOLD        ;B(0,J)
            PUSH        AX                ;4
            PUSH        AX                ;4
            PUSH        L_HOLD            ;L
            PUSH        BX                ;1
            PUSH        DX                ;M
            CALL        GINP
            FSTP        DWORD PTR [DI]


            ADD         DI,4              ;NEXT C
            ADD         SI,4              ;NEXT A
            LOOP        ROW_LOOP          ;NEXT ROW
            MOV         SI,M4_HOLD        ;SKIP TO NEXT COLUMN
            ADD         ADDRB_HOLD,SI     ;NEXT B
            DEC         N_HOLD
            JMP         COL_LOOP
;
DONE:
            MOV         SP,LOCAL_SPACE+2
            MOV         SS,LOCAL_SPACE
            POP         ES
            POP         BP
            FWAIT
            RET         12
MATMULT     ENDP
CSEG        ENDS
            END
```

MATMULT executes in about 211*l*n + 59*l*m*n microseconds. In the worst case, m = 1 and large l*n, MATMULT uses about 270 microseconds per element. Even though 80 percent of the 270 microseconds is overhead, MATMULT is still over 100 times faster than BASIC. By the time m is as large as 20, execution speed rises to about 70 microseconds per element, which is 80 percent of maximum hardware speed. Adaptation of MATMULT to double precision arguments is straightforward.

GINPROD allows us to easily create many variants of matrix multiplication. Suppose we want to multiply the transpose of a matrix A by a matrix B, as in C = A′B, where A is m by l and B is m by n. Row i of A′ is column i of A, so we can use GINPROD specifying a "skip" of 1 for A to specify a row of A′.

```
10 DEFINT I-N
20 DEFDBL S
30 DIM A(M-1,L-1),B(M-1,N-1),C(L-1,N-1)
35 I1=1 : ITYPE=4
40   FOR IROW=0 TO L-1
50      FOR JCOL=0 TO N-1
55 CALL GINPROD(A(0,IROW),B(0,JCOL),SUM,ITYPE,ITYPE,I1,I1,M)
60             REM SUM=0
70             REM      FOR K=0 TO M-1
80             REM      SUM=SUM+A(K,IROW)*B(K,JCOL)
90             REM      NEXT K
100       C(IROW,JCOL)=SUM
110       NEXT JCOL
120    NEXT IROW
```

A slightly simpler program could be written using INPROD rather than GINPROD, but the method here allows double precision matrices and is easily adaptable to problems such as C = AB′, which require the matrix to be processed by row rather than column.

Solving Systems of Linear Equations

This is a good place to pause in your reading. We spend the rest of this chapter on linear algebra and in writing BASIC programs for solving systems of linear equations and inverting matrices. Our next 8087 program doesn't appear until Chapter 11. If your main interest is the 8087 aspect of these problems, you should just quickly skim the rest of this chapter.

The next few pages move very fast. You can spend most of a course in college learning about linear equations. The next few pages are really more of a quick review than a proper introduction to the subject. If you're new to the topic—or if it's been a long time since you last saw the subject—spend some time playing with the BASIC programs. One of the nice things about exploring with a personal computer is that your "study" can be as fast or as slow as you please.

Equation Manipulation

Return now to our example of two linear equations in two unknowns. The equations to be satisfied are:

$$18 = 4x_1 + 2x_2$$
$$9 = 2x_1 - 2x_2$$

which can also be written

$$y = Ax$$

For a given y, what value of x makes both equations true simultaneously? We solve for x by making judicious use of the following theorems.

1. *If we multiply both sides of a true equation by a constant, the resulting equation is also true.*
2. *If we add one true equation to another, the resulting equation is also true.*
3. *We can always exchange the position of two equations.*

Clever application of these principles allows us to easily solve systems of linear equations. Consider applying the following transformations to our example system.

1. Multiply the top equation by $-1/2$ and add the result to the second equation. The transformed system looks like this:

$$18 = 4x_1 + 2x_2$$
$$0 = 0x_1 - 3x_2$$

2. By inspecting the bottom equation, we see that x_2 equals 0. Solving backwards, we set x_2 to zero in the top equation and see immediately that x_1 equals $18/4$, or 4.5.

Matrix Manipulation

These steps generalize to a two-step procedure for solving systems of linear equations in terms of matrices.

1. *Reduce* the system to triangular form. Multiply the first equation by a constant and add the result to the second equation so as to produce a zero in column 1, row 2. Multiply the first equation by a (different) constant and add the result to the third equation so as to produce a zero in column 1, row 3. Continue in this manner until the first column is all zeros below the diagonal.
   Now take the second equation, multiply it by a constant and add it to the third equation so as to produce a zero in column 2, row 3. Continue until the entire second column is zero below the diagonal. Apply this procedure repeatedly until the entire area below the diagonal equals zero. This sort of matrix, with all zeros below the diagonal is called *upper triangular*.
2. *Back substitute*. Take the transformed version of A and y and solve for x by

$$x_n = y_n/A_{n,n}$$
$$x_{n-1} = (y_{n-1} - A_{n-1,n}\, x_n)/A_{n-1,n-1}$$

and so forth.

Let's look at what our sample system looks like in terms of matrices. We start with the original A and y.

$$A = \begin{bmatrix} 4 & 2 \\ 2 & -2 \end{bmatrix} \qquad y = \begin{bmatrix} 18 \\ 9 \end{bmatrix}$$

Now we begin the reduction process. Our first step multiplies the top row of A and y by $-\frac{1}{2}$ and adds the result to the second row giving us new values of A and y.

$$A = \begin{bmatrix} 4 & 2 \\ 0 & -3 \end{bmatrix} \quad y = \begin{bmatrix} 18 \\ 0 \end{bmatrix}$$

You can see why A is said to be in "triangular form." The non-zero entries form a triangle on and above the diagonal.

Notice that A and y are changed. If you want to keep the original data intact, be certain to perform the reduction on a copy of the original matrices.

The second step is to back-substitute. The matrix equation $y = Ax$ still applies to the new versions of A and y. Starting at the bottom and working up we have

$$0 = (0)x_1 + (-3)x_2$$

so $x_2 = 0$. Now we can substitute this into the first equation.

$$18 = (4)x_1 + (2)0$$

X_1 equals $(18-0)/4$, or 4.5.

In theory, only one thing can go wrong with this procedure. Suppose that at some step the equation we are using to produce zeros below the diagonal has a zero as its own diagonal element. (This diagonal element is called the *pivot* element.) In this case, the equation cannot be used to eliminate the elements below it and the program stops. The solution to this problem is to exchange the offending equation with another so as to obtain a non-zero pivot. (Implementation of this solution is deferred until the next chapter.) If the entire column equals zero, the system of equations and the matrix A are said to be *singular*. The system of equations does not have a unique solution.

This method of solving linear systems is called *Gaussian elimination*. While not the best computational method (better ones are introduced in the next chapter), it is the most straightforward. The following BASIC program implements Gaussian elimination. Notice that the original contents of A and y are replaced by transformed values.

```
5   REM PROGRAM GAUSS
10  DEFINT I-N
20  DIM A(N-1,N-1),Y(N-1),X(N-1)
25     REM BE SURE A,Y AND N ARE DEFINED
30      FOR IEQ=0 TO N-1
40      IF A(IEQ,IEQ)=0 THEN PRINT "ZERO PIVOT AT",IEQ:STOP
50         FOR JROW=IEQ+1 TO N-1
60         FACTOR=-A(JROW,IEQ)/A(IEQ,IEQ)
70         Y(JROW)=Y(JROW)+FACTOR*Y(IEQ)
80            FOR K=IEQ TO N-1
90            A(JROW,K)=A(JROW,K)+FACTOR*A(IEQ,K)
100            NEXT K
110         NEXT JROW
120      NEXT IEQ
130 REM
140 REM A IS NOW UPPER TRIANGULAR
150 REM
160 X(N-1)=Y(N-1)/A(N-1,N-1)
170     FOR IEQ=(N-1)-1 TO 0 STEP -1
180     SUM=0
190       FOR K=IEQ+1 TO N-1
200       SUM=SUM+A(IEQ,K)*X(K)
210       NEXT K
220     X(IEQ)=(Y(IEQ)-SUM)/A(IEQ,IEQ)
230     NEXT IEQ
```

How long does it take to solve a system using Gaussian elimination? The outermost loop, the IEQ loop, is executed $N-1$ times. The next loop, the JROW loop, is done $N-1$ times for the first IEQ, $N-2$ for the second, and so forth. So the JROW loop is executed approximately $n^2/2$ times. The inner-most loop, K, executes N times per JROW for the first IEQ, $N-1$ times per JROW for the second IEQ, for a total of about $n^3/3$ operations. In total, the time required to solve a system of n equations is proportional to $n^3/3$, plus a small factor proportional to $n^2/2$.

The logical next step would be to prepare 8087 routines to speed up the program. Since better solution methods are proposed in the next chapter, introduction of more 8087 routines will be postponed until that point. However, here are a couple of suggestions in case you'd like to experiment.

Almost the entire execution time is spent in lines 80, 90, and 100. These lines multiply a row vector by a scalar and then add two row vectors. The routines prepared in Chapter 9 will only multiply and add column vectors. However, these routines could easily be modified to include a skip parameter, so as to work on row vectors. We might replace lines 80, 90, and 100 with lines something like this:

```
25    DIM XTRAROW(N-1):IONE=1
85    K=(N-1)-IEQ+1
95    CALL MULTSC(A(IEQ,IEQ),FACTOR,XTRAROW(0),N,IONE,K)
105   CALL VADD(A(JROW,IEQ),XTRAROW(0),A(JROW,0),N,IONE,N,K)
```

Lines 180-200 might be replaced with GINPROD for some further gain.

Using BASIC, solving a system of equations takes about $12500n^3/3$ microseconds. Solving a 50-equation system uses over eight minutes of computer time. Replacing the inner-most loop with 8087 routines as suggested will reduce execution time to about $100n^3/3$ microseconds. That knocks solution time for a 50-equation system down to about five seconds.

Solving Multiple Linear Systems

We frequently want to solve a number of linear systems, sharing a common A matrix but having different y vectors. In place of a single n by 1 column vector y, we can arrange m column vectors into an n by m matrix Y. The solutions can be placed in an n by m matrix X. The entire set of linear equations are represented in this way by the matrix equation

$$Y = AX$$

Examination of the Gaussian elimination routine shows that all the hard work, that is the order n^3 work, involves only the A matrix. If we blindly apply the program above, execution time will be of order mn^3. The revision below keeps the transformation of y and backsolving for x out of the innermost loop.

```
10   DEFINT I-N
20   DIM A(N-1,N-1),Y(N-1,M),X(N-1,M)
25    REM BE SURE A,Y,N, AND M ARE DEFINED
30     FOR IEQ=0 TO N-1
40     IF A(IEQ,IEQ)=0 THEN PRINT "ZERO PIVOT AT",IEQ:STOP
50      FOR JROW=IEQ+1 TO N-1
60      FACTOR=-A(JROW,IEQ)/A(IEQ,IEQ)
70       FOR LEQ=0 TO M-1
80       Y(JROW,LEQ)=Y(JROW,LEQ)+FACTOR*Y(IEQ,LEQ)
90       NEXT LEQ
100      FOR K=IEQ TO N-1
110      A(JROW,K)=A(JROW,K)+FACTOR*A(IEQ,K)
120      NEXT K
130     NEXT JROW
140    NEXT IEQ
150  REM
160  REM A IS NOW UPPER TRIANGULAR
170  REM
180   FOR LEQ=0 TO M-1
190   X(N-1,LEQ)=Y(N-1,LEQ)/A(N-1,N-1)
200    FOR IEQ=(N-1)-1 TO 0 STEP -1
210    SUM=0
220     FOR K=IEQ+1 TO N-1
230     SUM=SUM+A(IEQ,K)*X(K,LEQ)
240     NEXT K
250    X(IEQ,LEQ)=(Y(IEQ,LEQ)-SUM)/A(IEQ,IEQ)
```

```
260     NEXT IEQ
270   NEXT LEQ
```

This version of Gaussian elimination executes in time proportional to n^3 plus mn^2. For moderately large m and n, this means an improvement factor of roughly m over repeated Gaussian elimination! Notice that lines 70-90 are ripe for replacement by 8087 row operations.

Space Efficient Gaussian Elimination

The Gaussian elimination program above solves multiple linear systems quickly, but requires a great deal of storage, since 2*m*n locations are allocated for Y and X. We frequently want to solve systems sequentially, so that only a single y and x need be stored.

Gaussian elimination transforms y. As you can see in lines 70-90 above, the same factors are used to transform every column of Y. If we save the factors, we can, at a later stage, transform as many different y's as we like.

At each step in the reduction, all the (lower) elements of y are transformed. Suppose we save all the factors, labeling the factors from the first step f_{00}, f_{10}, f_{20}, and so forth. The second step produces one less factor. We label these f_{11}, f_{21}, f_{31}, and so forth. Arranging the columns of factors into a matrix, we get

$$F = \begin{bmatrix} 1 & 0 & 0 & 0 & 0 & 0 \\ f_{10} & 1 & 0 & 0 & 0 & 0 \\ f_{20} & f_{21} & 1 & 0 & 0 & 0 \\ \cdot & \cdot & \cdot & 1 & 0 & 0 \\ \cdot & \cdot & \cdot & \cdot & 1 & 0 \\ \cdot & \cdot & \cdot & \cdot & \cdot & 1 \end{bmatrix}$$

The matrix of factors is *lower triangular* with ones along the diagonal. We need a convenient place to store F for later use. As we reduce A, the area below the diagonal fills with zeros. Since this lower part of A would otherwise go to waste, we'll use it to store the part of F below the diagonal, and remember that the remaining part of F is ones and zeros.

Suppose we label the transformed vector y, "y*." The reduction process transforms y according to the following rules:

$$\begin{aligned} y^*_0 &= y_0 \\ y^*_1 &= y_1 + f_{10}y^*_0 \\ y^*_2 &= y_2 + f_{20}y^*_0 + f_{21}y^*_1 \\ y^*_3 &= y_3 + f_{30}y^*_0 + f_{31}y^*_1 + f_{32}y^*_2 \end{aligned}$$

and so forth.

The first step of our space efficient program is to reduce A to upper triangular form and store the factors in A's lower triangle. Then, each time we want to find x for a new y, we generate a new y* from the stored factors and back substitute. The next set of BASIC code takes this approach.

```
5      REM PROGRAM GAUSS-SE (SPACE EFFICIENT)
10     DEFINT I-N
20     DIM A(N-1,N-1),Y(N-1),X(N-1),YSTAR(N-1)
25       REM BE SURE A,Y, AND N ARE DEFINED
30         FOR IEQ=0 TO N-1
40         IF A(IEQ,IEQ)=0 THEN PRINT "ZERO PIVOT AT",IEQ:STOP
50           FOR JROW=IEQ+1 TO N-1
60           FACTOR= -A(JROW,IEQ)/A(IEQ,IEQ)
70             FOR K=IEQ TO N-1
80             A(JROW,K)=A(JROW,K)+FACTOR*A(IEQ,K)
90             NEXT K
100          A(JROW,IEQ)=FACTOR
110          NEXT JROW
120        NEXT IEQ
130    REM
140    REM A IS NOW UPPER TRIANGULAR
150    REM
160    YSTAR(0)=Y(0)
170        FOR IEQ=0 TO (N-1)-1
180        SUM=0
190          FOR K=0 TO IEQ-1
200          SUM=SUM+A(IEQ+1,K)*YSTAR(K)
210          NEXT K
220        YSTAR(IEQ+1)=Y(IEQ+1)+SUM
230        NEXT IEQ
240    X(N-1)=YSTAR(N-1)/A(N-1,N-1)
250        FOR IEQ=(N-1)-1 TO 0 STEP -1
260        SUM=0
270          FOR K=IEQ+1 TO N-1
280          SUM=SUM+A(IEQ,K)*X(K)
290          NEXT K
300        X(IEQ)=(YSTAR(IEQ)-SUM)/A(IEQ,IEQ)
310        NEXT IEQ
```

Lines 160-310 can be repeated for other y vectors as needed. Notice that lines 190-210 are really forming an inner product and could be replaced with 8087 code.

In the next chapter, we will discuss more advanced methods of solving linear systems.

Matrix Inversion

Suppose we were faced with the scalar equation

$$y = Ax$$

and were asked to solve for x given y. We might write the answer as

$$x = y/A$$

or as

$$x = A^{-1}y$$

For a scalar equation, A^{-1}, pronounced "A inverse," is just $1/A$. The question arises as to whether there is not a matrix we could label "A^{-1}," such that $x = A^{-1}y$. There is indeed such a matrix.

First, define the *identity matrix* as a square matrix with ones along the diagonal and zeros off the diagonal. For example, if I is the 3 by 3 identity matrix, then

$$I = \begin{bmatrix} 1 & 0 & 0 \\ 0 & 1 & 0 \\ 0 & 0 & 1 \end{bmatrix}$$

The identity matrix is analogous to a one in scalar multiplication. The identities $IX = X$ and $XI = I$ hold for the identity matrix and any conformable matrix X. For scalars, we say that A^{-1} is the inverse of A if $AA^{-1} = 1$. Analogously, for matrices we say

A^{-1} is the matrix inverse of A if $AA^{-1} = I$.

(Note we are restricting our attention to square matrices. For a square matrix, not only does $AA^{-1} = I$, so does $A^{-1}A$.)

How do we "invert" a matrix? The equation $I = AA^{-1}$ has precisely the same form as the matrix equation $Y = AX$, where I is Y and A^{-1} is X. We can use our BASIC program above to reduce A to upper triangular form and then back substitute for each column of the identity matrix. Because of the special form of the identity matrix we can calculate y* without creating each y.

Assume we have executed the reduction part of the previous program. The code below replaces lines 160 on, to calculate A^{-1} in AINV.

```
160    DIM AINV(N-1,N-1)
170      FOR LEQ=0 TO N-1
180        FOR IEQ=0 TO LEQ-1
190        YSTAR(IEQ)=0
200        NEXT IEQ
210      YSTAR(LEQ)=1
220      FOR IEQ=LEQ TO (N-1)-1
230      SUM=0
240        FOR K=0 TO IEQ
250        SUM=SUM+A(IEQ+1,K)*YSTAR(K)
260        NEXT K
270      YSTAR(IEQ+1)=SUM
280      NEXT IEQ
290      AINV(N-1,LEQ)=YSTAR(N-1)/A(N-1,N-1)
300        FOR IEQ=(N-1)-1 TO 0 STEP -1
```

```
310       SUM=0
320        FOR K=IEQ+1 TO N-1
330        SUM=SUM+A(IEQ,K)*AINV(K,LEQ)
340        NEXT K
350       AINV(IEQ,LEQ)=(YSTAR(IEQ)-SUM)/A(IEQ,IEQ)
360       NEXT IEQ
370      NEXT LEQ
```

We now have a "complete" set of routines to solve systems of linear equations and invert matrices. But these routines still leave a few things to be desired.

- They stop if they hit a zero pivot.
- They would be a lot faster if written in 8087 code.
- They would be more accurate if higher precision arithmetic were used, but we do not want to sacrifice too much storage space.

In the next chapter, we remedy these faults . . . and learn a few new tricks.

11

Linear Systems and Matrix Inversion: More Advanced Computational Techniques

By the end of the last chapter, we had created a set of procedures for solving systems of linear equations and for handling the related operation of matrix inversion. These methods followed the logic of "school room" techniques. The methods we develop in this chapter are perhaps less familiar, but they lend themselves well to highly accurate and highly efficient 8087 implementation.

Our goals for this chapter are:

- Fix the "zero pivot" problem.
- Express the solution to a system of linear equations in terms of inner products, in order to take full advantage of the 8087's design.
- Move our procedures from BASIC to 8087 code.

The Cookbook—Chapter 11

Program:	**GAUSS-PP**
Purpose:	Solve linear equations by Gaussian elimination with partial pivoting.
Input:	A—N by N coefficient matrix. Y—N vector.

	YSTAR—N vector; scratch space.
	N—number of rows and columns of A.
Output:	X—N vector; X solves equations Y=AX.
	A—A replaced with permuted Gaussian reduction.
	INDEX—N vector showing row swaps.
Language:	BASIC.

Program:	**CROUT-PP**
Purpose:	Perform Crout decomposition with partial pivoting.
Input:	A—N by N coefficient matrix.
	N—number of rows and columns of A.
Output:	A—A replaced with permuted Gaussian reduction.
	INDEX—N vector showing row swaps.
Language:	BASIC.

Program:	**PIV**
Purpose:	Perform pivot step in Crout decomposition.
Input:	A—N by N coefficient matrix.
	INDEX—integer N vector of row permutations.
	TYPEA—integer giving length of element of A.
	DIAG—integer index of column to be searched.
	N—integer number of rows and columns of A.
Output:	INDEX—updated to reflect new pivot.
Language:	8087/8088 assembly language.
Note:	NEAR procedure called by PIVOT and CROUTP.

Program:	**XINP**
Purpose:	Inner product with permuted column.
Input:	A—N vector.
	B—permuted N vector.
	INDEX—integer N vector of row permutations for B.
	TYPE—integer giving length of element of A,B.
	SKIPA—integer "skip factor" (see text) for A.
	N—integer number of elements of A,B.
Output:	8087 register ST; ST=inner product A,B.
Language:	8087/8088 assembly language.
	Note: NEAR procedure called by XINPROD and CROUTP.

Program:	**XINPROD**
Purpose:	Inner product with permuted column.
Call:	CALL XINPROD(A(I,0),A(0,K),SUM,INDEX(0), TYPE,SKIPA,N).
Input:	A—N vector.
	B—permuted N vector.
	INDEX—integer N vector of row permutations for B.
	TYPE—integer giving length of element of A,B.

	SKIPA—integer "skip factor" (see text) for A.
	N—integer number of elements of A,B.
Output:	SUM—double precision scalar; sum = inner product A,B.
Language:	8087/8088 assembly language.
Note:	Requires NEAR procedure XINP.
Program:	**PIVOT**
Purpose:	Perform pivot step in Crout decomposition.
Call:	CALL PIVOT(A(0,K),INDEX(0),TYPE,K,N).
Input:	A—N by N coefficient matrix.
	INDEX—integer N vector of row permutations.
	TYPE—integer giving length of element of A.
	K—integer index of column to be searched.
	N—integer number of rows and columns of A.
Output:	INDEX—updated to reflect new pivot.
Language:	8087/8088 assembly language.
Note:	Requires NEAR procedure PIV.
Program:	**CROUTP**
Purpose:	Perform Crout decomposition with partial pivoting.
Input:	A—N by N coefficient matrix.
	TYPE—integer giving length of element of A.
	N—integer number of rows and columns of A.
Output:	INDEX—integer N vector of row permutations.
	IER—integer error flag, IER = −1 if A singular.
Language:	8087/8088 assembly language.
Note:	NEAR procedure called by REDUCE.
	Requires NEAR procedures XINP and PIV.
Program:	**REDUCE**
Purpose:	Perform Crout decomposition with partial pivoting.
Call:	CALL REDUCE(A(0,0),INDEX(0),TYPE,IER,N).
Input:	A—N by N coefficient matrix.
	TYPE—integer giving length of element of A.
	N—integer number of rows and columns of A.
Output:	INDEX—integer N vector of row permutations.
	IER—integer error flag, IER = −1 if A singular.
Language:	8087/8088 assembly language.
Note:	Requires NEAR procedures CROUTP.
Program:	**SOLP**
Purpose:	Solve system of linear equations after Crout decomposition with partial pivoting.
Input:	A—N by N matrix reduced by CROUTP with partial pivoting.
	Y—N vector.
	N—number of rows and columns of A.
	INDEX—N vector showing row swaps.
Output:	X—N vector; X solves equations Y = AX.
Language:	BASIC.

Program: **SOL**
Purpose: Solve system of linear equations after Crout decomposition with partial pivoting.
Input: A—N by N matrix reduced by CROUTP with partial pivoting.
Y—N vector.
INDEX—N vector showing row swaps.
TYPEA—integer giving length of element of A.
TYPEY—integer giving length of element of Y.
TYPEX—integer giving length of element of X.
N—integer number of rows and columns of A.
Output: X—N vector; X solves equations Y = AX.
Language: 8087/8088 assembly language.
Note: NEAR procedure called by SOLVE.

Program: **SOLVE**
Purpose: Solve system of linear equations after Crout decomposition with partial pivoting.
Call: CALL SOLVE(A(0,0),Y(0),X(0),INDEX(0),TYPEA, TYPEY,TYPEX,N).
Input: A—N by N matrix reduced by CROUTP with partial pivoting.
Y—N vector.
INDEX—N vector showing row swaps.
TYPEA—integer giving length of element of A.
TYPEY—integer giving length of element of Y.
TYPEX—integer giving length of element of X.
N—integer number of rows and columns of A.
Output: X—N vector; X solves equations Y = AX.
Language: 8087/8088 assembly language.
Note: Requires NEAR procedure SOL.

Program: **INV**
Purpose: Invert matrix.
Call: CALL SOLVE(A(0,0),AINV(0,0),SCRATCH(0), INDEX(0),IER,TYPEA,N).
Input: A—N by N matrix.
SCRATCH—single precision N vector of scratch space.
TYPEA—integer giving length of element of A,AINV.
N—integer number of rows and columns of A.
Output: AINV—N by N matrix; inverse of A.
A—A replaced by Crout reduction.
INDEX—integer N vector, permutations of reduced A.
IER—integer error flag, IER = −1 if A singular.
Language: 8087/8088 assembly language.
Note: Requires NEAR procedures CROUTP and SOL.

Our original program for Gaussian elimination stops if it hits a zero diagonal, or "pivot," element. A zero pivot may indicate a "mathematical," not "just a computational," problem, because the system of equations may not have a unique solution. Consider the following linear system as an example.

$$y_1 = 2x_1 + 4x_2$$
$$y_2 = 4x_1 + 8x_2$$

The "A" matrix is originally

$$\begin{bmatrix} 2 & 4 \\ 4 & 8 \end{bmatrix}$$

After one step of Gaussian elimination, the reduced matrix looks like this:

$$\begin{bmatrix} 2 & 4 \\ 0 & 0 \end{bmatrix}$$

In addition, we have saved the FACTOR, -2.

At the next attempted step of Gaussian elimination, the program finds that $A_{2,2}$ equals zero, and therefore stops with the error message "ZERO PIVOT AT 2." The problem is a mathematical one. The matrix A is *singular*, so the pair of equations does not have a unique solution. In fact, an infinite set of combinations of x_1 and x_2 solve the system if y_2 is twice y_1. No solution exists if y_2 isn't exactly twice y_1.

Consider the following rather different pair of equations.

$$y_1 = 0x_1 + 1x_2$$
$$y_2 = 1x_1 + 0x_2$$

The "A" matrix is originally

$$\begin{bmatrix} 0 & 1 \\ 1 & 0 \end{bmatrix}$$

Our Gaussian elimination routine hits a zero pivot—and stops—on the very first step. This example demonstrates a computational, rather than a mathematical, problem. By inspection, the solution to the system is $x_1 = y_2$ and $x_2 = y_1$. The solution to the computational problem is simple. We just reorder the equations so that the diagonal elements aren't zero. Instead of solving the system as originally specified, we work on

$$y_2 = 1x_1 + 0x_2$$
$$y_1 = 0x_1 + 1x_2$$

with the "A" matrix

$$\begin{bmatrix} 1 & 0 \\ 0 & 1 \end{bmatrix}$$

Gaussian elimination proceeds smoothly as long as we keep track of the order in which the equations are solved.

These two examples illustrate the general rules for dealing with zero pivot elements.

1. *If a zero pivot is encountered in equation i, exchange the equation i with an equation below it that does not have a zero in column i.*
2. *If all the remaining equations have a zero in column i, the matrix is singular.*
3. *Keep a record of all equation exchanges, so that we can later "unswap" the equations, if desired.*

In practice, we add two further steps.

4. *Rather than actually exchanging the equations, create an array INDEX such that INDEX(I) is the original number of the equation that now belongs in row i.*

Just as a zero pivot stops the program by creating an infinite FACTOR, so too, a very small pivot creates a very large FACTOR and tends to generate sizable round-off error. Accuracy can be considerably enhanced by using the largest possible pivot.

5. *Instead of exchanging equations only when a zero pivot is encountered (as required by rule 1), search the remainder of column i for the element, A(J,I), with the largest absolute value and exchange rows i and j.*

The implementation of Gaussian elimination with rules 2 through 5 is called *Gaussian elimination with partial pivoting*. The BASIC code below rewrites the Gaussian elimination program of the previous chapter to include partial pivoting. Notice that instead of row I, we now reference row INDEX(I), but column j remains column j.

```
5       REM PROGRAM GAUSS-PP
100     DEFINT I-N
200     DIM A(N-1,N-1),Y(N-1),X(N-1),YSTAR(N-1), INDEX(N-1)
210       FOR IEQ=0 TO N-1
220       INDEX(IEQ)=IEQ
230       NEXT IEQ
300       FOR IEQ=0 TO N-1
310       REM NOW SWAP ROWS
320       GOSUB 5000
330       SWAP INDEX(IEQ),INDEX(IBIGGEST)
340       IEQX=INDEX(IEQ)
400       IF A(IEQX,IEQ)=0 THEN PRINT "SINGULAR MATRIX",IEQ:STOP
500         FOR JROW=IEQ+1 TO N-1
510         JROWX=INDEX(JROW)
600         FACTOR=-A(JROWX,IEQ)/A(IEQX,IEQ)
700           FOR K=IEQ TO N-1
800           A(JROWX,K)=A(JROWX, K)+FACTOR*A(IEQX,K)
900           NEXT K
1000        A(JROWX,IEQ)=FACTOR
1100        NEXT JROW
1200      NEXT IEQ
1300    REM
1400    REM A IS NOW UPPER TRIANGULAR
```

```
1500   REM
1600   YSTAR(0)=Y(INDEX(0))
1700     FOR IEQ=1 TO N-1
1710     IEQX=INDEX(IEQ)
1800     SUM=0
1900       FOR K=0 TO IEQ-1
2000       SUM=SUM+A(IEQX,K)*YSTAR(K)
2100       NEXT K
2200     YSTAR(IEQ)=Y(IEQX)+SUM
2300     NEXT IEQ
2310     IN=INDEX(N-1)
2400     X(N-1)=YSTAR(N-1)/A(IN,N-1)
2500     FOR IEQ=(N-1)-1 TO 0 STEP -1
2510     IEQX=INDEX(IEQ)
2600     SUM=0
2700       FOR K=IEQ+1 TO N-1
2800       SUM=SUM+A(IEQX,K)*X(K)
2900       NEXT K
3000     X(IEQ)=(YSTAR(IEQ)-SUM)/A(IEQX,IEQ)
3100     NEXT IEQ
3200   STOP
5000   REM SUBROUTINE TO FIND LARGEST ELEMENT IN COLUMN
5100   BIGGEST=ABS(A(INDEX(IEQ),IEQ)
5200   IBIGGEST=IEQ
5300     FOR I=IEQ+1 TO N-1
5400     PIV=ABS(A(INDEX(I),IEQ))
5500     IF PIV>BIGGEST THEN BIGGEST=PIV:IBIGGEST=I
5600     NEXT I
5700   RETURN
```

This program performs the same number of multiplications and additions as simple Gaussian elimination, but will run a little more slowly due to increased overhead. The time spent selecting pivot rows is an order n^2 operation, and is therefore negligible compared to the basic reduction operation.

We've fixed the "zero pivot" problem. Before moving on to the chapter's other goals, we need to discuss some more mathematics. If you're more interested in "how" than "why," skip ahead to the programs. It will help to look at the BASIC programs before the 8087 programs, since the former are easier to follow.

The Theory of the "LU Decomposition"

A number of advanced methods of solving systems of linear equations, and consequently of matrix inversion, rely on the principle of "LU decomposition." This principle states that a square matrix A can be factored into a lower triangular matrix L and an upper triangular matrix U such that L times U equals A. There are many such decompositions. A particular method is arrived at by our choice of restrictions on the contents of L or U.

LU methods all work in three steps. Suppose the initial problem is

$y = Ax$

1. Factor A into L and U. This decomposition is an order n^3 operation. Now we have

   $y = (LU)x = L(Ux)$

   While LU is a square matrix, Ux is a column vector.
2. Solve the following system of equations for y^*. Solution of an upper (or lower) triangular system of equations is an order n^2 operation.

   $y = Ly^*$

   Since $y^* = L^{-1}y$, we next
3. Solve, the order n^2 problem

   $y^* = Ux$

Does this look like a roundabout method? It really isn't, it only seems that way. For example, the reduction process of Gaussian elimination leaves us with an upper triangular matrix that we might call U. If we add a diagonal with all ones to the set of factors we store along the way, we have a lower triangular matrix that we might call L. A bit of calculation will show you that LU indeed equals A. Further, solving for y^* and x in the Gaussian elimination programs are exactly steps 2 and 3 above. So Gaussian elimination is actually a particular example of using an LU decomposition.

The Crout Decomposition

The most useful LU method for the 8087 is called the *Crout decomposition*. (The Crout decomposition is a member of the family called "compact" methods.) The defining characteristic of the Crout decomposition is that U has all ones along the diagonal. So this LU decomposition looks like this:

$$L = \begin{bmatrix} L_{0,0} & 0 & 0 & \cdot & \cdot & 0 \\ L_{1,0} & L_{1,1} & 0 & & & \cdot \\ L_{2,0} & L_{2,1} & L_{2,2} & & & \cdot \\ \cdot & \cdot & \cdot & & & \\ \cdot & \cdot & \cdot & & & \\ \cdot & \cdot & \cdot & & & 0 \\ L_{N-1,0} & L_{N-1,1} & \cdot & \cdot & \cdot & L_{N-1,N-1} \end{bmatrix}$$

$$U = \begin{bmatrix} 1 & U_{0,1} & U_{0,2} & \cdot & \cdot & \cdot & U_{0,N-1} \\ 0 & 1 & U_{1,2} & & & & U_{1,N-1} \\ 0 & 0 & 1 & & & & \cdot \\ \cdot & & & & & & \cdot \\ \cdot & & & & & & \cdot \\ \cdot & & & & & & U_{N-2,N-1} \\ 0 & 0 & \cdot & \cdot & \cdot & 0 & 1 \end{bmatrix}$$

Notice the special pattern in which the rows of L match up with the columns of U. The inner product of row 0 of L and column 0 of U, which equals $A_{0,0}$, is just $L_{0,0}$. Moving down to the second row of L we see that $L_{1,0}$ equals $A_{1,0}$, and so forth. In this way, the entire first column of L is defined.

Now multiply the first row of L with the second column of U. We find $L_{0,0}$ times $U_{0,1}$ equals $A_{0,1}$. Since we already know $L_{0,0}$, we can solve for $U_{0,1}$ directly. Moving on to the third column of U gets us $U_{0,2}$ in the same manner. In this way the entire first row of U is defined.

Having defined the first column of L and the first row of U, we move on to the second column of L and the first row of U. In effect, the Crout procedure marches down the diagonal of the matrix. At each step, the portion of the column of L hanging down from the diagonal and the portion of the row of U sticking out to the right, are defined. To conserve space, we reuse A to store L and U. The following BASIC program performs a CROUT decomposition.

```
10    DEFINT I-N
20    DEFDBL S
30    DIM A(N-1,N-1)
40      FOR K=0 TO N-1
50      IF A(K,K)=0 THEN PRINT "ZERO PIVOT",K:STOP
60      REM FILL IN COLUMN OF L
70        FOR I=K TO N-1
80        SUM=0
90          FOR L=0 TO K-1
100         SUM=SUM+A(I,L)*A(L,K)
110         NEXT L
120       A(I,K)=A(I,K)-SUM
130       NEXT I
140     REM FILL IN ROW OF U
150       FOR J=K+1 TO N-1
160       SUM=0
170         FOR L=0 TO K-1
180         SUM=SUM+A(K,L)*A(L,J)
190       NEXT L
200       A(K,J)=(A(K,J)-SUM)/A(K,K)
210       NEXT J
220     NEXT K
```

Do you see why the Crout decomposition is so well suited to the 8087? Lines 80-110 and 160-190 form inner products between a portion of a column of L and a portion of a row of U! By using INPROD or GINPROD we take full advantage of the 8087's speed. Of probably greater importance, since the inner products are accumulated in temporary real precision, we can store a matrix in single or double precision and still get almost all the accuracy of 80-bit storage.

If you'd like to get a better handle on the logic of the Crout decomposition, you might try reducing the following 2 by 2 matrix into upper and lower triangular matrices.

$$A = \begin{bmatrix} 3 & 6 \\ 4 & 2 \end{bmatrix}$$

You should end up with these two matrices:

$$L = \begin{bmatrix} 3 & 0 \\ 4 & -6 \end{bmatrix} \qquad U = \begin{bmatrix} 1 & 2 \\ 0 & 1 \end{bmatrix}$$

Note that our program stores both L and U in place of A.

$$A \text{ reduced} = \begin{bmatrix} 3 & 2 \\ 4 & -6 \end{bmatrix}$$

The "zero pivot" problem has returned with this version of Crout decomposition. We adapt this program to include partial pivoting by exchanging rows just before filling each row of U. The next BASIC program illustrates Crout decomposition with partial pivoting.

```
5       REM PROGRAM CROUT-PP
100     DEFINT I-N
200     DEFDBL S
300     DIM A(N-1,N-1),INDEX(N-1),Y(N-1)
310       FOR I=0 TO N-1
320       INDEX(I)=I
330       NEXT I
400       FOR K=0 TO N-1
600       REM FILL IN COLUMN OF L
700         FOR I=K TO N-1
710         IX=INDEX(I)
800         SUM=0
900           FOR L=0 TO K-1
910           LX=INDEX(L)
1000          SUM=SUM+A(IX,L)*A(LX,K)
1100          NEXT L
1200        A(IX,K)=A(IX,K)-SUM
1300        NEXT I
1310    REM SWAP ROWS
1320    GOSUB 5000
```

```
1330  SWAP INDEX(K),INDEX(KBIGGEST)
1400  REM FILL IN ROW OF U
1410  KX=INDEX(K)
1420  IF A(KX,K)=0 THEN PRINT "SINGULAR MATRIX",K:STOP
1500    FOR J=K+1 TO N-1
1600    SUM=0
1700      FOR L=0 TO K-1
1710      LX=INDEX(L)
1800      SUM=SUM+A(KX,L)*A(LX,J)
1900      NEXT L
2000    A(KX,J)=(A(KX,J)-SUM)/A(KX,K)
2100    NEXT J
2200  NEXT K
3000  STOP
5000  REM SUBROUTINE TO FIND LARGEST ELEMENT IN COLUMN
5100  BIGGEST=ABS(A(INDEX)(K),K))
5200  KBIGGEST=K
5300    FOR I=K+1 TO N-1
5400    PIV=ABS(A(INDEX)(I),K))
5500    IF PIV>BIGGEST THEN BIGGEST=PIV:KBIGGEST=I
5600    NEXT I
5700  RETURN
```

This program effectively takes the original A, permutes A by swapping rows as indicated in INDEX, and then replaces A with the Crout decomposition of the permuted A. In the solution phase, we'll have to undo the row swaps.

8087 Routines for Solving Systems of Linear Equations

The time has finally arrived to prepare high-speed 8087 routines for solving systems of linear equations and for matrix inversion. Three routines based on the Crout decomposition with partial pivoting appear below. REDUCE reduces a matrix to its LU decomposition. Given the reduced matrix and the vector y, SOLVE calculates x, as in y = Ax. INV inverts a matrix in one step.

For maximum flexibility, we write a series of 8087 internal procedures, and then add external procedures that may be called from BASIC. Our first procedure, PIV, finds the largest element of a column, indexed by INDEX, and exchanges indexes to accomplish partial pivoting.

```
;SUBROUTINE PIV(A,INDEX,TYPEA,DIAG,N)
; ASSUMPTIONS: A IS ADDRESS OF N-ARRAY IN DATA SEGMENT
;              INDEX IS AN INTEGER N-ARRAY
;              TYPEA,DIAG,N ARE INTEGERS
;              NOTE THIS PROCEDURE CANNOT BE CALLED FROM
               BASIC
;              IT FINDS ITS ARGUMENTS ON THE STACK
;              NOT THEIR ADDRESSES
```

```
;
;               THERE MUST BE AT LEAST 2 FREE LOCATIONS ON
;               THE 8087 STACK AND AT LEAST 14 FREE BYTES ON
;               THE MEMORY STACK
;               THE LAST 2 WORDS OF LOCAL_SPACE MUST ALSO BE
                 FREE
;
;               PIV A SEARCHES FROM DIAG
;               TO THE BOTTOM FOR THE ELEMENT LARGEST IN
;               ABSOLUTE VALUE. PIV EXCHANGES THE INDEXES OF
;               DIAG AND THIS ELEMENT
;
;               A IS AN N-VECTOR PERMUTED ACCORDING TO INDEX
;
;
          ASSUME    CS:CSEG,ES:ESEG
PIV       PROC      NEAR
          PUSH      BP
          MOV       BP,SP
;SINCE THIS IS A NEAR PROCEDURE, ARGUMENTS BEGIN AT [BP]+4
          PUSH      AX
          PUSH      BX
          PUSH      CX
          PUSH      DX
          PUSH      SI
          PUSH      DI
          MOV       CX,[BP]+4           ;CX=N
          MOV       SI,[BP]+12          ;SI=ADDR(A)
          MOV       DI,[BP]+10          ;DI=ADDR(INDEX)
          MOV       DX,[BP]+6           ;DX=DIAG
          ADD       DI,DX
          ADD       DI,DX               ;DI=ADDR(INDEX(DIAG))
KBIGGEST EQU LOCAL_SPACE_LAST-2         ;KEEP BIGGEST FOUND
          MOV       KBIGGEST,DI         ;ASSUME FIRST IS
                                         BIGGEST
          SUB       CX,DX               ;CX=N-DIAG,
          DEC       CX                  ; # OF ELEMENTS TO
                                         CHECK
          MOV       AX,[BP]+8           ;AX=TYPEA
          MUL       WORD PTR [DI]       ;AX=TYPEA*INDEX(DI)
          MOV       BX,AX
          CMP       WORD PTR [BP]+8,4   ;IS A SINGLE?
          JNE       A_DOUBLE
          FLD       DWORD PTR [SI][BX]  ;LOAD SINGLE
          JMP       LOADED_ONE
A_DOUBLE: FLD       QWORD PTR [SI][BX]  ;LOAD DOUBLE
LOADED_ONE:
          FABS
          JCXZ      DONE
COMP_LOOP:
          ADD       DI,2                ;NEXT INDEX
          MOV       AX,[BP]+8           ;AX=TYPEA
```

```
            MUL         WORD PTR [DI]       ;AX=TYPEA*INDEX(DI)
            MOV         BX,AX
            CMP         WORD PTR [BP]+8,4   ;IS A SINGLE?
            JNE         AI_DOUBLE
            FLD         DWORD PTR [SI][BX]  ;LOAD SINGLE
            JMP         COMPARE
AI_DOUBLE:  FLD         QWORD PTR [SI][BX]  ;LOAD DOUBLE
COMPARE:
            FABS
            FCOM                            ;COMPARE NEW TO
                                             BIGGEST
STATUS_WORD EQU LOCAL_SPACE_LAST-4          ;SCRATCH SPACE
            FSTSW       STATUS_WORD
            FWAIT
            MOV         AH,BYTE PTR STATUS_WORD+1
            SAHF
            JB          LESS_OR_NONCOMPARABLE
;HERE IF NEW IS GREATER THAN OR EQUAL TO BIGGEST
            FSTP        ST(1)               ;MOVE NEW DOWN STACK
            MOV         KBIGGEST,DI
            JMP         NEXT_ELEMENT
                                            ;BIGGEST IS STILL
LESS_OR_NONCOMPARABLE:                       CHAMP
            FSTP        ST(0)

NEXT_ELEMENT:
            LOOP        COMP_LOOP
;SWAP INDEX(DIAG) AND INDEX(KBIGGEST)
            MOV         DX,[BP]+6           ;DX=DIAG
            MOV         DI,[BP]+10          ;DI=ADDR(INDEX)
            ADD         DI,DX
            ADD         DI,DX               ;DI=ADDR(INDEX(DIAG))
            MOV         AX,[DI]             ;AX=INDEX(DIAG)
            MOV         BX,KBIGGEST         ;BX=ADDR(INDEX
                                             (KBIGGEST))
            XCHG        AX,[BX]
            XCHG        AX,[DI]
DONE:
            FSTP        ST(0)               ;CLEAR ELEMENT OFF
                                             STACK
            POP         DI
            POP         SI
            POP         DX
            POP         CX
            POP         BX
            POP         AX
            POP         BP
            RET         10
PIV         ENDP
```

Procedure PIV takes roughly 80 microseconds per element. When used for partial pivoting, PIV searches n, n-1, n-2, and so forth elements at successive calls. Quite roughly then, in solving a system of n equations, we spend about $80n^2/2$ microseconds in PIV. For a large matrix, PIV might take up half a second. If you'd like an exercise in array addressing techniques, rewrite PIV replacing the MUL instruction in COMP_LOOP with appropriate SHL (SHift Left) instructions. You should be able to speed up PIV by about 25 percent.

Most of the work of the Crout decomposition is a series of inner products. Unfortunately, the rows are permuted according to INDEX, so we can't use procedure GINP. GINP assumes that columns are stored sequentially, while ours are "scrambled." Procedure XINP does an inner product with indexed columns.

```
;SUBROUTINE XINP(A(I,0),A(0,J),INDEX,TYPE,SKIPA,N)
; ASSUMPTIONS: A(I,0) IS THE ADDRESS OF ROW I
;              A(0,J) IS THE ADDRESS OF COLUMN J
;              INDEX IS THE ADDRESS OF INTEGER ARRAY INDEX
;              TYPE,SKIPA,N ARE INTEGERS
;              NOTE THIS PROCEDURE CANNOT BE CALLED FROM
                BASIC
;              IT FINDS ITS ARGUMENTS ON THE STACK
;              NOT THEIR ADDRESSES
;
;              THERE MUST BE AT LEAST 2 FREE LOCATIONS ON
;              THE 8087 STACK AND AT LEAST 14 FREE BYTES ON
;              THE MEMORY STACK
;
;              XINP RETURNS THE INNER PRODUCT OF THE FIRST N
;              ELEMENTS OF ROW I AND COLUMN J ON THE
;              8087 STACK
;
;              XINP TAKES EVERY SKIPA ELEMENT OF A(I,0) AND
;              INDEXES THE ELEMENTS OF A(0,J)
;
          ASSUME     CS:CSEG
XINP      PROC       NEAR
          PUSH       BP
          MOV        BP,SP

;SINCE THIS IS A NEAR PROCEDURE, ARGUMENTS BEGIN AT [BP]+4
          PUSH       AX
          PUSH       BX
          PUSH       CX
          PUSH       DX
          PUSH       SI
          PUSH       DI
          FLDZ                          ;SET RUNNING SUM=0
          JCXZ       DONE
          MOV        SI,[BP]+14         ;SI=ADDR(A(I,0))
          MOV        DI,[BP]+10         ;DI=ADDR(INDEX)
;IF TYPE IS SINGLE PRECISION SET CX=2 ELSE SET CX=3
```

```
; USE CX FOR SHIFTING BELOW
          MOV       CX,3                 ;ASSUME TYPE DOUBLE
          CMP       WORD PTR [BP]+8,4    ;IS TYPE SINGLE?
          JNE       NOT_SINGLE
          MOV       CX,2                 ;YES, TYPE IS SINGLE
NOT_SINGLE:
          MOV       AX,[BP]+6            ;AX=SKIP
          SHL       AX,CL                ;AX=A ELEMENT DISTANCE
          CMP       WORD PTR [BP]+4,0    ;N LE 0?
          JLE       DONE
XINP_LOOP:
;FIRST GET READY FOR COLUMN
          MOV       BX,[DI]              ;BX=INDEX(L)
          SHL       BX,CL                ;BX=TYPE*INDEX(L)
          ADD       BX,[BP]+12           ;BX=A(INDEX(L),L)

          CMP       CL,2                 ;IS A SINGLE?
          JNE       A_DOUBLE
          FLD       DWORD PTR [SI]       ;LOAD SINGLE ROW
                                          ELEMENT
          JMP       MULT_B
A_DOUBLE: FLD       QWORD PTR [SI]       ;LOAD DOUBLE COL
                                          ELEMENT
MULT_B:
          CMP       CL,2                 ;IS A SINGLE?
          JNE       A_DOUBLE2
          FMUL      DWORD PTR [BX]       ;MULTIPLY SINGLE
          JMP       NEXT_ELEMENT
A_DOUBLE2: FMUL     QWORD PTR [BX]       ;MULTIPLY DOUBLE

NEXT_ELEMENT:
          FADDP     ST(1),ST             ;SUM=SUM+ROW(L)*COL(L)
          ADD       SI,AX                ;NEXT ROW ELEMENT
          ADD       DI,2                 ;NEXT INDEX
          DEC       WORD PTR [BP]+4      ;DECREMENT COUNT(NOTE N
          CMP       WORD PTR [BP]+4,0    ; WAS IN TEMP LOCATION)
          JG        XINP_LOOP

DONE:
          POP       DI
          POP       SI
          POP       DX
          POP       CX
          POP       BX
          POP       AX
          POP       BP
          RET       12
XINP      ENDP
```

Like most of our inner product routines, XINP uses about 59 microseconds per element. Notice that we went to the trouble of using the shift rather than the multiply. It actually takes the 8088 longer to multiply two integers than it takes the 8087 to multiply single precision numbers.

If we multiplied rather than shifted, the 8087 would have to wait idly while the 8088 calculated the next address.

Essentially all of the hard computational work of the Crout decomposition is done by XINP. Because it is a NEAR procedure, XINP cannot be called directly from BASIC. Procedure XINPROD, below, is a FAR procedure, callable from BASIC, that calls XINP for us and then returns the inner product as a double precision result. It's also convenient to be able to use PIV, even though PIV is only called n times as compared to the n^2 calls to XINP, so we also include a FAR procedure, PIVOT.

```
;SUBROUTINE XINPROD(A(I,0),A(0,J),SUM,INDEX,TYPE,SKIPA,N)
; ASSUMPTIONS: A(I,0),A(0,J),INDEX ARE ADDRESSES TO BE PASSED
;               TO XINP
;              TYPE,SKIPA,N ARE ADDRESSES OF INTEGERS WHOSE
;               VALUES SHOULD BE PASSED TO XINP
;              XINP RETURNS THE RESULT ON THE TOP OF STACK
;
;              IT SHOULD BE PLACED IN DOUBLE PRECISION SUM
;
  XINP CALLS THE INTERNAL SUBROUTINE XINP
;
            PUBLIC      XINPROD
            ASSUME      CS:CSEG,ES:ESEG
XINPROD     PROC        FAR
            PUSH        BP
            MOV         BP,SP

;SET UP STACK AREA IN ESEG
            PUSH        ES
            CALL        NEXT
NEXT:       POP         AX
            SUB         AX,(OFFSET NEXT)-(OFFSET FIRST_INST)
            MOV         CL,4
            SHR         AX,CL
            MOV         BX,CS
            ADD         BX,ESEG
            SUB         BX,CSEG
            ADD         AX,BX
            MOV         ES,AX
;
            MOV         LOCAL_SPACE,SS
            MOV         LOCAL_SPACE+2,SP
            MOV         AX,ES
            MOV         SS,AX
            MOV         SP,OFFSET STACK_TOP
;
;SET UP CALL PARAMETERS
            PUSH        DS:[BP]+18          ;ADDR(A(I,0))
            PUSH        DS:[BP]+16          ;ADDR(A(0,J))
            PUSH        DS:[BP]+12          ;ADDR(INDEX)
            MOV         BX,DS:[BP]+10       ;BX=ADDR(TYPE)
            PUSH        [BX]                ;TYPE
```

```
        MOV     BX,DS:[BP]+8    ;BX=ADDR(SKIPA)
        PUSH    [BX]            ;SKIPA
        MOV     BX,DS:[BP]+6    ;BX=ADDR(N)
        PUSH    [BX]            ;N
;
        CALL    XINP
        MOV     SP,LOCAL_SPACE+2
        MOV     SS,LOCAL_SPACE
        MOV     BX,[BP]+14      ;BX=ADDR(SUM)
        FSTP    QWORD PTR [BX]  ;STORE SUM
        POP     ES
        POP     BP
        FWAIT
        RET     14
XINPROD ENDP




;SUBROUTINE PIVOT(A(0,K),INDEX,TYPE,K,N)
; ASSUMPTIONS: A(I,0),INDEX ARE ADDRESSES TO BE PASSED
;                TO PIVOT
;              TYPE,K,N ARE ADDRESSES OF INTEGERS WHOSE
;                VALUES SHOULD BE PASSED TO XINP
;
; PIVOT CALLS THE INTERNAL SUBROUTINE PIV
;
        PUBLIC  PIVOT
        ASSUME  CS:CSEG,ES:ESEG
PIVOT   PROC    FAR
        PUSH    BP
        MOV     BP,SP
;SET UP STACK AREA IN ESEG
        PUSH    ES
        CALL    NEXT
NEXT:   POP     AX
        SUB     AX,(OFFSET NEXT)-(OFFSET FIRST_INST)
        MOV     CL,4
        SHR     AX,CL
        MOV     BX,CS
        ADD     BX,ESEG
        SUB     BX,CSEG
        ADD     AX,BX
        MOV     ES,AX
;
        MOV     LOCAL_SPACE,SS
        MOV     LOCAL_SPACE+2,SP
        MOV     AX,ES
        MOV     SS,AX
        MOV     SP,OFFSET STACK_TOP
;
```

```
;SET UP CALL PARAMETERS
            PUSH        DS:[BP]+14        ;ADDR(A(0,K))
            PUSH        DS:[BP]+12        ;ADDR(INDEX)
            MOV         BX,DS:[BP]+10     ;BX=ADDR(TYPE)
            PUSH        [BX]              ;TYPE
            MOV         BX,DS:[BP]+8      ;BX=ADDR(K)
            PUSH        [BX]              ;K
            MOV         BX,DS:[BP]+6      ;BX=ADDR(N)
            PUSH        [BX]              ;N
;
            CALL        PIV
            MOV         SP,LOCAL_SPACE+2
            MOV         SS,LOCAL_SPACE
            POP         ES
            POP         BP
            RET         10
PIVOT       ENDP
```

With XINPROD and PIVOT in hand, we need only replace the appropriate lines of the BASIC program with CALL statements. The new version of the BASIC program appears below.

```
100     DEFINT I-N
200     DEFDBL S
300     DIM A(N-1,N-1),INDEX(N-1)
310       FOR I=0 TO N-1
320       INDEX(I)=I
330       NEXT I
340       ITYPE=4
400       FOR K=0 TO N-1
600       REM FILL IN COLUMN OF L
700         FOR I=K TO N-1
710         IX=INDEX(I)
800         SUM=0
900           REM FOR L=0 TO K-1
910           REM LX=INDEX(L)
1000          REM SUM=SUM+A(IX,L)*A(LX,K)
1100          REM NEXT L
1150        CALL XINPROD(A(IX,0),A(0,K),SUM,INDEX(0),ITYPE,N,K)
1200        A(IX,K)=A(IX,K)-SUM
1300        NEXT I
1310    REM SWAP ROWS
1320    REM GOSUB 5000
1330    REM SWAP INDEX(K),INDEX(KBIGGEST)
1350    CALL PIVOT(A(0,K),INDEX(0),TYPE,K,N)
1400    REM FILL IN ROW OF U
1410    KX=INDEX(K)
1420    IF A(KX,K)=0 THEN PRINT "SINGULAR MATRIX",K:STOP
1500      FOR J=K+1 TO N-1
1600      SUM=0
1700        REM FOR L=0 TO K-1
1710        REM LX=INDEX(L)
```

```
1800      REM SUM=SUM+A(KX,L)*A(LX,J)
1900      REM NEXT L
1950     CALL XINPROD(A(KX,0),A(0,J),SUM,INDEX(0),ITYPE,N,K)
2000     A(KX,J)=(A(KX,J)-SUM)/A(KX,K)
2100     NEXT J
2200    NEXT K
5000    REM SUBROUTINE TO FIND LARGEST ELEMENT IN COLUMN
5100    REM BIGGEST=ABS(A(INDEX(K),K))
5200    REM KBIGGEST=K
5300     REM FOR I=K+1 TO N-1
5400     REM PIV=ABS(A(INDEX(I),K))
5500     REM IF PIV>BIGGEST THEN BIGGEST=PIV:KBIGGEST=I
5600     REM NEXT I
5700    REM RETURN
```

XINP does most of the hard work of Crout reduction. For large n, most execution time is spent doing the inner products, so the BASIC code above is quite efficient. Lines 700−1300 and 1500−2100 are executed n^2 times. For moderate n, these lines may take up a substantial amount of time. In procedure CROUTP we put everything together into an 8087 program for Crout reduction with partial pivoting.

```
;SUBROUTINE CROUTP(A,INDEX,IER,TYPE,N)
; ASSUMPTIONS: A IS THE ADDRESS OF AN N BY N MATRIX
;              INDEX IS THE ADDRESS OF AN INTEGER N-ARRAY
;              IER IS THE ADDRESS OF AN INTEGER
;              TYPE,N ARE INTEGERS
;              NOTE THIS PROCEDURE CANNOT BE CALLED FROM
                BASIC
;              IT FINDS ITS ARGUMENTS ON THE STACK
;              NOT THEIR ADDRESSES
;
;              CROUTP REPLACES A WITH THE CROUT LU
                DECOMPOSITION
;              OF THE PERMUTATION OF A RETURNED IN INDEX
;
;              AT EXIT IER=-1 IF MATRIX IS SINGULAR, ELSE
                IER=0;
          ASSUME    CS:CSEG
CROUTP    PROC      NEAR
          PUSH      BP
          MOV       BP,SP
;SINCE THIS IS A NEAR PROCEDURE, ARGUMENTS BEGIN AT [BP]+4
          PUSH      AX                  ;THESE ARE
                                         UNNECESSARY
          PUSH      BX
          PUSH      CX
          PUSH      DX
          PUSH      SI
          PUSH      DI                  ;BUT GOOD FORM
;
```

```
            MOV         BX,[BP]+8              ;BX=ADDR(IER)
            MOV         WORD PTR [BX],0        ;IER=0
;FIRST SET INDEX(I)=I
            MOV         CX,[BP]+4              ;CX=N
            MOV         DI,[BP]+10             ;DI=ADDR(INDEX)
            MOV         AX,0
INDEX_LOOP:
            MOV         [DI],AX                ;INDEX(I)=I
            INC         AX
            ADD         DI,2
            LOOP        INDEX_LOOP
;
;IF TYPE IS SINGLE PRECISION SET CX=2 ELSE SET CX=3
; USE CX FOR SHIFTING BELOW
            MOV         CX,3                   ;ASSUME TYPE DOUBLE
            CMP         WORD PTR [BP]+6,4      ;IS TYPE SINGLE?
            JNE         NOT_SINGLE
            MOV         CX,2                   ;YES, TYPE IS SINGLE
NOT_SINGLE:
;OUTERMOST LOOP IS FOR K=0 TO N-1
            MOV         SI,0                   ;KEEP K IN SI
;
;
MAJOR_LOOP:
            MOV         AX,[BP]+4              ;AX=N
            MUL         SI                     ;AX=N*K
            SHL         AX,CL                  ;AX=TYPE*N*K
            MOV         DX,AX
            ADD         DX,[BP]+12             ;DX=ADDR(A(0,K))
;FILL IN COLUMN OF L
;MOVE THROUGH INDEX(I) FOR I=K TO N-1
;
COUNT EQU LOCAL_SPACE+4                        ;SCRATCH SPACE FOR
                                                COUNTS
;
            MOV         AX,[BP]+4              ;AX=N
            SUB         AX,SI                  ;AX=N-K
            MOV         COUNT,AX               ;COUNT=N-K
;
            MOV         DI,[BP]+10             ;DI=ADDR(INDEX(0))
            ADD         DI,SI
            ADD         DI,SI                  ;DI=ADDR(INDEX(I))
L_LOOP:
;CALL XINP(A(INDEX(I),0),A(0,K),INDEX,TYPE,N,K)
;
            MOV         BX,[DI]                ;BX=INDEX(I)
            SHL         BX,CL                  ;BX=BEGINNING OF ROW
            ADD         BX,[BP]+12             ;BX=ADDR(A(INDEX(I),0))
            PUSH        BX
            PUSH        DX                     ;ADDR(A(0,K))
            PUSH        [BP]+10                ;ADDR(INDEX)
            PUSH        [BP]+6                 ;TYPE
```

```
           PUSH       [BP]+4                ;N
           PUSH       SI                    ;K
           CALL       XINP
;GET ADDRESS OF A(INDEX(I),K)
           MOV        BX,[DI]               ;BX=INDEX(I)
           SHL        BX,CL                 ;BX=TYPE*K
           ADD        BX,DX                 ;BX=ADDR(A(INDEX(I),K))
;CALCULATE A(INDEX(I),K)-SUM FOR SINGLE OR DOUBLE PRECISION
           CMP        CX,2                  ;SINGLE?
           JNE        A_DOUBLE
           FSUBR      DWORD PTR [BX]        ;ST=A(INDEX(I),K)-SUM
           FSTP       DWORD PTR [BX]        ;A(INDEX(I),K)=ST
           JMP        NEXT_COL_ELEMENT
;
A_DOUBLE:  FSUBR      QWORD PTR [BX]        ;ST=A(INDEX(I),K)-SUM
           FSTP       QWORD PTR [BX]        ;A(INDEX(I),K)=ST

           JMP        NEXT_COL_ELEMENT
;
NEXT_COL_ELEMENT:
           ADD        DI,2                  ;NEXT INDEX(I)
           DEC        COUNT
           CMP        COUNT,0
           JG         L_LOOP

;
;
;CALL PIV(A(0,K),INDEX,TYPE,K,N)
           PUSH       DX                    ;ADDR(A(0,K))
           PUSH       [BP]+10               ;ADDR INDEX
           PUSH       [BP]+6                ;TYPE
           PUSH       SI                    ;K
           PUSH       [BP]+4                ;N
           CALL       PIV
;********CHECK FOR SINGULAR MATRIX
;IS A(INDEX(K),K)=0???
;
STATUS_WORD EQU LOCAL_SPACE+6
;
           MOV        DI,[BP]+10            ;DI=ADDR(INDEX)
           ADD        DI,SI
           ADD        DI,SI                 ;DI=ADDR(INDEX(K))
           MOV        DI,[DI]               ;DI=INDEX(K)
           SHL        DI,CL                 ;DI=TYPE*INDEX(K)
           ADD        DI,DX                 ;DI=ADDR(A(INDEX(K),K)
;
           CMP        CX,2                  ;SINGLE?
           JNE        A_DOUBLE2
           FLD        DWORD PTR [DI]        ;LOAD A(INDEX(K),K)
                                            ;AND LEAVE IT ON
                                             STACK
           JMP        TEST_FOR_ZERO
A_DOUBLE2: FLD        QWORD PTR [DI]
```

```
 TEST_FOR_ZERO:
          FTST
          FSTSW      STATUS_WORD
          FWAIT
          MOV        AH,BYTE PTR STATUS_WORD+1
          SAHF
          JC         NOT_SINGULAR         ;JUMP IF C3=0
          JNZ        NOT_SINGULAR         ;OR   IF C0=0

;SINGULAR MATRIX
          MOV        BX,[BP]+8            ;BX=ADDR(IER)
          MOV        WORD PTR [BX],-1     ;IER=-1
          JMP        DONE

NOT_SINGULAR:
;FILL IN ROW OF U
;MOVE J THROUGH K+1 TO N-1
          MOV        AX,[BP]+4            ;AX=N
          SUB        AX,SI                ;AX=N-K
          MOV        DI,[BP]+10           ;DI=ADDR(INDEX)
          ADD        DI,SI
          ADD        DI,SI                ;DI=ADDR(INDEX(K))
          MOV        DI,[DI]              ;DI=INDEX(K)
          SHL        DI,CL                ;DI=TYPE*INDEX(K)
          ADD        DI,[BP]+12           ;DI=ADDR(A(INDEX)K),0))
;
          MOV        AX,SI                ;AX=K
          MUL        WORD PTR [BP]+4      ;AX=N*K
          SHL        AX,CL                ;AX=TYPE*N*K
;
          MOV        DX,[BP]+4            ;DX=N
          SUB        DX,SI                ;DX=N-K
          MOV        COUNT,DX
U_LOOP:   DEC        COUNT                ;COUNT=COUNT-1
          CMP        COUNT,0
          JLE        END_U_LOOP
;
          MOV        BX,[BP]+4            ;BX=N
          SHL        BX,CL                ;BX=TYPE*N
          ADD        AX,BX                ;AX=TYPE*N*J
;
;CALL XINP(A(INDEX(K),0),A(0,J),INDEX,TYPE,N,K)
          PUSH       DI                   ;ADDR(A(INDEX(K),0))
          MOV        BX,[BP]+12           ;BX=ADDR(A(0,0)
          ADD        BX,AX
          PUSH       BX                   ;ADDR A(0,J)
          PUSH       [BP]+10              ;ADDR INDEX
          PUSH       [BP]+6               ;TYPE
          PUSH       [BP]+4               ;N
          PUSH       SI                   ;K
          CALL       XINP
;CALCULATE (A(INDEX(K),J)-SUM)/A(INDEX(K),K)
; FOR SINGLE OR DOUBLE PRECISION
```

```
;NOTE THAT SUM IS IN ST
;AND A(INDEX(K),K) IN ST(1)
           MOV       BX,DI                ;BX=ADDR(A(INDEX(K),0))
           ADD       BX,AX                ;BX=ADDR(A(INDEX(K),J))
           CMP       CX,2                 ;SINGLE?
           JNE       A_DOUBLE3
           FSUBR     DWORD PTR [BX]       ;ST=A(INDEX(K),J)-SUM
           FDIV      ST,ST(1)             ;ST=ST/A(INDEX(K),K)
           FSTP      DWORD PTR [BX]       ;A(INDEX(I),K)=ST
           JMP       NEXT_ROW_ELEMENT
;
A_DOUBLE3:
           FSUBR     QWORD PTR [BX]       ;ST=A(INDEX(K),J)-SUM
           FDIV      ST,ST(1)             ;ST=ST/A(INDEX(K),K)
           FSTP      QWORD PTR [BX]       ;A(INDEX(I),K)=ST
;
NEXT_ROW_ELEMENT:
           JMP       U_LOOP
;
END_U_LOOP:
           FSTP      ST(0)                ;CLEAR ST
;READY FOR NEXT K
           INC       SI
           CMP       SI,WORD PTR [BP]+4 ;K=N?
           JGE       DONE
           JMP       MAJOR_LOOP
;
DONE:
           POP       DI
           POP       SI
           POP       DX
           POP       CX
           POP       BX
           POP       AX
           POP       BP
           RET       10
CROUTP     ENDP
```

All we need now is a procedure to call CROUTP from BASIC. We'll call this procedure REDUCE. Procedure REDUCE is called by

```
CALL REDUCE(A(0,0),INDEX(0),TYPE,IER,N)
```

where A is the N by N matrix of coefficients. INDEX is an integer array returning the row permutations. TYPE, IER, and N are integers. TYPE indicates whether A is single or double precision. IER returns 0 if the matrix is nonsingular and -1 if the matrix is singular. REDUCE replaces A with its Crout reduction with partial pivoting.

```
;SUBROUTINE REDUCE(A(0,0),INDEX(0),TYPE,IER,N)
; ASSUMPTIONS: A(0,0),INDEX(0),IER ARE ADDRESSES TO BE PASSED
;                 TO CROUTP
```

```
;              TYPE,N ARE ADDRESSES OF INTEGERS WHOSE
;               VALUES SHOULD BE PASSED TO CROUTP
;
; REDUCE CALLS THE INTERNAL SUBROUTINE CROUTP
;
          PUBLIC      REDUCE
          ASSUME      CS:CSEG,ES:ESEG
REDUCE    PROC        FAR
          PUSH        BP
          MOV         BP,SP

;SET UP STACK AREA IN ESEG
          PUSH        ES
          CALL        NEXT
NEXT:     POP         AX
          SUB         AX,(OFFSET NEXT)-(OFFSET FIRST_INST)
          MOV         CL,4
          SHR         AX,CL
          MOV         BX,CS
          ADD         BX,ESEG
          SUB         BX,CSEG
          ADD         AX,BX
          MOV         ES,AX
;
          MOV         LOCAL_SPACE,SS
          MOV         LOCAL_SPACE+2,SP
          MOV         AX,ES
          MOV         SS,AX
          MOV         SP,OFFSET STACK_TOP
;
;SET UP CALL PARAMETERS
          PUSH        DS:[BP]+14       ;ADDR(A(0,0))
          PUSH        DS:[BP]+12       ;ADDR(INDEX)
          PUSH        DS:[BP]+8        ;ADDR(IER)
          MOV         BX,DS:[BP]+10    ;BX=ADDR(TYPE)
          PUSH        [BX]             ;TYPE
          MOV         BX,DS:[BP]+6     ;BX=ADDR(N)
          PUSH        [BX]             ;N
;
          CALL        CROUTP
          MOV         SP,LOCAL_SPACE+2
          MOV         SS,LOCAL_SPACE
          POP         ES
          POP         BP
          RET         10
REDUCE    ENDP
```

Back Substitution After a Crout Reduction

REDUCE leaves the LU decomposition in A and the order of row permutation in INDEX. Temporarily setting aside the question of INDEXing, we face a computationally straightforward problem of solving $y = LUx$ for x. We do this in two steps. First, solve $y = Ly^*$ for y^*. Second, solve $y^* = Ux$ for x.

Examination of the triangular matrices above shows the simple form for solving triangular systems of equations. For a lower triangular system,

$$y_0 = L_{0,0}y^*_0$$

$$y_1 = L_{1,0}y^*_0 + L_{1,1}y^*_1$$

$$y_2 = L_{2,0}y^*_0 + L_{2,1}y^*_1 + L_{2,2}y^*_2$$

and so forth.

Turning these equations around we can solve directly for y^*.

$$y^*_0 = y_0/L_{0,0}$$

$$y^*_1 = (y_1 - L_{1,0}y^*_0)/L_{1,1}$$

$$y^*_2 = (y_2 - (L_{2,0}y^*_0 + L_{2,1}y^*_1))/L_{2,2}$$

and so forth.

For an upper triangular system we have:

$$y^*_{n-1} = U_{n-1,n-1}x_{n-1}$$

$$y^*_{n-2} = U_{n-2,n-2}x_{n-2} + U_{n-2,n-1}x_{n-1}$$

$$y^*_{n-3} = U_{n-3,n-3}x_{n-3} + U_{n-3,n-2}x_{n-2} + U_{n-3,n-1}x_{n-1}$$

and so forth.

As we turn these equations around to solve for x, remember that $U_{i,i}$ equals 1 after the Crout reduction.

$$x_{n-1} = y^*_{n-1}$$

$$x_{n-2} = (y^*_{n-2} - U_{n-2,n-1}x_{n-1})$$

$$x_{n-3} = (y^*_{n-3} - (U_{n-3,n-2}x_{n-2} + U_{n-3,n-1}x_{n-1}))$$

and so forth.

The following BASIC code takes a Crout reduced matrix A and a column vector X and solves for X.

```
10    DEFINT I-N
20    DEFDBL S
30    DIM A(N-1,N-1),YSTAR(N-1),Y(N-1),X(N-1)
40    REM SOLVE LOWER TRIANGULAR SYSTEM FOR YSTAR
50      FOR I=0 TO N-1
60      SUM=0
70        FOR J=0 TO I-1
80        SUM=SUM+A(I,J)*YSTAR(J)
90        NEXT J
100     YSTAR(I)=(Y(I)-SUM)/A(I,I)
```

```
110      NEXT I
120     REM SOLVE UPPER TRIANGULAR SYSTEM FOR X
130      FOR I=N-1 TO 0 STEP -1
140      SUM=0
150       FOR J=I+1 TO N-1
160       SUM=SUM+A(I,J)*X(J)
170       NEXT J
180      X(I)=YSTAR(I)-SUM
190      NEXT I
```

Notice that solving the lower triangular and upper triangular system are both order n^2 operations. Once order n^3 operations have been performed to reduce A, each new y can be solved for x at the expense of only order n^2 additional operations. Notice that lines 60-90 and 140-170 form inner products. We could use GINPROD here.

REDUCE performs row permutations in the process of generating a triangular form. Our next set of BASIC code "undoes" the INDEXing and also makes explicit use of GINPROD.

```
2500    REM PROGRAM SOLP
2600   ITYPE=4
2700   I1=1
2800   REM USE X FOR SCRATCH SPACE, RATHER THAN "Y*"
2900   REM SOLVE LOWER TRIANGULAR SYSTEM FOR YSTAR
3000      FOR I=0 TO N-1
3100      NUM=I
3200      CALL GINPROD(A(INDEX(I),0),X(0),SUM,ITYPE,ITYPE,N,I1,
        NUM)
3300      X(I)=(Y(INDEX(I))-SUM)/A(INDEX(I),I)
3400    NEXT I
3500    REM SOLVE UPPER TRIANGULAR SYSTEM FOR X
3600      FOR I=N-1 TO 0 STEP -1
3700      IP=I+1
3800      NUM=N-IP
3900    REM CALL GINPROD(A(INDEX(I),IP),X(IP),SUM,
        ITYPE,ITYPE,N,I1,NUM)
4000    X(I)=X(I)-SUM
4100    NEXT I
```

The BASIC program is easily recoded into an 8087 NEAR procedure, SOL, which can be called from BASIC by the external procedure SOLVE.

```
;SUBROUTINE SOL(A,Y,X,INDEX,TYPEA,TYPEY,TYPEX,N)
; ASSUMPTIONS: A,Y,X,INDEX ARE ADDRESSES
;              TYPEA,TYPEY,TYPEX,N ARE INTEGERS
;              NOTE THIS PROCEDURE CANNOT BE CALLED FROM
;               BASIC
;              IT FINDS ITS ARGUMENTS ON THE STACK
;              NOT THEIR ADDRESSES
;
;              SOL SOLVES Y=AX FOR X, WHERE A AND INDEX
;               RESULT
```

```
;               FROM A CROUT DECOMPOSITION WITH PARTIAL
;                PIVOTING
            ASSUME    CS:CSEG
SOL         PROC      NEAR
            PUSH      BP
            MOV       BP,SP
            PUSH      AX
            PUSH      BX
            PUSH      CX
            PUSH      DX
            PUSH      SI
            PUSH      DI
;TAKE CARE OF LOWER TRIANGLE
;FOR I=0 TO N-1
            MOV       CX,[BP]+4             ;CX=N
            CMP       CX,0
            JG        AROUND
            JMP       DONE
AROUND:     MOV       SI,0                  ;KEEP I IN SI
            MOV       DI,[BP]+12            ;DI=ADDR(INDEX(0))
L_LOOP:
;CALL GINP(A(INDEX(I),0),X(0),TYPEA,TYPEX,N,1,I)
            MOV       AX,[DI]               ;AX=INDEX(I)
            MUL       WORD PTR [BP]+10      ;AX=TYPEA*INDEX(I)
            ADD       AX,[BP]+18            ;AX=ADDR(A(INDEX(I),0))
            PUSH      AX
            PUSH      [BP]+14               ;X(0)
            PUSH      [BP]+10               ;TYPEA
            PUSH      [BP]+6                ;TYPEX
            PUSH      [BP]+4                ;N
            MOV       BX,1
            PUSH      BX                    ;1
            PUSH      SI
            CALL      GINP
;SUM IS NOW IN ST
;X(I)=(Y(INDEX(I))-SUM)/A(INDEX(I),I)
            MOV       BX,[DI]               ;BX=INDEX(I)
            SHL       BX,1
            SHL       BX,1                  ;BX=4*INDEX(I)
            CMP       WORD PTR [BP]+8,4     ;IS Y SINGLE?
            JNE       Y_DOUBLE
            ADD       BX,[BP]+16            ;BX=ADDR(Y(INDEX(I)))
            FSUBR     DWORD PTR [BX]        ;ST=Y(INDEX(I))-SUM
            JMP       DO_DIV
Y_DOUBLE:   SHL       BX,1                  ;BX=8*INDEX(I)
            ADD       BX,[BP]+16            ;BX=ADDR(Y(INDEX(I)))
            FSUBR     QWORD PTR [BX]        ;ST=Y(INDEX(I))-SUM
;
DO_DIV:
;AX HAS ADDR(A(INDEX(I),0)), SO ADD TYPEA*N*I
            MOV       BX,AX                 ;BX=ADDR(A(INDEX(I),0))
            MOV       AX,SI                 ;AX=I
```

```
            MUL         WORD PTR [BP]+4    ;AX=N*I
            SHL         AX,1
            SHL         AX,1               ;AX=4*N*I
            CMP         WORD PTR [BP]+10,4 ;IS A SINGLE?
            JNE         A_DOUBLE
            ADD         BX,AX              ;BX=ADDR(A(INDEX(I),I))
            FDIV        DWORD PTR [BX]     ;(Y(I)-SUM)/A(INDEX(I),I)
            JMP         DO_STORE
A_DOUBLE:   SHL         AX,1               ;AX=8*N*I
            ADD         BX,AX              ;BX=ADDR(A(INDEX(I),I))
            FDIV        QWORD PTR [BX]     ;(Y(I)-SUM)/A(INDEX(I),I)
;
DO_STORE:   MOV         BX,SI              ;BX=I
            SHL         BX,1
            SHL         BX,1               ;BX=4*I
            CMP         WORD PTR [BP]+6,4  ;IS X SINGLE?
            JNE         X_DOUBLE
            ADD         BX,[BP]+14         ;BX=ADDR(X(I))
            FSTP        DWORD PTR [BX]     ;STORE X(I)
            JMP         L_BOTTOM
X_DOUBLE:   SHL         BX,1               ;BX=8*I
            ADD         BX,[BP]+14         ;BX=ADDR(X(I))
            FSTP        QWORD PTR [BX]     ;STORE X(I)
L_BOTTOM:
            INC         SI                 ;I=I+1
            ADD         DI,2               ;NEXT INDEX
            LOOP        GOTO_L_LOOP
            JMP         U_TOP
GOTO_L_LOOP: JMP L_LOOP
;
U_TOP:
;TAKE CARE OF UPPER TRIANGLE
;FOR I=N-1 TO 0 STEP -1
            MOV         SI,[BP]+4          ;KEEP I IN SI
            MOV         DI,[BP]+12         ;DI=ADDR(INDEX(0))
            ADD         DI,SI
            ADD         DI,SI              ;DI=ADDR(INDEX(N))
U_LOOP:
;CALL GINP(A(INDEX(I),I+1),X(I+1),TYPEA,TYPEX,N,1,N-I-1)
            DEC         SI                 ;I=I-1
            SUB         DI,2               ;NEXT INDEX
            MOV         AX,SI              ;AX=I
            INC         AX                 ;AX=I+1
            MUL         WORD PTR [BP]+4    ;AX=N*(I+1)
            ADD         AX,[DI]            ;AX=INDEX(I)+N*(I+1)
            SHL         AX,1
            SHL         AX,1               ;AX=4*AX
            CMP         WORD PTR [BP]+10,4 ;IS A SINGLE?
            JE          A_SINGLE
            SHL         AX,1               ;AX=8*(. . .)
A_SINGLE:   ADD         AX,[BP]+18         ;AX=ADDR(A(INDEX(I),
                                            I+1))
```

```
            PUSH      AX
            MOV       BX,SI                  ;BX=I
            INC       BX                     ;BX=I+1
            SHL       BX,1
            SHL       BX,1                   ;BX=4*(I+1)
            CMP       WORD PTR [BP]+6,4      ;IS X SINGLE?
            JE        X_SINGLE
            SHL       BX,1                   ;BX=8*(I+1)
X_SINGLE:   ADD       BX,[BP]+14             ;BX=ADDR(X(I+1))
            PUSH      BX                     ;NOTE: LEAVE ADDR IN
                                              BX
            PUSH      [BP]+10                ;TYPEA
            PUSH      [BP]+6                 ;TYPEX
            PUSH      [BP]+4                 ;N
            MOV       DX,1
            PUSH      DX                     ;1
            MOV       DX,[BP]+4              ;DX=N
            SUB       DX,SI
            DEC       DX                     ;DX=N-(I+1)
            PUSH      DX
            CALL      GINP
;
;X(I)=X(I)-SUM
;NOTE BX STILL POINTS TO X(I+1)
            SUB       BX,[BP]+6              ;BX=ADDR(X(I))
            CMP       WORD PTR [BP]+6,4      ;ONCE AGAIN, IS X
                                              SINGLE?
            JNE       X_DOUBLE2
            FSUBR     DWORD PTR [BX]         ;ST=X(I)-SUM
            FSTP      DWORD PTR [BX]         ;STORE X(I)
            JMP       U_BOTTOM
X_DOUBLE2:  FSUBR     QWORD PTR [BX]         ;ST=X(I)-SUM
            FSTP      QWORD PTR [BX]         ;STORE X(I)
U_BOTTOM:
            CMP       SI,0                   ;DONE YET?
            JLE       DONE
            JMP       U_LOOP
;
DONE:
            POP       DI
            POP       SI
            POP       DX
            POP       CX
            POP       BX
            POP       AX
            POP       BP
            FWAIT
            RET       16
SOL         ENDP
```

```
;SUBROUTINE SOLVE(A(0,0),Y(0),X(0),INDEX(0),TYPEA,TYPEY,TYPEX,N)
; ASSUMPTIONS: A(0,0),Y(0),X(0),INDEX(0) ARE ADDRESSES
;               TO BE PASSED TO XINP
;              TYPEA,TYPEY,TYPEX,N ARE ADDRESSES OF INTEGERS
;
;               WHOSE VALUES SHOULD BE PASSED TO XINP
;
; SOLVE CALLS THE INTERNAL SUBROUTINE SOL
;
          PUBLIC    SOLVE
          ASSUME    CS:CSEG,ES:ESEG
SOLVE     PROC      FAR
          PUSH      BP
          MOV       BP,SP
;SET UP STACK AREA IN ESEG
          PUSH      ES
          CALL      NEXT
NEXT:     POP       AX
          SUB       AX,(OFFSET NEXT)-(OFFSET FIRST_INST)
          MOV       CL,4
          SHR       AX,CL
          MOV       BX,CS
          ADD       BX,ESEG
          SUB       BX,CSEG
          ADD       AX,BX
          MOV       ES,AX
;
          MOV       LOCAL_SPACE,SS
          MOV       LOCAL_SPACE+2,SP
          MOV       AX,ES
          MOV       SS,AX
          MOV       SP,OFFSET STACK_TOP
;
;SET UP CALL PARAMETERS
          PUSH      DS:[BP]+20        ;ADDR(A(0,0))
          PUSH      DS:[BP]+18        ;ADDR(Y(0))
          PUSH      DS:[BP]+16        ;ADDR(X(0))
          PUSH      DS:[BP]+14        ;ADDR(INDEX(0))
          MOV       BX,DS:[BP]+12     ;BX=ADDR(TYPEA)
          PUSH      [BX]              ;TYPEA
          MOV       BX,DS:[BP]+10     ;BX=ADDR(TYPEY)
          PUSH      [BX]              ;TYPEY
          MOV       BX,DS:[BP]+8      ;BX=ADDR(TYPEX)
          PUSH      [BX]              ;TYPEX
          MOV       BX,DS:[BP]+6      ;BX=ADDR(N)
          PUSH      [BX]              ;N
;
          CALL      SOL
          MOV       SP,LOCAL_SPACE+2
          MOV       SS,LOCAL_SPACE
          POP       ES
```

```
            POP         BP
            RET         16
SOLVE       ENDP
```

Matrix Inversion

One good reason for creating procedures from modular programs is the ease with which the subroutines may be rearranged. It is now quite easy to prepare a matrix inversion subroutine. Since matrix inversion is equivalent to solving a system of equations n times (first for a "y vector" 1,0,0, . . ., then for 0,1,0,0 . . ., and so forth.), we can use CROUTP and SOL to create a new subroutine INV.

INV is called by

```
CALL INV(A(0,0),AINV(0,0),SCRATCH(0),INDEX(0),IER,TYPEA,N)
```

A initially contains the n by n matrix to be inverted. When INV returns, A contains the Crout decomposition, with permutation index in INDEX; AINV contains A^{-1}. IER equals 0 if A is nonsingular and -1 otherwise. INV calls CROUTP to reduce A. It then sets up a "y column," in vector SCRATCH, n times, and calls SOL to fill in the columns of the inverse matrix, AINV.

```
;SUBROUTINE INV(A(0,0),AINV(0,0),SCRATCH(0),INDEX(0),IER,TYPEA,N)
; ASSUMPTIONS: A,AINV ARE N BY N MATRICES OF TYPE TYPEA
;              SCRATCH IS SINGLE PRECISION
;              INDEX,TYPEA,N ARE INTEGERS
;
; INV INVERTS A INTO AINV
;
            PUBLIC      INV
            ASSUME      CS:CSEG,ES:ESEG
INV         PROC        FAR
            PUSH        BP
            MOV         BP,SP

;SET UP STACK AREA IN ESEG
            PUSH        ES
            CALL        NEXT
NEXT:       POP         AX
            SUB         AX,(OFFSET NEXT)-(OFFSET FIRST_INST)
            MOV         CL,4
            SHR         AX,CL
            MOV         BX,CS
            ADD         BX,ESEG
            SUB         BX,CSEG
            ADD         AX,BX
            MOV         ES,AX

            MOV         LOCAL_SPACE,SS
            MOV         LOCAL_SPACE+2,SP
```

```
            MOV         AX,ES
            MOV         SS,AX
            MOV         SP,OFFSET STACK_TOP
;
            MOV         BX,DS:[BP]+6           ;BX=ADDR(N)
            MOV         CX,[BX]                ;CX=N
            CMP         CX,0
            JG          ARND
            JMP         DONE
ARND:
;CALL CROUTP(A,INDEX,IER,TYPE,N)
;SET UP CALL PARAMETERS
            PUSH        DS:[BP]+18             ;ADDR(A(0,0))
            PUSH        DS:[BP]+12             ;ADDR(INDEX(0))
            PUSH        DS:[BP]+10             ;ADDR(IER)
            MOV         BX,DS:[BP]+8           ;BX=ADDR(TYPEA)
            PUSH        [BX]                   ;TYPEA
            PUSH        CX                     ;N
;
            CALL        CROUTP
;WAS IT SINGULAR
            MOV         BX,DS:[BP]+10          ;BX=ADDR(IER)
            CMP         WORD PTR [BX],0        ;IER=0?
            JE          ARNDB
            JMP         DONE
ARNDB:
;
;SOLVE FOR COLUMNS I=0 TO N-1
          MOV         SI,0                   ;KEEP I IN SI
INV_LOOP:
;CLEAR SCRATCH
            MOV         BX,DS:[BP]+6
            MOV         CX,[BX]                  ;CX=N
            MOV         BX,DS:[BP]+14            ;BX=ADDR(SCRATCH(0))
ZERO_LOOP:
            MOV         WORD PTR [BX],0
            MOV         WORD PTR [BX]+2,0        ;SCRATCH(J)=0
            ADD         BX,4                     ;J=J+1
            LOOP        ZERO_LOOP
;NOW FILL IN APPROPRIATE 1
            MOV         BX,SI                    ;BX=I
            SHL         BX,1
            SHL         BX,1                     ;BX=4*I
            ADD         BX,WORD PTR DS:[BP]+14
                                                 ;BX=ADDR(SCRATCH(I))
            FLD1                                 ;PUSH 1.0 ONTO STACK
            FSTP        DWORD PTR [BX]           ;STORE INTO MEMORY
;
;GET ADDRESS OF AINV(0,I)
            MOV         BX,DS:[BP]+6             ;BX=ADDR(N)
            MOV         AX,[BX]                  ;AX=N
            MUL         SI                       ;AX=N*I
```

```
            MOV         BX,DS:[BP]+8            ;ADDR(TYPEA)
            MUL         WORD PTR [BX]           ;AX=TYPEA*N*I
            ADD         AX,DS:[BP]+16           ;AX=ADDR(AINV(0,I))
;CALL  SOL(A,SCRATCH,AINV(0,I),INDEX,TYPEA,4,TYPEA,N)
            PUSH        DS:[BP]+18              ;ADDR(A(0,0))
            PUSH        DS:[BP]+14              ;ADDR(SCRATCH(0))
            PUSH        AX                      ;ADDR(AINV(0,I))
            PUSH        DS:[BP]+12              ;ADDR(INDEX(0))
            MOV         BX,DS:[BP]+8            ;BX=ADDR(TYPEA)
            PUSH        [BX]                    ;TYPEA
            MOV         AX,4
            PUSH        AX                      ;4
            PUSH        [BX]                    ;TYPEA
            MOV         BX,DS:[BP]+6
            PUSH        [BX]                    ;N
;
            CALL        SOL
;
            INC         SI                      ;I=I+1
            MOV         BX,DS:[BP]+6            ;BX=ADDR(N)
            CMP         SI,[BX]                 ;SI>N?
            JGE         DONE
            JMP         INV_LOOP
;
DONE:
            MOV         SP,LOCAL_SPACE+2
            MOV         SS,LOCAL_SPACE
            POP         ES
            POP         BP
            RET         14
INV         ENDP
```

Of Linear Things Not Covered Above

Two chapters and hundreds of lines of code will have to suffice as an introduction to matrix methods. Before moving on, it's worth listing a few of the things not covered here. This is also a good point to pause for a review of some general themes in programming the 8087.

The routines in these two chapters will do just about every ordinary thing you usually need to do with a matrix. However, if you have really large problems, you may soon develop an interest in extraordinary procedures. Everything you need to know about the 8087 is included here, but there are many sophisticated algorithms that we haven't even touched upon. These algorithms appear in many excellent books on numerical computation. Two exceptional books are:

Elementary Numerical Analysis, by S. D. Conte, McGraw-Hill.
Introduction to Matrix Computations, by G. W. Stewart, Academic Press.

One of the best ways to learn more about the "tricks" of numerical programming is to browse through the documentation of a large numerical programming subroutine library. Such a "library collection" can usually be found at your local college computer center. The *IMSL* library is particularly good. You will find an excellent applied discussion of numerical methods and the IMSL library in (this book is moderately advanced):

Numerical Methods, Software, and Analysis, by John R. Rice, McGraw-Hill.

The procedures in this and the last chapter provide the basic foundation for matrix programming. Some advanced topic areas not covered here include:

- *Matrices with a lot of zeros*. Problems in the natural sciences often give rise to special forms of matrices. For example, if we know a matrix is triangular, we can avoid processing the zeros. That would double the speed of matrix multiplication. As we've seen, taking advantage of the shape of a triangular matrix can improve the speed of matrix inversion or solving a system of equations by a factor of n. Other special forms include the "diagonal matrix," in which all off-diagonal elements are zero; the "band matrix," which is zero except for elements close to the diagonal; and the general designation of a "sparse matrix." Sparse matrices, which often arise from solving systems of differential equations, may be 99 percent zeros. Special storage techniques, in which only the nonzero elements are stored, must be used to work with sparse matrices.
- *Matrices with special mathematical properties*. Sometimes the mathematics of a problem supply special information about the structure of the numbers stored in a matrix. For example, many problems give rise to a *symmetric* matrix, one in which $A_{i,j}$ equals $A_{j,i}$. You can double the speed of many matrix operations by taking advantage of symmetry. Symmetric matrices are especially common in statistical work.
- *Super-high accuracy methods*. One of the lessons of numerical programming is that mathematically correct procedures don't always give the mathematically correct answer when executed on a computer with finite precision. One place this lesson is often learned is in the reduction of a matrix to triangular form. We picked the Crout reduction with partial pivoting because it is particularly well suited to the 8087's high-precision, temporary real format internal registers. Nonetheless, you may eventually want to learn about other methods, including *iterative* techniques, which are much slower, but which can be much more accurate.
- *Advanced numerical methods for special problems*. Scientists use so much computer time solving matrix problems that special matrix algorithms have been developed for a number of different problems. These algorithms are more accurate and/or faster than the general purpose matrix routines presented in this chapter. If much of your computing concentrates in a narrow area, then it's probably worth investigating

these special algorithms. (The references given above should get you started.) It is frequently true that the bulk of the computation in such algorithms lies in forming inner products. Therefore, you may find that you can easily code an appropriate algorithm in BASIC while using INPROD or GINPROD, from Chapter 10, or XINPROD, from this Chapter, to drive the 8087.

8087 Matrix Program Review

1. Expect assembly language programs to be 10 times as long as their BASIC counterparts. Writing large programs in assembler is time consuming and error prone. In fact, the expense in programming time may be prohibitive. (Even if the time is "free," because it's your own.)
2. 8087 assembly language programs may be 100, or more, times faster than BASIC programs. In fact, when attempting large problems in BASIC, the expense in computer time may be prohibitive. (Even if the time is "free," because the computer is already paid for.)
3. *Optimize the inner-most loop.* Worry about optimizing, for speed and for accuracy, the equivalent of the inner-most FOR/NEXT loop. For matrix operations, this usually means having an inner product routine carefully hand-coded for the 8087. We chose Crout decomposition over Gaussian elimination for two reasons. First, the inner product specification allowed accumulation in a high-precision register even if the overall operation is only single precision. Second, this specification allows us, if we wish, to code just the inner product routine in assembler and leave the shell of the program in BASIC.
4. Never invert a matrix when you really need only solve a system of equations. Reducing a matrix is an order n^3 operation. Inverting a reduced matrix requires an additional order n^3 operations, while solving a system of equations only requires an additional order n^2 operations. A series of solutions is best obtained with one call to REDUCE and several calls to SOLVE, not one call of INV and several MATMULTs. The principle exception to this rule occurs when the inverse matrix itself has an important interpretation, as it frequently does in statistical applications.
5. The 8088 can do most bookkeeping faster than the 8087 can do floating point arithmetic, so most 8088 operations run in parallel with the 8087's speed as the limiting factor. An exception is the integer multiply used in addressing matrix elements. It pays to keep integer multiplication out of inner-most loops. Sometimes multiplication can be avoided by adding to a location counter at each loop. At other times, a "left shift" can be substituted for each multiply-by-2. (Not coincidentally, Intel made the multiply instruction on its newer processors, the 188 and 186, three times as fast as on the original 8088 and 8086.)

6. Counter testing can be done at either the top or the bottom of a loop. The choice is largely a matter of style. (Loops which use the 8088 LOOP instruction test more naturally at the bottom.) Some of the programs in the last two chapters test at the top and some test at the bottom, so that you can see both methods. Ordinarily, it's good programming practice to choose one style or the other and stick to it.

7. Subroutine calls, subroutine relocation code, and a few other instruction sequences are very repetitive. If you use the MACRO assembler, you might want to replace these sequences with macros.

8. To conserve storage, the routines here reduce a matrix "in place." If you need to save the original matrix, make a copy first using GCOPY from Chapter 9.

Onward, Non-linearly

We set aside matrix operations here, and move on to non-linear operations in Chapter 12. If you'd like some practical applications of our matrix routines, skip ahead to the discussion of statistical computing in Chapter 14.

12

Advanced Instruction Set

In this chapter, we pick up and complete the task laid aside at the end of Chapter 6, our description of the 8087 instruction set. Describing the use of the most advanced instructions is rather long and technical; on a first reading you may want to proceed directly to the next chapter.

The Cookbook—Chapter 12

Program:	**LN**
Purpose:	Natural logarithm (base e).
Input:	8087 register ST; requires ST>0.
Output:	8087 register ST; new ST = log(old ST).
Language:	8087/8088 assembly language.
Note:	NEAR procedure.
Program:	**LOG10**
Purpose:	Common logarithm (base 10).
Input:	8087 register ST; requires ST>0.
Output:	8087 register ST; new ST = $\log_{10}$(old ST).
Language:	8087/8088 assembly language.
Note:	NEAR procedure.
Program:	**TWO2THEZ**
Purpose:	Raises 2 to the power Z.
Input:	Z in 8087 register ST.
Output:	8087 register ST; new ST = $2^{(\text{old ST})}$.
Language:	8087/8088 assembly language.
Note:	NEAR procedure.
Program:	**EXP**
Purpose:	Raises e to the power X.
Input:	X in 8087 register ST.

Output: 8087 register ST; new ST = $e^{(\text{old ST})}$.
Language: 8087/8088 assembly language.
Note: NEAR procedure.

Program: **TEN2THEX**
Purpose: Raises 10 to the power X.
Input: X in 8087 register ST.
Output: 8087 register ST; new ST = $10^{(\text{old ST})}$.
Language: 8087/8088 assembly language.
Note: NEAR procedure.

Program: **Y2THEX**
Purpose: Raises Y to the power X.
Input: X in 8087 register ST.
Y in 8087 register ST(1).
Output: 8087 register ST; new ST = $(\text{old ST})^{(\text{old ST(1)})}$.
Language: 8087/8088 assembly language.
Note: NEAR procedure.

Program: **TANGENT**
Purpose: Compute tangent.
Input: 8087 register ST (angle in radians).
Output: 8087 register ST; new ST = tan(old ST).
Language: 8087/8088 assembly language.
Note: NEAR procedure.

Program: **SINE**
Purpose: Compute sine.
Input: 8087 register ST (angle in radians).
Output: 8087 register ST; new ST = sin(old ST).
Language: 8087/8088 assembly language.
Note: NEAR procedure.

Program: **COSINE**
Purpose: Computer cosine
Input: 8087 register ST (angle in radians)
Output: 8087 register; new ST=cos (old ST).
Language: 8087/8088 assembly language.
Note: NEAR procedure.

Program: **ARCTAN**
Purpose: Compute arctangent.
Input: 8087 register ST.
Output: 8087 register ST; new ST = arctan(old ST).
Language: 8087/8088 assembly language.
Note: NEAR procedure.

This chapter is divided into four sections. The first two sections finish describing the arithmetic and constant instructions. The last two sections present the *transcendental* and *processor control* instructions. A number of examples are included for the more intricate operations.

Arithmetic Instructions

Four arithmetic instructions remain to be discussed. Remember that the instruction timings shown below are for an IBM PC or equivalent. (We discussed the relative speed of the IBM AT in Chapter 6.)

FRDINT {ST} 9 microseconds

FRDINT (round to integer) rounds the element on top of the 8087 stack to an integer. (The number continues to be represented as a temporary real; after an FRDINT the temporary real number has an integer value.) The 8087 offers four rounding modes: *round to nearest*, *round down*, *round up*, and *chop* (round toward zero). Round to nearest is the default mode.

FSCALE {ST,ST(1)} 7 microseconds

FSCALE (scale by powers of two) adds the value found in ST(1) to the exponent of ST. This effectively multiplies the top of stack element by 2 to the power contained in ST(1). Since the exponent field is an integer, the value in ST(1) should be an integer as well. If ST(1) is not an integer, the value is rounded toward zero before being added to the exponent in ST. The scale factor in ST(1) must be between -32768 and 32768 (2^{15}). If the scale factor is out of range or a non-integer value between -1 and $+1$, the result is undefined. For safety, load ST(1) from a word integer. Notice that FSCALE provides an extremely fast way to multiply or divide numbers by a power of 2.

FPREM {ST,ST(1)} 25 microseconds

FPREM (partial remainder) divides the stack top by ST(1) and places the *remainder* back in the stack top. (We explain use of the name "partial" below.) The result is exact with no loss of precision. FPREM (in effect) repeatedly subtracts ST(1) from ST and leaves the remainder in ST. When no more subtractions can be done without getting a negative difference, FPREM quits. Thus, if ST initially holds X, at completion of FPREM ST holds $X-(q \times ST(1))$, where q is an integer.

FPREM will, however, only reduce the difference in magnitude between ST and ST(1) by 2^{64}. If the difference is greater than this, repeated executions are necessary. (The 8087 doesn't allow itself to be interrupted in the middle of an instruction. Some programs might want to interrupt the 8087 in a bit of a hurry, so FPREM was designed to work part way through a modular division problem at each execution.) At each step, the "partial remainder" is left in ST. At the end of each execution, three possible comparisons exist between ST and ST(1). If ST<ST(1), the remainder is in ST. If ST=ST(1), the remainder is 0. If ST>ST(1), then ST has only the partial remainder and FPREM should be repeated. FPREM sets bit C2 of the status word when it needs to be repeated and clears the bit when it has completed. FPREM also places the least-significant three bits of the quotient, q, in bits C0, C3, and C1, which is quite useful in analyzing periodic functions, such as sine, cosine, and tangent. For example, if all C0, C3, and C0 equal zero, then the quotient is a multiple of eight. If C1 alone equals one, then the quotient is one greater than a multiple of eight. (Why eight? Because trigonometric calculations are based on dividing a circle into eight parts.) Table 12.1 describes the possible bit patterns.

Table 12-1. Condition Code Bits After FPREM.

Least Significant Bits of Quotient	*C0*	*C3*	*C1*
0	0	0	0
1	0	0	1
2	0	1	0
3	0	1	1
4	1	0	0
5	1	0	1
6	1	1	0
7	1	1	1

The most important use of FPREM is in bringing arguments into the valid range for the transcendental instructions. Examples using FPREM are given in the section "Trigonometric Functions," below.

FXTRACT {ST} 10 microseconds

FXTRACT (extract exponent and significand) separates out the exponent and significand of the top of stack element. The exponent replaces the top of stack element and the significand is then *pushed* onto the stack. (Both are represented as temporary reals.) If ST originally held zero, both exponent and significand are zero. Note that FXTRACT is the logical inverse of FSCALE.

Constant Instructions

The 8087 has seven useful constants "hardwired in." These constants have full temporary real accuracy (over 19 decimal digits). Use of a constant instruction saves about eight microseconds and considerable nuisance as compared to retrieving data from memory.

The constants are zero, one, pi, and four logarithmic values.

FLDZ {ST} 3 microseconds

FLDZ (load zero) *pushes* 0.0 onto the stack.

FLD1 {ST} 4 microseconds

FLD1 (load one) *pushes* 1.0 onto the stack.

FLDPI {ST} 4 microseconds

FLDPI (load pi) *pushes* pi onto the stack.

FLDL2T {ST} 4 microseconds

FLDL2T (load $\log_2 10$) *pushes* $\log_2 10$ onto the stack.

FLDL2E {ST} 4 microseconds

FLDL2E (load $\log_2 e$) *pushes* $\log_2 e$ onto the stack. (e is the base of the natural logarithms.)

FLDLG2 {ST} 4 microseconds

FLDLG2 (load common logarithm of 2) *pushes* $\log_{10} 2$ onto the stack.

FLDLN2 {ST} 4 microseconds

FLDLN2 (load natural logarithm of 2) *pushes* $\log_e 2$ onto the stack.

Transcendental Instructions

Five transcendental instructions are provided on the 8087. Two of these instructions are used for logarithmic calculations, one for exponentiation, and two for trigonometric calculations. The five instructions provide *core calculations* for a much larger set of transcendental operations. We have written this section in two parts. In the first part we describe the five instructions. In the second part we present a series of 8087 NEAR procedures that can be used for the most common transcendental functions.

The transcendental instructions require valid (normalized) arguments and require that the arguments be within range. Further, the *transcendental instructions do not check their arguments. Invalid arguments may produce erroneous results.*

F2XM1 {ST} 100 microseconds

F2XM1 (2 to the X, minus 1) takes the stack top as X, calculates $2^X - 1$, and places the answer back in the stack top. X must be between 0 and ½, inclusive. While calculating $2^X - 1$ instead of 2^X seems peculiar at first, this method allows much more accuracy when X is small. For example, $2^{0.000001}$ is approximately 1.000000693. Subtracting one allows the 8087 to report, in this case, about seven extra significant digits.

Below, we show how to use F2XM1 to calculate exponents to bases other then two.

FYL2X {ST,ST(1)} 190 microseconds

FYL2X (Y times $\log_2$ X) calculates Y $\times$ $\log_2$ X, where X is in ST and Y in ST(1). The stack is *popped*, eliminating X, and the answer then replaces Y in the new top of stack. X must be strictly positive.

Below, we show how to use FYL2X to calculate logarithms using bases other than two.

FYL2XP1 {ST,ST(1)} 170 microseconds

FYL2XP1 (Y times $\log_2$ (X+1)) takes X from the stack top, Y from ST(1), and calculates Y $\times$ $\log_2$ (1+X). X is popped and the result replaces Y on the new stack top. The absolute value of X must be greater than zero and less than SQRT(2)/2. FYL2XP1 should be used in preference to FYL2X when the argument is very close to one.

FPTAN {ST} 90 microseconds

FPTAN (partial tangent) calculates tan(theta), where theta is in the stack top. The argument theta is restricted to the range 0 < theta < pi/4. The answer is in the form of a ratio Y/X. Y replaces theta and X is *pushed* onto the stack.

We can translate from tangent to sine and cosine by use of standard trigonometric identities. (See "Trigonometric Functions", below.)

FPATAN {ST,ST(1)} 130 microseconds

FPATAN (partial arctangent) calculates arctan (Y/X) where X is taken from ST and Y from ST(1). Y and X must observe the inequality 0 < Y < X < infinity. FPATAN *pops* the stack and then places the answer in the new stack top, replacing Y.

FPATAN serves as a base for calculating all the inverse trigonometric functions.

In the following sections, we create a number of "super instructions." Each "super instruction" is an 8087/8088 NEAR procedure that computes a common mathematical function. The procedures all assume that the calling routine has provided necessary scratch space and defined required constants. The calling routine should look something like the following.

```
;CALLING ROUTINE FOR "SUPER-INSTRUCTIONS"
CSEG        SEGMENT     'CODE'
            ASSUME      CS:CSEG,ES:ESEG
; WE SHOULD SAVE ANY REGISTERS AS REQUIRED
            MOV         AX,ESEG          ;POINT TO SCRATCH
                                          AREAS
            MOV         ES,AX
            MOV         SS,AX
            MOV         SP,OFFSET STACK_TOP
            CALL        SUPER-INSTRUCTION
CSEG        ENDS
```

```
ESEG        SEGMENT      'DATA'
STATUS_WORD              DW          ?
CONTROL_WORD             DW          ?
CONTROL_WORD_TEMP        DW          ?
HALF                     DD          3F000000H
MINUS2                   DW          -2
SIGN_STORE               DB          ?
REALLY_COS               DB          ?
LOCAL_SPACE              DW          10 DUP(?)
STACK_AREA               DW          50 DUP(?)
STACK_TOP                EQU         THIS WORD
ESEG        ENDS
            END
```

The diskette prepared for this book includes routines to call each of the "super-instructions" from BASIC.

Logarithms

The 8087 hardware calculates logarithms for log base two. Most mathematical applications require natural logarithms, log base e, or common logarithms, log base 10. These are easily calculated using the fundamental identity for changing the base of a logarithm. Suppose we want the log of X base n, and only know how to calculate logarithms using base two.

$$\log_n X = \log_n 2 \times \log_2 X$$

In this case n is e or 10. The following "super instructions" assume X is on the stack top, that $0 < X <$ infinity, and that the stack is not too deep to be pushed at least once more. X is replaced with its logarithm.

```
;   NATURAL LOG {ST}                               197 MICROSECONDS
;SUBROUTINE LN
LN          PROC       NEAR
            FLDLN2               ;PUSH LOG BASE E OF 2
            FXCH                 ;SWAP ST,ST(1)
            FYL2X                ;POP AND REPLACE ST WITH NATURAL
                                  LOG
            RET
LN          ENDP

;   COMMON LOG {ST}                                197 MICROSECONDS
;SUBROUTINE LOG10
LOG10       PROC       NEAR
            FLDLG2               ;PUSH LOG BASE E OF 10
            FXCH                 ;SWAP ST,ST(1)
            FYL2X                ;POP AND REPLACE ST WITH NATURAL
                                  LOG
            RET
LOG10       ENDP
```

Exponentiation

The 8087 hardware provides the instruction F2XM1 for raising 2 to the power X. Mathematical calculations often require e^X, 10^X, and y^X. These are easily calculated using the fundamental identity for changing the base of an exponent. Suppose we want y^X and only know how to calculate 2^X.

$$y^X = 2^{(X \times \log_2 y)}$$

Exponentiation routines would be simple if we had an instruction to raise 2 to an arbitrary power. Since F2XM1 only accepts arguments between 0 and ½, we need a super-instruction to perform the operation 2^Z for an arbitrary Z. The 8087 instruction set is organized to make this a relatively easy operation, though a bit of planning is required. We actually have two hardware operations for taking a power of two. F2XM1 accepts exponents between 0 and ½. FSCALE accepts any integer exponent. We'll pick Z_1 and Z_2 such that Z_1 is an integer and Z_2 is a positive fraction. If Z_2 is greater than ½, we'll subtract ½ from Z_2 and then multiply the answer by $2^{1/2}$. (This is all easier than it sounds.) The algorithm works as follows:

1. Let Z_1 equal the greatest integer less than or equal to Z. This is a little messy since we need to *round down* Z. In order to accomplish this, we need to change the 8087 rounding control by using the load control word, FLDCW, and store control word, FSTCW instructions; instructions we don't officially meet until the next section.
2. Let $Z_2 = Z - Z_1$. Note that Z_2 is guaranteed to be positive.
3. Is $Z_2 > 1/2$? If so, subtract ½ and make note of the fact.
4. Raise 2 to the Z_2 and scale by Z_1.
5. If we subtracted ½ from Z_2 above, now multiply the result by $2^{1/2}$.

```
;2 TO THE Z {ST}                                         295 MICROSECONDS
;SUBROUTINE TWO2THEZ
;
;THIS ROUTINE ASSUMES THAT THE FOLLOWING MEMORY LOCATIONS
;HAVE BEEN DEFINED
; STATUS_WORD      2 BYTES
; CONTROL_WORD 2 BYTES
; CONTROL_WORD_TEMP 2 BYTES
; HALF HAS 0.5 IN SHORT-REAL FORMAT
;
;Z IS ASSUMED TO BE FOUND IN ST
; THERE MUST BE AT LEAST 2 FREE STACK LOCATIONS
TWO2THEZ    PROC      NEAR
            PUSH      AX                     ;SAVE AX
            FSTCW     CONTROL_WORD           ;SAVE CONTROL WORD SO
                                              WE CAN
                                             ;RESTORE IT LATER
            FSTCW     CONTROL_WORD_TEMP       ;USE TEMP TO CHANGE
                                             ;ROUNDING CONTROL(RC)
```

```
        FWAIT
        AND     CONTROL_WORD_TEMP,0F3FFH ;CLEAR OUT RC
                                           BITS
        OR      CONTROL_WORD_TEMP,00400H ;RC=ROUND-DOWN
        FLDCW   CONTROL_WORD_TEMP ;SET TO ROUND DOWN
        FLD     ST(0)             ;PUSH COPY OF Z ONTO
                                   ST
        FRNDINT                   ;OK, ST=Z1, ST(1)=Z
        FLDCW   CONTROL_WORD      ;RETURN THINGS TO NORMAL
        FSUB    ST(1),ST          ;ST(1)(Z2)=Z-Z1
        FXCH                      ST=Z2, ST(1)=Z1
        FLD     HALF              ;LOAD 1/2 ONTO THE
                                   STACK
        FXCH                      ;ST=Z2 ST(1)=1/2
        FPREM                     ;ST HAS Z2 OR Z2=1/2
                                  ;C1=1 IN THE LATTER
                                   CASE
        FSTSW   STATUS_WORD
        FWAIT
                                  ;NOW WE'VE GOT FLAGS
                                   SET
        FSTP    ST(1)             ;GET RID OF THE 1/2
        F2XM1                     ;ST=(2 TO THE ST)-1
        FLD1
        FADDP   ST(1),ST
        TEST    BYTE PTR STATUS_WORD+1,00000010B
                                  ;ST HAS Z2 IF BIT 1 ON
        JZ      WAS_Z2            ;OTHERWISE IT WAS
                                   Z2-1/2
        FLD1                      ;SO,
        FADD    ST,ST(0)          ;MULTIPLY BY THE
        FSQRT                     ;SQUARE ROOT OF 2
        FMULP   ST(1),ST
;
WAS_Z2:                           ;WE JUST NEED TO SCALE
        FSCALE                    ;NOTICE WE DIDN'T
                                   CHECK
                                  ;FOR OVER OR UNDERFLOW
        FSTP    ST(1)
        POP     AX
        RET
TWO2THEZ ENDP
```

This may all seem like going to some trouble, but it does speed things up quite a bit over not having an 8087. How much? Try rewriting our super instruction "2 to the Z" in BASIC without the 8087. You'll find that one minute of 8087 exponentiation takes just about an hour with compiled BASIC and about three hours with interpreted BASIC.

Of course, we aren't actually interested in raising two to some power all that often. With the TWO2THEZ firmly in hand, it's easy to provide new super-instructions for e^X, 10^X, and y^X.

```
    ;EXP(X) {ST}                                    322 MICROSECONDS
EXP         PROC        NEAR
            FLDL2E                  ;PUSH LOG E BASE 2
            FMULP       ST(1),ST    ;ST=X TIMES LOG E BASE 2
            CALL        TWO2THEZ    ;ST=EXP(X)
            RET
EXP         ENDP


    ;10 TO THE X {ST}                                322 MICROSECONDS
TEN2THEX    PROC        NEAR
            FLDL2T                  ;PUSH LOG 10 BASE 2
            FMULP       ST,ST(1)    ;ST=X TIMES LOG 10 BASE 2
            CALL        TWO2THEZ    ;ST=10 TO THE X
            RET
TEN2THEX    ENDP

    ;Y TO THE X {ST(1),ST}                           482 MICROSECONDS
;ASSUMES Y IS POSITIVE IN {ST}
;ASSUMES X IN ST(1)
Y2THEX      PROC        NEAR
            FYL2X                   ;ST=Y TIMES LOG X BASE 2
            CALL        TWO2THEZ    ;ST=Y TO THE X
            RET
Y2THEX      ENDP
```

Trigonometric Functions

The tangent function provides the base for calculating all the common trigonometric functions. FPTAN calculates the tangent for arguments between 0 and pi/4. Computation of a trigonometric function involves three broad steps. First, prologue code is used to bring the argument within range of the FPTAN instruction. Second, the FPTAN instruction is applied. Third, epilogue code is used to correct the result of FPTAN. The trigonometric identities used are described in the code below.

```
;TANGENT  {ST}                                       370 MICROSECONDS
;THETA IN ST IS ASSUMED TO BE A VALID NUMBER
;THERE MUST BE AT LEAST 2 FREE STACK LOCATIONS
;THIS ROUTINE ASSUMES THAT THE FOLLOWING MEMORY
;LOCATIONS HAVE BEEN DEFINED:
;STATUS_WORD    2 BYTES
;SIGN_STORE     1 BYTE
;MINUS2         2 BYTES INITIALIZED TO -2
;
TANGENT     PROC        NEAR
            PUSH        AX
            PUSH        BX
;FIRST CHECK FOR A NEGATIVE ARGUMENT
```

```
; NOTE TAN(-X)=-TAN(X)
        MOV     SIGN_STORE,0        ;ASSUME POSITIVE
        FTST
        FSTSW   STATUS_WORD
        FWAIT
        MOV     AH,BYTE PTR STATUS_WORD+1
        SAHF
        JNC     NON_NEGATIVE
        MOV     SIGN_STORE,-1       ;ITS NEGATIVE
        FABS                        ;NOW POSITIVE
NON_NEGATIVE:
;NOW GET ST BETWEEN 0 AND PI/4
        FILD    MINUS2              ;LOAD -2
        FLDPI                       ;LOAD PI
        FSCALE                      ;GOT PI/4
        FSTP    ST(1)               ;DUMP -2
        FXCH
; NOW X IS IN ST AND PI/4 IN ST(1)
RANGE:
        FPREM
        FSTSW   STATUS_WORD
        FWAIT
        MOV     AH,BYTE PTR STATUS_WORD+1
        SAHF
        JP      RANGE               ;THIS TESTS BIT C2
;AT THIS POINT AH HAS THE STATUS BITS
;NOW LETS SEE IF THE REMAINDER WAS EXACTLY ZERO
        FTST
        FSTSW   STATUS_WORD
        FWAIT
;IT WAS ZERO IF C3=1 AND C0=0
;IF ZERO, SET BX=-1, ELSE BX=0
        MOV     BX,0
        AND     BYTE PTR STATUS WORD+1,01000001B
        CMP     BYTE PTR STATUS_WORD+1,01000001B
        JNE     NOT_ZERO
        MOV     BX,-1
NOT_ZERO:
;THERE ARE FOUR POSSIBILITIES GIVEN ST NOW HAS X MOD PI/4

;OCTANT   C3  C1   CALCULATE              IF ZERO
;0,4      0   0    FPTAN(ST)                0
;1,5      0   1    1/FPTAN(PI/4 - ST)       1
;2,6      1   0    -1/FPTAN(ST)           INFINITY
;3,7      1   1    -FPTAN(PI/4 - ST)        -1
;
;FIRST CHECK BIT C1 AND TAKE FPTAN
        TEST    AH,10B              ;IS C1 ON
        JZ      C1ISOFF             ;JUMP IF OFF
        CMP     BX,0                ;ST EXACTLY ZERO?
        JNE     STOANDC1            ;JUMP IF YES
```

```
            FSUBP       ST(1),ST            ;NOW PI/4-ST
            FPTAN
            JMP         TANDONE
STOANDC1:
            FSTP        ST                  ;POP ST
            FSTP        ST                  ; AND PI/4
            FLD1                            ;LOAD RATIO 1 TO 1
            FLD1
            JMP         TANDONE
C1ISOFF:
            FSTP        ST(1)               ;GET RID OF PI/4
            CMP         BX,0                ;ST EXACTLY ZERO?
            JNE         STOANDNOC1          ;JUMP IF YES
            FPTAN
            JMP         TANDONE
STOANDNOC1:
            FSTP        ST                  ;DUMP ST
            FLDZ                            ;LOAD RATIO 0 TO 1
            FLD1
TANDONE:
;PUT C1 XOR C3 IN BX
            MOV         BX,0                ;ASSUME C3 OFF
;IF C3 IS ON THEN CHANGE SIGNS
            TEST        AH,01000000B
            JZ          NOC3                ;JUMP IF OFF
            FCHS
            MOV         BX,1                ;NOTE C3 ON
NOC3:
;IS C1 ON ?
            TEST        AH,10B
            JZ          NOC1                ;JUMP IF OFF
            XOR         BX,1
            JMP         RECIP
NOC1:       XOR         BX,0
RECIP:
;IF BX=1 THEN WE WANT RECIPROCAL OF RATIO
            CMP         BX,1
            JNE         NORECIP
            FXCH
NORECIP:    FDIVP       ST(1),ST            ;THAT'S IT
;DID WE ORIGINALLY CHANGE SIGN?
            CMP         SIGN_STORE,0
            JE          LEAVE_POS
            FCHS
LEAVE_POS:
            POP         BX
            POP         AX
            RET
TANGENT     ENDP
```

Sine and cosine functions are also calculated using FPTAN. Since a cosine is just a sine rotated 90 degrees, we build the cosine routine to make use of the code for sines.

```
;SINE     {ST}                                  513 MICROSECONDS
;THETA IN ST IS ASSUMED TO BE A VALID NUMBER
;THERE MUST BE AT LEAST 3 FREE STACK LOCATIONS
;THIS ROUTINE ASSUMES THAT THE FOLLOWING MEMORY
;LOCATIONS HAVE BEEN DEFINED:
;STATUS_WORD   2 BYTES
;SIGN_STORE    1 BYTE
;MINUS2        2 BYTES INITIALIZED TO -2
;REALLY_COS    1 BYTE
SINE        PROC       NEAR
            PUSH       AX
            PUSH       BX
;FIRST CHECK FOR A NEGATIVE ARGUMENT
; NOTE SIN(-X)=-SIN(X)
            MOV        SIGN_STORE,0       ;ASSUME POSITIVE
            FTST
            FSTSW      STATUS_WORD
            FWAIT
            MOV        AH,BYTE PTR STATUS_WORD+1
            SAHF
            JNC        NON_NEGATIVE
            MOV        SIGN_STORE,-1      ;ITS NEGATIVE
            FABS                          ;NOW POSITIVE

NON_NEGATIVE:
            MOV        REALLY_COS,0       ;SINE, NOT COSINE
COS_ENTRY:
;NOW GET ST BETWEEN 0 AND PI/4
            FILD       MINUS2             ;LOAD -2
            FLDPI                         ;LOAD PI
            FSCALE                        ;GOT PI/4
            FSTP       ST(1)              ;DUMP -2
            FXCH

; NOW X IS IN ST AND PI/4 IN ST(1)
RANGE:
            FPREM
            FSTSW      STATUS_WORD
            FWAIT
            MOV        AH,BYTE PTR STATUS_WORD+1
            SAHF
            JP         RANGE              ;THIS TESTS BIT C2

;AT THIS POINT AH HAS THE STATUS BITS

;IF WE ARE REALLY DOING COSINE, WE NEED TO ADD TWO TO THE
 OCTANT
            CMP        REALLY_COS,0
            JE         ITS_SINE
;ADD INTO C3 AND CARRY INTO C0
            XOR        AH,01000000B
            TEST       AH,01000000B
            JNZ        NOCARRY
            XOR        AH,1B
```

```
NOCARRY:
ITS_SINE:
;NOW LETS SEE IF THE REMAINDER WAS EXACTLY ZERO
          FTST
          FSTSW     STATUS_WORD
          FWAIT

;IT WAS ZERO IF C3=1 AND C0=0
;IF ZERO, SET BX=-1, ELSE BX=0
          MOV       BX,0
          AND       BYTE PTR STATUS_WORD+1,01000001B
          CMP       BYTE PTR STATUS_WORD+1,01000001B
          JNE       NOT_ZERO
          MOV       BX,-1

NOT_ZERO:
;THERE ARE FOUR POSSIBILITIES GIVEN ST NOW HAS X MOD PI/4
;OCTANT    C3  C1   CALCULATE         IF ZERO
;0         0   0    SIN(ST)             0
;1         0   1    COS(PI/4 - ST)        SQRT(2)/2
;2         1   0    COS(ST)               1
;3         1   1    SIN(PI/4 - ST)    SQRT(2)/2
;
; OCTANTS 4-7 ARE JUST LIKE 0-3 ONLY NEGATIVE
;NOTE: IF TAN(THETA)=X/Y, THEN
;          SIN(THETA)=X/SQRT(X*X+Y*Y)
;          COS(THETA)=Y/SQRT(X*X+Y*Y)
;
;FIRST CHECK BIT C1 AND TAKE FPTAN
          TEST      AH,10B            ;IS C1 ON
          JZ        C1ISOFF           ;JUMP IF OFF
          CMP       BX,0              ;ST EXACTLY ZERO?
          JNE       ST0ANDC1          ;JUMP IF YES
          FSUBP     ST(1),ST          ;NOW PI/4-ST
          FPTAN
          JMP       SINDONE
ST0ANDC1:
          FSTP      ST                ;POP ST
          FSTP      ST                ; AND PI/4
          FLD1                        ;LOAD RATIO 1 TO 1
          FLD1
          JMP       SINDONE

C1ISOFF:
          FSTP      ST(1)             ;GET RID OF PI/4
          CMP       BX,0              ;ST EXACTLY ZERO?
          JNE       ST0ANDNOC1        ;JUMP IF YES
          FPTAN
          JMP       SINDONE
ST0ANDNOC1:
          FSTP      ST                ;DUMP ST
          FLDZ                        ;LOAD RATIO 0 TO 1
          FLD1
```

```
SINDONE:
;IS C1 XOR C3 TRUE?
          MOV       BX,0                ;ASSUME C3 OFF

;IF C3 IS ON
          TEST      AH,01000000B
          JZ        NOC3                ;JUMP IF OFF
          MOV       BX,1                ;NOTE C3 ON
NOC3:
;IS C1 ON ?
          TEST      AH,10B
          JZ        NOC1                ;JUMP IF OFF
          XOR       BX,1
          JMP       DOSINE
NOC1:     XOR       BX,0
DOSINE:
;IF BX=1 THEN WE WANT WANT COSINE FUNCTION
          CMP       BX,1
          JNE       SINFUNC
          FXCH
SINFUNC:
;ST(1)=X, ST(0)=Y
;SIN(THETA)=X/SQRT(X*X+Y*Y)
          FMUL      ST(0),ST(0)         ;ST(0)=Y*Y
          FLD       ST(1)               ;ST(0)=X
          FMUL      ST(0),ST(0)         ;ST(0)=X*X
          FADDP     ST(1),ST(0)         ;ST(0)=X*X+Y*Y
          FSQRT
          FDIVP     ST(1),ST(0)
;
;IS BIT C0 ON?
          TEST      AH,1B
          JZ        C0OFF
          NOT       SIGN_STORE
C0OFF:
;DO WE NEED TO CHANGE SIGN?

          CMP       SIGN_STORE,0
          JE        LEAVE_POS
          FCHS
LEAVE_POS:
          POP       BX
          POP       AX
          RET
SINE      ENDP

;COSINE   {ST}                                   510 MICROSECONDS
;THETA IN ST IS ASSUMED TO BE A VALID NUMBER
;THERE MUST BE AT LEAST 3 FREE STACK LOCATIONS
;THIS ROUTINE USES THE SINE ROUTINE
COSINE    PROC      NEAR
          PUSH      AX
          PUSH      BX
```

```
            FABS
            MOV         SIGN_STORE,0        ;ITS POSITIVE NOW
            MOV         REALLY_COS,-1
            JMP         COS_ENTRY
COSINE      ENDP
```

For further explanation of trigonometric calculations and for programs which perform sophisticated error checking, see

Getting Started With the Numeric Data Processor, by Bill Rash, Intel Corporation, Application Note AP-113.

Inverse Trigonometric Functions

The 8087 instruction FPATAN performs the core calculations for the inverse trigonometric functions: Arctan, Arcsin, Arccos, Arccot, Arccsc, and Arcsec. Just as FPTAN produces a result in the form Y/X, so FPATAN accepts an argument in the form Y/X. The inverse trigonometric functions require somewhat less programming, because the argument range is less restricted for FPATAN than for FPTAN. (The direct trigonometric functions are periodic, where the inverse trigonometric functions aren't.) For FPATAN, we need only assure that the arguments obey the relation $0 < Y < X <$ infinity. Thus to compute Arctan(Z) we need to check seven cases: Z equal 0, Z positive or negative and ABS(Z) less than, equal to, or greater than 1. We bring Z into the proper range by using the identities:

$$\text{Arctan}(Z) = -\text{Arctan}(-Z)$$
$$\text{Arctan}(Z) = \text{pi}/2 - \text{Arctan}(1/Z)$$

```
;ARCTAN   {ST}                                  351 MICROSECONDS
;ST IS ASSUMED TO BE A NORMAL NUMBER
;THERE MUST BE AT LEAST 3 FREE STACK LOCATIONS
;THIS ROUTINE ASSUMES THAT THE FOLLOWING MEMORY
;LOCATIONS HAVE BEEN DEFINED:
;STATUS_WORD   2 BYTES
;SIGN_STORE    1 BYTE
ARCTAN     PROC       NEAR
           PUSH       AX
;THE FIRST PROBLEM IS TO CHECK FOR A ZERO OR
;      NEGATIVE ARGUMENT
           MOV        SIGN_STORE,0      ;ASSUME NON-NEGATIVE
           FTST
           FSTSW      STATUS_WORD
           FWAIT
           MOV        AH,BYTE PTR STATUS_WORD+1
           SAHF
           JA         POSITIVE
           JZ         ZERO              ;ASSUME ITS ZERO
           JMP        NEGATIVE
```

```
ZERO:
;ARCTAN(0)=0
          FSTP      ST(0)
          FLDZ
          JMP       DONE
NEGATIVE:      ;DEAL WITH A NEGATIVE ARGUMENT USING IDENTITY
;ARCTAN(-X)=-ARCTAN(X)
          FCHS
          MOV       SIGN_STORE,-1

POSITIVE:                          ; HOW DOES 1 COMPARE TO
                                    X
          FLD1
          FCOM
          FSTSW     STATUS_WORD
          FWAIT
          MOV       AH,BYTE PTR STATUS_WORD+1
          SAHF
          JA        Z_LT_1
          JC        Z_GT_1
;EXACTLY 1 RETURN ARCTAN(1)=PI/4
          FCHS                     ;ST NOW=-1
          FADD      ST(0),ST(0)    ;ST=-2
          FLDPI
          FSCALE                   ;ST NOW PI/4
          FSTP      ST(1)
          JMP       RESTORE_SIGN
Z_GT_1:
;USE IDENTITY ATAN(X)=PI/2 - ATAN(1/X)
          FXCH                     ;ST=Z,ST(1)=1
          FPATAN
          FLD1                     ;NOW ADJUST BY PI/2
          FCHS
          FLDPI
          FSCALE
          FSTP      ST(1)
          FSUBRP    ST(1),ST
          JMP       RESTORE_SIGN
Z_LT_1:
          FPATAN                   ;ST=1,ST(1)=Z
RESTORE_SIGN:
          TEST      SIGN_STORE,0FFH
          JZ        DONE
          FCHS
DONE:
          POP       AX
          RET
ARCTAN    ENDP
```

Processor Control Instructions

Sixteen instructions are used to examine and control the internal status of the 8087. We make regular use of the instructions that manipulate the *status word* and the *control word*. In particular, these instructions are used for examining the results of comparisons and for setting the controls, such as for rounding, on the 8087. Most of the other instructions are needed for writing system programs. We discuss these briefly for completeness. The processor control instruction FSTSW (store status word) was discussed in Chapter 6.

- As we mentioned in Chapter 5, the 287 electronically synchronizes most instructions (unlike the 8087, which requires a WAIT instruction). However, processor control instructions are not synchronized electronically. The assembler will automatically generate the necessary WAIT instructions for processor control instructions for both the 8087 and the 287. (For system programming purposes, it is possible to prevent automatic generation of WAIT instructions by using the "no-wait" form of the processor control instructions. For example, FNSTCW rather than FSTCW. None of the programs in this book need "no-wait" instructions.)

FLDCW word-integer 4 microseconds

FLDCW (load control word) loads a word from a two-byte memory location into the 8087's internal control word register. FLDCW is used, for example, to change the 8087 rounding control.

FSTCW word-integer 5 microseconds

FSTCW (store control word) stores the 8087 control word at the two-byte destination location. We used FSTCW earlier to save a clean copy of the control word before changing rounding control. Later we used FLDCW to restore the control word to its original state.

FWAIT

FWAIT is actually an 8088, not an 8087, instruction. (The FWAIT mnemonic generates the 8088 WAIT instruction.) FWAIT halts the 8088 until the 8087 completes its current instruction. FWAIT should be coded before any 8088 instruction that references a memory location being read from or written to by the 8087. During an FWAIT, the 8088 checks the 8087 once per microsecond, and resumes execution as soon as the 8087 is free.

The description of the remaining processor control instructions is included for completeness. None of these instructions are necessary for the programs in this book.

The following two instructions are useful in writing subroutines because they allow a subroutine to save a copy of the 8087's internal state and then restore it.

FSAVE memory — 44 microseconds

FSAVE (save state) copies all internal 8087 information into a 94-byte area in memory. It then reinitializes the processor by executing an FINIT (see below). Figure 12.1 illustrates the layout of the memory save area.

The save area for the 287 running in *Virtual Protected Address Mode* has a very slightly different layout from the one shown in Figure 12.1. In Protected Mode, the two words holding the instruction pointer (6 and 8) hold the instruction pointer offset and the CS segment address. The two words holding the operand pointer (10 and 12) hold the operand offset and segment addresses. These differences are relevant only to the system programmer.

The reinitialization feature of FSAVE can cause undesired side effects, such as unintentionally resetting rounding control. The control word is easily restored by following "FSAVE memory" with "FLDCW memory."

FRSTOR memory — 44 microseconds

FRSTOR (restore state) reloads the 8087 state from the 94-byte area in memory, effectively "undoing" a previous FSAVE.

FSAVE and FRSTOR provide a mechanism by which a subroutine can use the 8087 and then return it to its original state. BASIC requires us to protect certain 8088 registers in an analogous way. (That's why many of our routines started with "PUSH BP" and ended with "POP BP.") Use of FSAVE/FRSTOR may or not be required, depending on the conventions of a given language translator. Note that the following code can be used to save and restore onto the 8088 stack.

```
SUB    SP,94
MOV    BP,SP
FSAVE  [BP]
    .
    .
    .
MOV    BP,SP
FRSTOR [BP]
ADD    SP,94
```

FINIT — 1 microsecond

FINIT (initialize processor) resets the 8087. The initialized conditions are described in Figure 12.2.

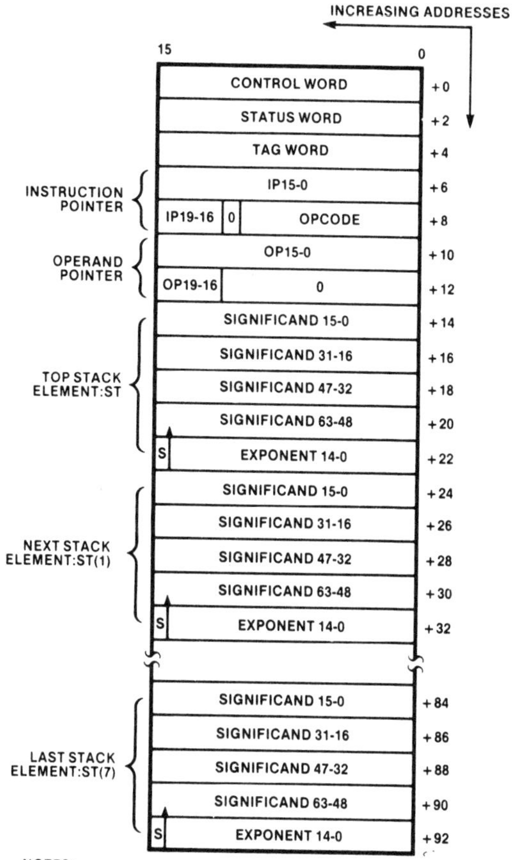

NOTES:
S = Sign
Bit 0 of each field is rightmost, least significant bit of corresponding register field.
Bit 63 of significand is integer bit (assumed binary point is immediately to the right).

Figure 12.1. Memory layout for 8087 internal state. (Used with permission of Intel Corporation.)

FSETPM — 1 microsecond

FSETPM (set Protected mode) is available only on the 287, not the 8087. FSETPM places the 287 in *Virtual Protected Address Mode*. The 287 can be returned to *Real Mode* only by a hardware reset. In particular, the FINIT instruction will not affect the address mode of the 287.

Interrupt and Exception-handling Instructions

Normally, we allow exceptions to be masked; that is, the 8087 hardware handles computational errors automatically. If a given exception type is unmasked, the 8087 will interrupt the 8088 when the exception occurs.

Field	Value	Interpretation
Control Word		
Infinity Control	0	Projective
Rounding Control	00	Round to nearest
Precision Control	11	64 bits
Interrupt-enable Mask	1	Interrupts disabled
Exception Masks	111111	All exceptions masked
Status Word		
Busy	0	Not busy
Condition Code	????	(Indeterminate)
Stack Top	000	Empty stack
Interrupt Request	0	No interrupt
Exception Flags	000000	No exceptions
Tag Word		
Tags	11	Empty
Registers	N.C.	Not changed
Exception Pointers		
Instruction Code	N.C.	Not changed
Instruction Address	N.C.	Not changed
Operand Address	N.C.	Not changed

Figure 12.2. 8087 initial conditions. (Used with permission of Intel Corporation.)

In this way, a computational error can be processed by user- or system-specified exception-handling software. If the 8088 is handling a task with higher priority than accepting 8087 "messages," 8087 interrupts can be disabled with the FDISI instruction.

FDISI — 1 microsecond

FDISI (disable interrupts) disables interrupts on the 8087 by setting the interrupt enable mask bit in the control word. FDISI is ignored on the 287. 8087 programs that rely on FDISI almost certainly must be rewritten to function properly on a 287. Fortunately, FDISI is used almost exclusively by system programmers.

FENI — 1 microsecond

FENI (enable interrupts) enables interrupts on the 8087 by clearing the interrupt enable mask bit in the control word. FENI is ignored on the 287. As with FDISI, 8087 programs that rely on FENI almost certainly must be rewritten to function properly on a 287. Fortunately, FENI too is used almost exclusively by system programmers.

FCLEX — 1 microsecond

FCLEX (clear exceptions) clears the exception flags, the interrupt request flag, and the busy flag in the status word. FCLEX is principally used by exception-handling routines after an exception has been taken care of. If the exception were not cleared before returning control to the 8087, a second interrupt request would be issued immediately.

FSTENV memory — 11 microseconds

FSTENV (store environment) stores the control, status, and tag words, and the exception pointers in a 12-byte memory area, so that these items may be examined by an exception handling routine. FSTENV stores a subset of the information stored by FSAVE and operates with considerably greater speed. Figure 12.3 illustrates the layout of the save area.

The 12-byte environment area for the 287 running in *Virtual Protected Address Mode* has a very slightly different layout from the one shown in Figure 12.3. In Protected Mode, the two words holding the instruction pointer (6 and 8) hold the instruction pointer offset and the CS segment address. The two words holding the operand pointer (10 and 12) hold the operand offset and segment addresses. (Note this is the same change as made for FSTOR.) These differences are relevant only to the system programmer.

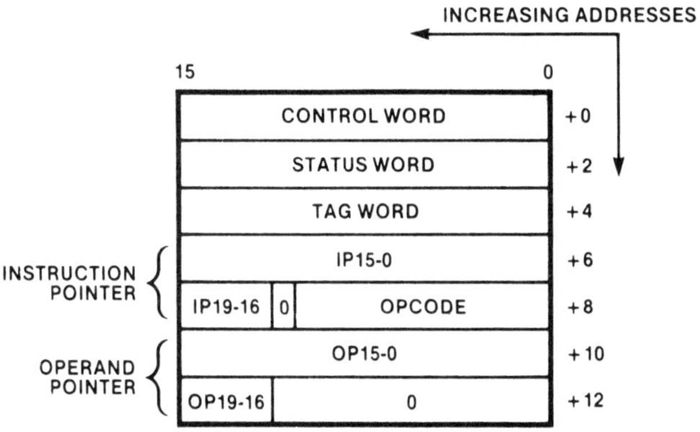

Figure 12.3. Memory layout for 8087 internal "environment" information. (Used with permission of Intel Corporation.)

FLDENV memory — 10 microseconds

FLDENV (load environment) loads the control, status, and tag words, and the exception pointers from a 12-byte memory area, as in Figure 12.3.

FINCSTP — 2 microseconds

FINCSTP (increment stack pointer) increments the 8087 stack pointer. Do not use this instruction to pop the stack, since it does not mark ST as empty. Use FSTP ST(0) instead.

FDECSTP 2 microseconds

FDECSTP (decrement stack pointer) decrements the 8087 stack pointer.

FFREE ST(i) 2 microseconds

FFREE (free register) marks the indicated register as empty.

FNOP 3 microseconds

FNOP (no operation) executes an FST ST,ST(0) in order to do nothing.

Advanced Instruction Set Summary

This chapter has seen much intricate detail. It took, for example, about 90 instructions to calculate a tangent even though the 8087 has a built-in "tangent" instruction. (If you think it took a lot of work this way, try writing a tangent instruction using only 8088 code!)

It is more difficult to build a small set of assembly language modules for non-linear problems than it is for linear problems. This is a place which really calls for an 8087-compatible language translator. (The non-linear programs in the next chapter are written in BASIC for this reason.) Nonetheless, it is instructive to see just how much improvement we can expect from the 8087.

Without the 8087, compiled BASIC requires about 26,800 microseconds to calculate a double precision tangent. Our assembly language program uses about 460 microseconds. Even using a poor 8087-compatible translator, you can look for an order of magnitude speed improvement on non-linear operations.

13

Non-Linear Methods

Given a non-linear function, y = f(x), how do we find the value of x that makes y equal to zero? The value that makes y equal one? What value of x gives the maximum possible value of the function? Answers to these and related questions are the subject of this chapter. BASIC's DEF FN statement makes it easy to define an algebraic formula as a function, f(x). For example, suppose we wish to explore the function

$$y = 17-(x-12)^2$$

We write this in BASIC as

```
10     DEFDBL Y,X
20     DEF FNY(X)=17-(X-12)^2
```

Of course, this particular function could be coded in assembly language in only a few minutes. A really complicated function might take some time. Worse, every time we need to work with a new function, we would need to write a new assembly language routine. Non-linear programs call for use of a high-level language. We use BASIC due to its widespread availability for personal computers.

In this chapter we discuss:

- Numerical differentiation
- Numerical integration
- Solving a non-linear equation
- Non-linear optimization

For many readers, the most interesting topic may be "solving a non-linear equation." As the first sections of the chapter provide useful background material for solving non-linear equations, you should probably work through these sections as well.

For a concrete focus of the discussion which follows, look now at the chart of the function y=f(x). Figure 13.1 shows the plot of our sample function.

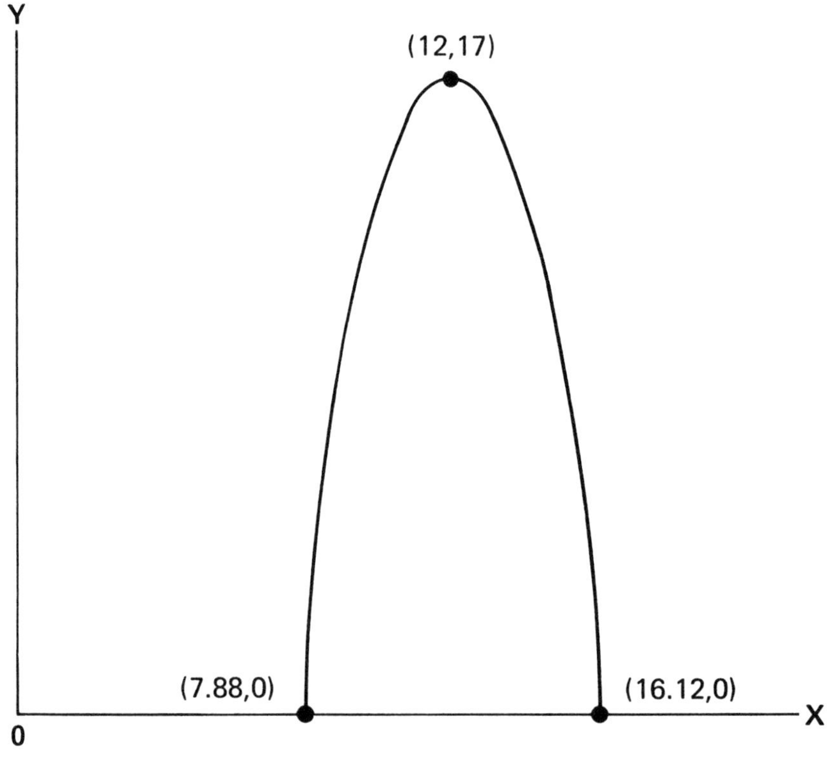

Figure 13.1. Graph of function $y = 17 - (x - 12)^2$.

This particular function equals zero at $x = 7.88$ and $x = 16.12$. It reaches its maximum value, 17.0, at $x = 12$.

Numerical Differentiation

The *derivative* of a function is the slope of the function at a particular point. To find the derivative graphically, draw a line tangent to the function at the point of interest and measure the ratio of the change in the vertical distance to the change in the horizontal distance, as in Figure 13.2.

The computer can't very well draw such a line (at least, not unless it knows the slope). Since the computer can easily evaluate the function, we approximate the tangent line by picking another point close to the point of interest and having the computer effectively "draw" a line to connect these two points. Figure 13.3 shows an "enlargement" of a small part of the function with just such a line.

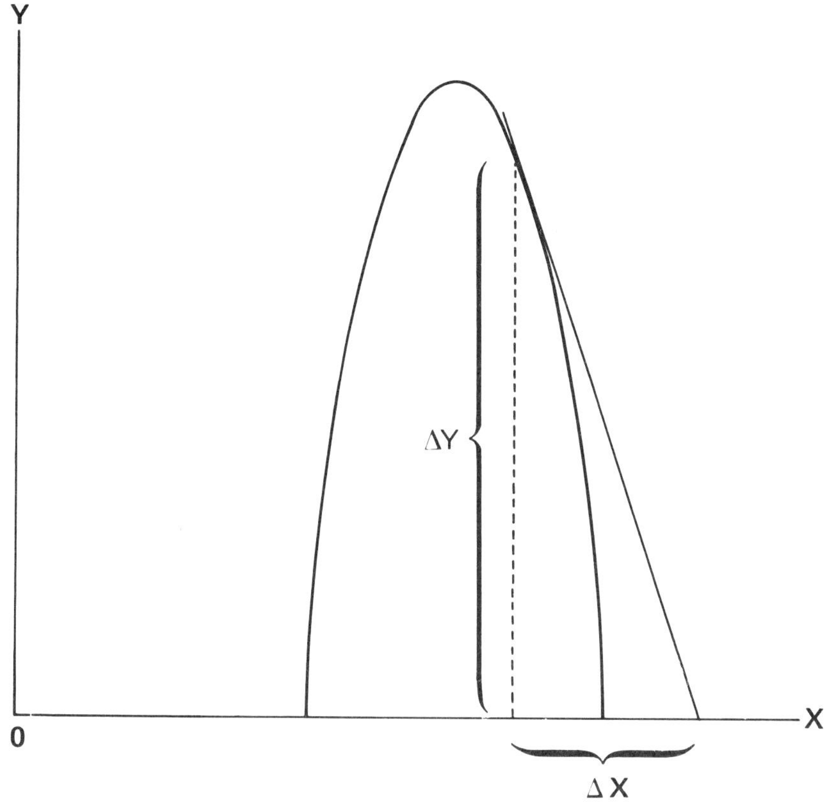

Figure 13.2. Tangent line.

The ratio of the vertical to the horizontal change is *approximately* the derivative of the function. If we pick the second point quite close to the first point, then the approximation will be quite accurate. How close do we need to be to assure some desired level of accuracy? The usual procedure is to evaluate the derivative once and then re-evaluate it with a closer second point. If the two answers lie within a distance "epsilon" of each other (that is, if they are no more than epsilon apart), then the answers are probably within epsilon of the true answer as well.

The following BASIC program evaluates the derivative of the function FNY at the point X0, assuming we require an answer accurate to within plus or minus EPS.

```
10      DEFDBL Y,X,F,E,D
20      DEF FNY(X)=17-(X-12)^2
30      REM SET X0 EPS ITLIM
40      X0=16
50      EPS=.001
60      ITLIM=100
70      DELTA=.01*X0
```

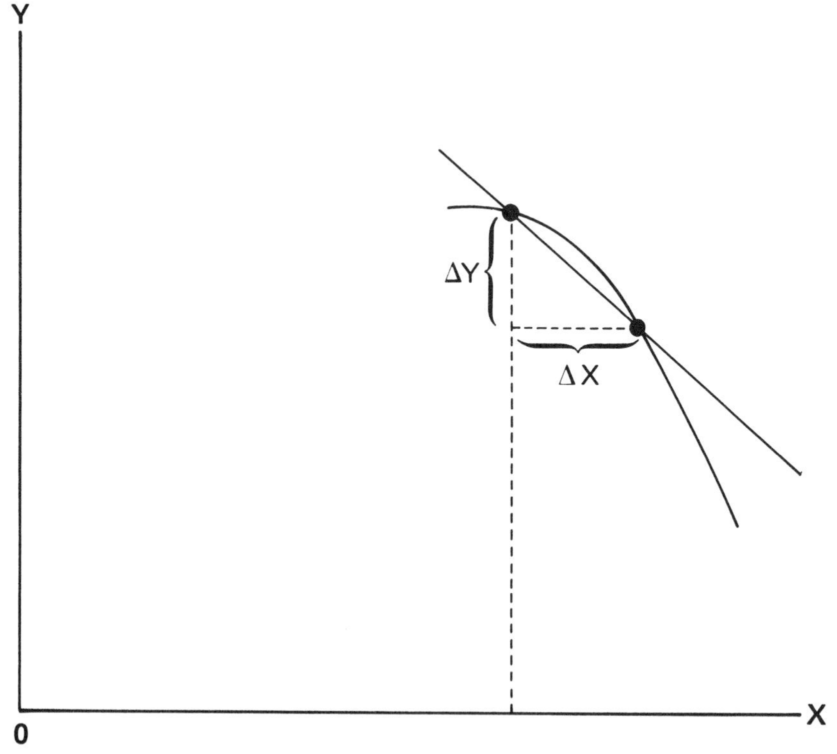

Figure 13.3. Enlarged view of tangent line.

```
80     FXO=FNY(XO)
90     DIFOLD=(FNY(XO+DELTA)-FXO)/DELTA
100    IT=1
110    REM LOOP UNTIL CONVERGENCE OR ITERATION LIMIT REACHED
120    DELTA=DELTA/2
130    DIF=(FNY(XO+DELTA)-FXO)/DELTA
140    IF ABS(DIF-DIFOLD) <EPS THEN 1000
150    IT=IT+1
160    IF IT>ITLIM THEN 2000
170    DIFOLD=DIF
180    GO TO 120
1000   REM CONVERGENCE ACHIEVED
1010   PRINT "DERIVATIVE AT ";XO;" IS ";DIF
1020   PRINT " AFTER ";IT;" ITERATIONS"
1030   STOP
2000   REM NO CONVERGENCE
2010   PRINT "FAILED TO CONVERGE AFTER ";ITLIM;" ITERATIONS"
2020   PRINT "APPROXIMATE DERIVATIVE AT ";XO;" IS ";DIF
2030   STOP
```

Always take the accuracy of this sort of numerical approximation with a grain of salt. It can happen that two successive approximations are close to one another without being equally close to the correct answer. Round-off error can also give results a false appearance of accuracy. The arithmetic operation at which computers are the least accurate is subtracting two numbers that are nearly equal in value, as in FNY(X0 + DELTA) – FNY(X0), for example.

By the way, you should always include an "iteration limit" in a program that otherwise relies on a mathematical condition to stop. Computer arithmetic is imperfect. With sufficient bad luck ("sufficient bad luck" means "sooner or later for sure"), your program will end up in an endless loop, if it doesn't have a guaranteed stopping mechanism.

The execution time for a non-linear program is roughly proportional to the number of function evaluations. That's why we evaluated FNY(X0) early in the program and saved the answer.

Numerical Integration

Integration is the inverse function of differentiation. Integration tells us the area under a curve between two points. The area under our sample function, from XLOWER to XUPPER, is shown in Figure 13.4.

We can approximate the area under the curve by drawing in rectangles as in Figure 13.5. The total area in all the rectangles is approximately the area under the curve. The more, and smaller, the rectangles we draw, the closer we come to the answer.

If we draw n rectangles, we make the width of each one one-nth of the distance between XLOWER and XUPPER. Since the area is just the height times the width, and since each of the n rectangles has the same width one-nth, we can find the area by just adding up the heights and multiplying the sum by the XUPPER-XLOWER. To obtain a more accurate answer, we cut each old rectangle in half and add new rectangles as in 13.6.

The following BASIC program integrates the function FNY.

```
10      DEFDBL Y,X,F,E,D,A
20      DEF FNY(X)=17-(X-12)>2
30      REM SET XLOWER XUPPER EPS ITLIM
40      XLOWER=9
50      XUPPER=13
60      EPS=.001
70      ITLIM=10
80      XWIDTH=(XUPPER-XLOWER)/2
90      FSUM=FNY(XLOWER)+FNY(XUPPER)
100     AREAOLD=FSUM*(XUPPER-XLOWER)
110     IT=1
120     N=2
```

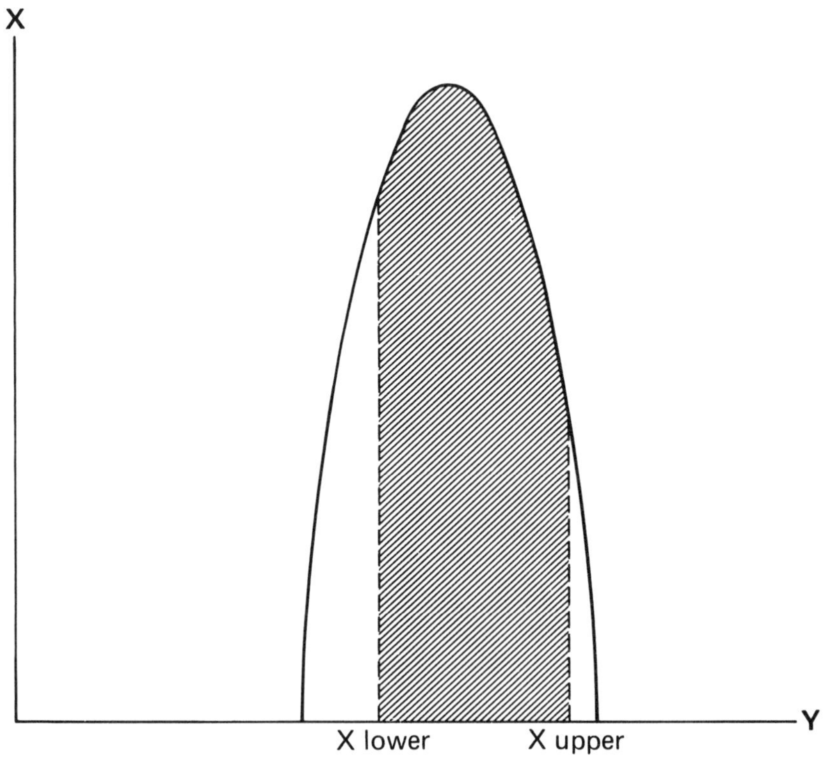

Figure 13.4. Area under function $y = 17 - (x - 12)^2$.

```
130   REM LOOP UNTIL CONVERGENCE OR ITERATION LIMIT REACHED
140   XWIDTH=XWIDTH/2
150   N=N*2
160   FSUM=0
170     FOR I=1 TO N STEP 2
180     X=XLOWER+XWIDTH*I
190     FSUM=FSUM+FNY(X)
200     NEXT I
210   AREA=FSUM*(XWIDTH)+(AREAOLD/2)
220   IF ABS(AREA-AREAOLD) <EPS THEN 1000
230   IT=IT+1
240   IF IT>ITLIM THEN 2000
250   AREAOLD=AREA
260   GO TO 140
1000  REM CONVERGENCE ACHIEVED
1010  PRINT "INTEGRAL FROM ";XLOWER;" TO";XUPPER;" IS ";AREA
1020  PRINT " AFTER ";IT;" ITERATIONS"
1030  STOP
2000  REM NO CONVERGENCE
```

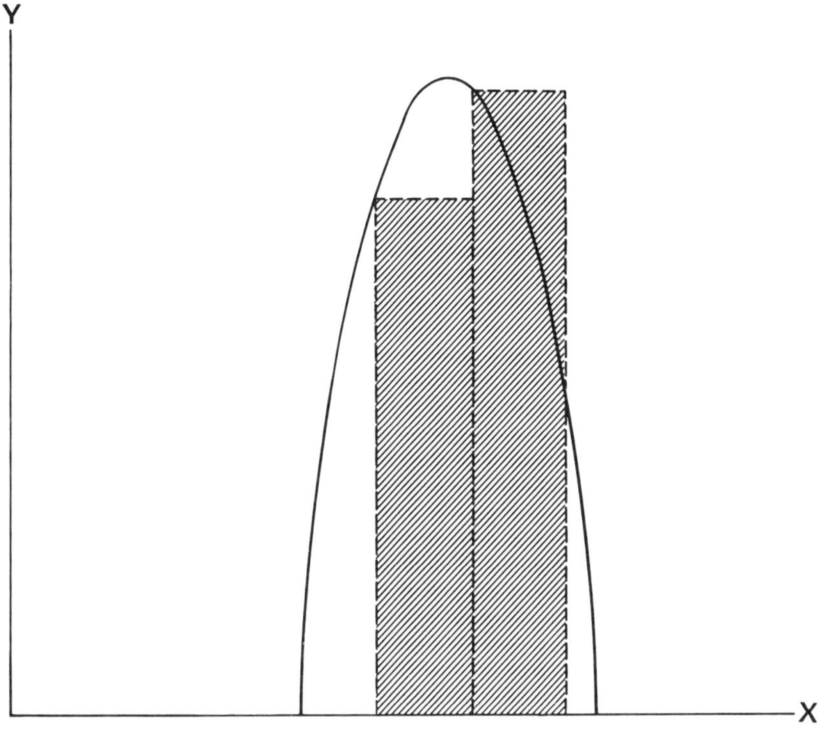

Figure 13.5. Approximation to area under function.

```
2010  PRINT "FAILED TO CONVERGE AFTER ";ITLIM;" ITERATIONS
2020  PRINT "APPROXIMATE INTEGRAL IS ";AREA
2030  STOP
```

Of course, one can usually use calculus in place of numerical computation. The formula for the derivative of our sample function is $24-2x$. The formula for the integral is $17x-(1/3)(x-12)^3$.

Derivatives can be found by applying the rules of calculus mechanically, so sometimes packaged programs actually figure out the formula for the derivative instead of using numerical methods. Integrals cannot be found by purely mechanical rules.

Solving a Non-linear Equation

Suppose we have a function $y=f(x)$ and know that the value of y is Y0. How can we find the value of x that produced Y0? Suppose that $Y0=0$ and look back at Figure 13.2. Start at the point (f(X0),X0). If the function

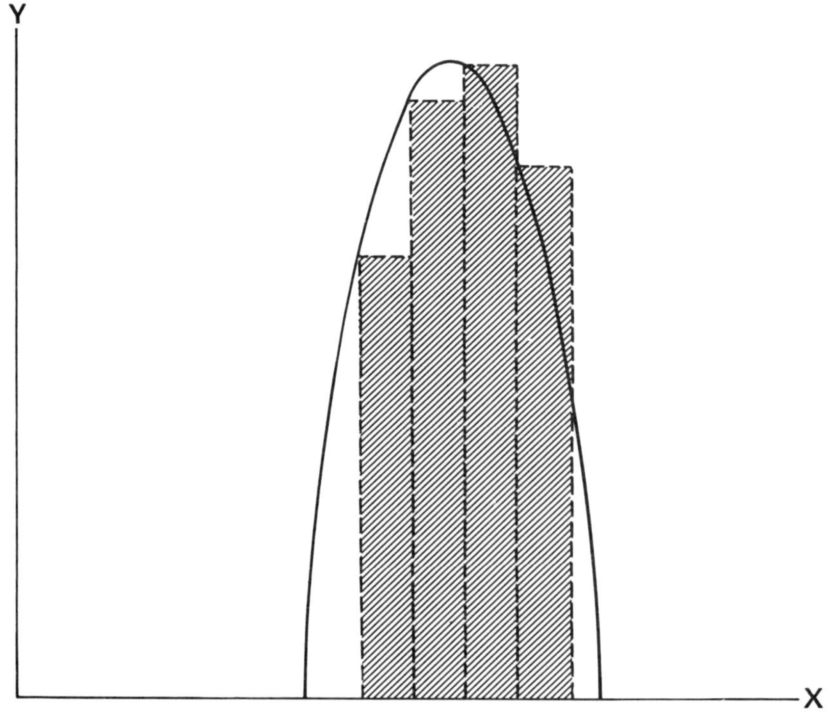

Figure 13.6. Refined approximation to area under function.

f(x) was actually a straight line, we could just run our finger down the tangent line until we hit the x axis at (0,X1). Since f(x) is not a straight line, when we hit the x-axis we actually get (f(X1),X1) instead. Now draw a tangent line from the new point and try again.

If the function f(x) is sufficiently smooth, this "shooting method" will usually converge to the correct point fairly quickly. However, sometimes after we shoot down the tangent, we are even further from the correct answer than we were originally. We'll add another rule to the procedure to prevent this. If our new guess is even further from the right spot then the initial guess, we cut in half the size of the step we took and try again. The BASIC program below implements this modified shooting method.

```
10      DEFDBL Y,X,F,E,D
20      DEF FNY(X)=17-(X-12)^2
30      DEF FNDIF(X)=(FNY((1+DEL)*X)-FNY(X))/(DEL*X)
40      REM SET YTARGET EPS DEL X0 ITLIM
50      YTARGET=0
60      DEL=.001
70      EPS=.01
```

```
80     X0=14
90     X=X0
100    ITLIM=20
110    STEPLIM=5
120    Y=FNY(X)
130    IT=1
140    ISTEP=0
150    STEPSIZE=1
160    XNEW=X+STEPSIZE*((YTARGET-Y)/FNDIF(X))
170    YNEW=FNY(XNEW)
180    IF ABS(YNEW-YTARGET)<EPS THEN 1000
190    IF ABS(YNEW-YTARGET)>ABS(Y-YTARGET) THEN 500
200    Y=YNEW
210    X=XNEW
220    IT=IT+1
230    IF IT>ITLIM THEN 2000
240    GOTO 140
500    REM REDUCE STEP SIZE
510    ISTEP=ISTEP+1
520    IF ISTEP>STEPLIM THEN 220
530    STEPSIZE=STEPSIZE/2
540    GOTO 160
1000   PRINT "SOLUTION IS ";XNEW;" AFTER ";IT;" ITERATIONS"
1010   STOP
2000   PRINT "FAILED TO CONVERGE AFTER ";ITLIM;" ITERATIONS"
2010   PRINT "APPROXIMATE ANSWER ";XNEW
2020   STOP
```

For the sample function, there are actually two correct answers for some values of YTARGET. This program only finds one, usually the closest to the initial starting point X0. In order to check for more than one solution, the program can be rerun with several different initial values.

Notice that the program uses DEF FNDIF to approximate the derivative. To increase the accuracy of the final solution, DEL should generally be reduced along with EPS. FNDIF could be redefined to give the exact derivative by using calculus. This would speed up the program a little by reducing the number of function evaluations and possibly also because of the greater accuracy of an exact derivative. On the other hand, figuring out analytic derivatives is more work for the user.

Non-linear Optimization

Suppose that y in our sample function described the profits of a small programming business as a function of the number of hours, x, spent typing on the keyboard of a personal computer. We would like to *maximize* this function, that is, find the value of x that gives us the highest possible value of y.

If you look back at Figure 13.1 you will see that at the highest point of the function the slope of the function is zero. In calculus terms, the derivative of a function equals zero at its maximum. (In logical terms, if a function is still going up, we should search further to the right; if it's going down, we've gone too far. Exactly at the maximum, the function must be going neither up nor down. Its slope must be zero.)

Finding the maximum of a function f(x) reduces to finding the point where the derivative of f(x) equals zero. The previous program will handle this quite nicely if we redefine the function calls to look at the derivative instead of the original function and the calls on the function for the derivative to look at the derivative of the derivative.

```
10    DEFDBL Y,X,F,E,D
20    DEF FNY(X)=17-(X-12)^2
30    DEF FNDIF(X)=(FNY((1+DEL)*X)-FNY(X))/(DEL*X)
35    DEF FNDDIF(X)=(FNDIF((1+DEL)*X)-FNDIF(X))/(DEL*X)
40    REM SET YTARGET EPS DEL X0 ITLIM
50    YTARGET=0
60    DEL=.001
70    EPS=.001
80    X0=14
90    X=X0
100   ITLIM=20
110   STEPLIM=5
120   Y=FNDIF(X)
130   IT=1
140   ISTEP=0
150   STEPSIZE=1
160   XNEW=X+STEPSIZE*((YTARGET-Y)/FNDDIF(X))
170   YNEW=FNDIF(XNEW)
180   IF ABS(YNEW-YTARGET)<EPS THEN 1000
190   IF ABS(YNEW-YTARGET)>ABS(Y-YTARGET) THEN 500
200   Y=YNEW
210   X=XNEW
220   IT=IT+1
230   IF IT>ITLIM THEN 2000
240   GOTO 140
500   REM REDUCE STEP SIZE
510   ISTEP=ISTEP+1
520   IF ISTEP>STEPLIM THEN 220
530   STEPSIZE=STEPSIZE/2
540   GOTO 160
1000  FM=FNY(XNEW)
1010  IF FM>=FNY((1+DEL)*XNEW) AND FM>=FNY((1-DEL)*XNEW) THEN
        1050
1020  PRINT "CAN'T FIND MAXIMUM"
1030  PRINT "STOPPED AT ";XNEW; "AFTER ";IT;" ITERATIONS
1040  STOP
1050  PRINT "MAXIMUM IS AT ";XNEW;" AFTER ";IT;" ITERATIONS
1060  PRINT "VALUE AT THE MAXIMUM IS ";FNY(XNEW)
1070  STOP
```

```
2000  PRINT "FAILED TO CONVERGE AFTER ";ITLIM;" ITERATIONS"
2010  PRINT "APPROXIMATE ANSWER ";XNEW
2020  STOP
```

Our BASIC program will find that the maximum, y=17, is found at X=12. Just as a non-linear function can have exactly one solution, no solution, or many solutions, in the same way a function can have one maximum, no maximum, or many maxima. The code at line 1000 checks for the possibility that the program located a point where the the derivative equals zero, but which is not a maximum. Such a point might be a minimum or an "inflection point." Even with this check, care on the part of the user is still a good idea. The program has no way to check whether it has found only a "local maximum," that is, whether there might be a point elsewhere that has an even higher value than the point found by the program.

Back to Linearity

In the next chapter, we build a small statistical analysis system and, in so doing, return to linear problems and to the use of assembly language modules.

14

Statistical Analysis and Program Canning

This chapter has two principle objectives: gaining an understanding of some of the basic techniques of programming for statistical analysis, and working through an example of how to make a "canned" program. This chapter will give you:

- Some basic methods for statistical analysis.
- Some practice in going from mathematical ideas to working programs.
- An adaptable "canned" program (which you can modify if you wish to add your own procedures).
- A complete, working multiple regression package.

The Cookbook—Chapter 14	
Program:	**8087 Statistical Analysis Program**
Purpose:	"Canned" program for multiple regression and other statistical analysis.
Input:	Interactive.
Output:	Interactive.
Language:	BASIC with 8087/8088 assembly language modules.

Statistical Analysis

Three of the basic procedures used in statistical analysis are descriptive statistics, correlation, and multiple regression. These methods are used to summarize data, to examine the relation between different events, and to make tests of scientific hypotheses. We discuss the use of these methods, and how to perform the necessary calculations, below.

One caveat first. The combination of sophisticated statistical methods and high-speed computers has made it possible to draw incorrect conclusions far more easily than at any time in the past. Almost any statistical procedure can be applied to almost any body of data. Just because we can do so does not mean we should. Various important mathematical caveats and warnings are omitted from the discussion below, since a thorough job would occupy a PhD course. We hope that the reader experienced in statistical analysis will not be offended—and that the reader first encountering statistical analysis will be careful.

Descriptive Statistics

Given repeated observations on an "event," such as the number of cars passing a certain intersection between 8:00 AM and 8:05 AM, we begin a statistical analysis by looking for simple ways to characterize the observed data. Assume we have made n observations. Call a typical datum, "x."

The very first question usually asked is "What was the average value of the data?" Calculating an average is simple. The *mean* of the data is the sum of all the data points divided by the number of observations. The mean of x is often written $\bar{x}$.

$$\bar{x} = \frac{x_1 + x_2 + \ldots + x_n}{n}$$

Next we would like to determine whether the observed data all lie close to one another or whether they are spread out over a wide range. The most common measurement is called the *variance*. Variance is a measure of the dispersion of data around its mean. Essentially, the variance is the average of the squared value of the difference between x and the mean of x. The variance can be calculated by subtracting the mean off of each datum, squaring this difference, summing the results, and dividing by $n-1$. (It turns out that, under reasonable assumptions, dividing by $n-1$ rather than n gives a more accurate average answer.)

$$\text{var}(x) = \frac{(x_1-\bar{x})^2 + (x_2-\bar{x})^2 + \ldots (x_n-\bar{x})^2}{(n-1)}$$

Closely related to the variance is the *standard deviation*. The standard deviation is the square root of the variance. The standard deviation is frequently a more convenient measure than the variance because it has the same units of measurement as the original data. If you multiply every piece of data by, say, 16, you also multiply the mean and the standard deviation by 16, while the variance is multiplied by 256. Thus if the original data is measured in pounds, then both mean and standard deviation are measured in pounds (and 16 times either is measured in ounces), while the variance is measured in the less familiar units of "pounds-squared."

The following rule gives a feeling for the "spread" of your data: If the data is drawn from a Normal ("bell curve") distribution, then about two-thirds of the data should lie in the range from one standard deviation below the mean to one standard deviation above the mean.

While these three descriptive statistics are probably the most common, there are many others you might also look at. What are the highest and lowest values of the data? What's the middle value? Does the data cluster around certain values? We'll stop at three: mean, variance, and standard deviation.

Correlation

Given two sets of data, x and y, we are frequently interested in whether the two sets of data tend to move together, to move in opposite directions, or whether the two appear to be unassociated. Statisticians use the *correlation coefficient* as a measure of association between two variables. Two variables that are exactly proportional to one another have a correlation coefficient of one. Two variables that are exactly proportional but that move in opposite directions have a correlation coefficient of minus one. A zero correlation coefficient usually indicates that knowing x tells you nothing about y, and vice versa.

The correlation coefficient is constructed as a ratio. The numerator measures how much x and y move together. The denominator measures how much each moves separately. The numerator is calculated as the average of the product of x minus x's mean and y minus y's mean. The numerator is the product of the standard deviations of x and y. (However, in this context we use n rather than $n-1$ in calculating the standard deviations.)

Guess what's back! Our friend from linear algebra—the inner product. (We promised you it was good for more than playing with systems of linear equations.) Think about calculating the numerator of the correlation coefficient. We begin the calculation by preparing two vectors, the first made up of each observation of x minus x's mean and the second made up similarly from y. The inner product of these vectors is the sum of the product of the elements. So the required average is just the inner product divided by n.

Actually, the same calculation can be done in a more simple form by avoiding the construction of the two vectors of deviations from the means. A little algebra will show that the required average can also be calculated as the inner product of x and y divided by n, minus n times the quantity the mean of x times the mean of y.

A little exercise for the reader: what's the correlation coefficient between x and y if the observations of x are all the same? The answer is that it doesn't make much sense to ask whether x and y move together if x doesn't move at all. Both the numerator and denominator of the correlation coefficient equal zero. We'll want to watch for this situation when programming in order to avoid "Division by zero" error messages.

Multiple Regression

Multiple regression must be far and away the most common statistical technique for equation estimation and forecasting. Suppose we have a sequence of observations on a variable to be explained, the *dependent* variable, y, and observations made at the same time on several explanatory, or *independent*, variables, x_1, x_2, and so forth. We might look for a linear relationship between the dependent and independent variables of the form:

$$y = b_0 + b_1x_1 + b_2x_2 + \ldots + b_kx_k + u$$

where u is an unobservable *error term*, indicative of the fact that x variables will not explain y perfectly. Regression may be interpreted in two ways: as either a statistical procedure or as a technique for fitting an equation to data.

The term "multiple regression" arises out of the statistical interpretation. We might posit that the equation above is a "true" equation in nature and that while we have observed a set of y's and x's, we have been unable to observe the u's. Given a certain set of statistical assumptions, multiple regression produces optimal estimates of the coefficients b_0 through b_k in the above equation. (The assumptions are fairly reasonable, but require more mathematics than we want to go into here.)

Further, given these statistical assumptions, we can test hypotheses about the coefficients. The coefficients produced by a multiple regression are estimates of the true values of b. The regression also produces a *standard error* for each estimated coefficient. There is a two out of three chance that the true coefficient lies in a band from one standard error below the estimated coefficient to one standard error above the estimated coefficient. Chances are about 19 out of 20 that the true coefficient lies in a band of plus or minus two standard errors around the estimated coefficient.

Suppose the true coefficient b_i is zero. This is equivalent to saying that the variable x_i has nothing do to with explaining y. If the estimated coefficient is far away from zero, in the sense of being many standard errors away, then it's unlikely that the true coefficient is zero. The ratio of an estimated coefficient to it's standard error is sometimes called the *t-statistic*. If the t-statistic of b_i is greater, in absolute value, than 2, there is only 1 chance in 20 that the variable x_i has nothing to do with explaining the variable y.

(All of the statements above are predicated on what are sometimes called the "Gauss-Markov" assumptions. See any good statistics or econometrics text for a thorough discussion of the role of various mathematical assumptions.)

The mathematics of regression is also known as *ordinary least squares*. We can regard the problem of estimating the coefficients in the preceding equation as a question of fitting the equation to the data, without regard to any statistical assumptions. The difference between the value of y and the value predicted by applying our estimated coefficients to the data x is called a *residual*. Ordinary least squares pick values for the coefficients that minimize the sum of the squared residuals.

In addition to the estimated coefficients, their associated standard errors and t-statistics, a multiple regression results in several auxiliary statistics. The R-squared is a "goodness of fit measure." The R-squared is the percentage of variation of y explained by the variables x. R-squared equals 1.0 for a perfect fit and 0.0 in the absence of any fit.

The standard error of the regression estimates the standard deviation of the error terms, u. The sum of squared residuals—which is just what it sounds like—is used in making various statistical tests.

We wrote b_0 above without any associated x variable. A constant term b_0 is equivalent to the coefficient on an x variable made up of all ones, which is how we calculate it in the program below. A regression should almost always have a constant term in it, but our program lets the user decide whether or not to include one.

Regression Formulas

Computation of a multiple regression is easily specified in matrix notation. Let y be a vector containing the values of y and X be a matrix where each column i is the values for x_i. If b is the vector of estimated coefficients then:

$$b = (X'X)^{-1}X'y$$

Remember from Chapter 9 that X' means the transpose of X.

Let SSR stand for the sum of squared residuals, s^2 for the square of the standard error of the regression, and R^2 for R squared. If there are n data points and k right-hand side variables (the constant counts as one of the k), we have

$$SSR = y'y - y'Xb$$
$$s^2 = SSR/(n\text{-}k)$$
$$R^2 = 1 - SSR/(y'y)$$

Algorithms for Computing Least Squares

You can see that the formula to compute the least squares coefficients simply requires a few matrix multiplications and one matrix inversion. It turns out that least squares is one of those problems in which the mathematical solution is straightforward, but accurate numerical computation is often difficult. We use the routines from Chapters 10 and 11 to do all the hard work, in particular INV to take care of the matrix inversion. These procedures are completely satisfactory in most cases. However, there are algorithms, specifically tailored to calculating least squares coefficients, which are sometimes far more accurate than and equally efficient as the general purpose routines we use. Discussion of these algorithms would carry us too far afield from the use of the 8087, but the references given in Chapter 11 will point you in the right direction. Chapter 5 of Stewart's *Introduction to Matrix Computations* is especially recommended. Be warned, the material is fairly advanced.

Canned Programs

If you flip to the end of this chapter, you'll find a complete listing of our "8087 Statistical Analysis Program." You may be struck immediately by the fact that the program is several hundred lines long. The code is lengthy despite the fact that this is a "plain vanilla" program, and despite the fact that all the important mathematics can be specified in only a few lines. (The source code for a commercial, mainframe statistic's package would be anywhere from 10,000 to a few hundred thousand lines long.)

Computer scientists use the name "modular programming" to describe the technique of breaking up a large problem into several smaller ones, each of which can be dealt with independently. Our canned program is composed of 19 "modules." The modules are classified according to whether they provide a user service, such as regression; a user utility, such as data entry; or a system service, such as program initialization. Because the program is broken up into small parts in this way, a new service could be added for the user with little or no modification to the existing modules. The modules in the program listing are:

User service:
- Descriptive statistics—Module 9
- Correlation—Module 10
- Multiple Regression—Module 11

User utilities:
- Catalog data in memory—Module 3
- Display data—Module 4
- Enter data—Module 5
- Edit data—Module 6

Save data to disk—Module 7
Retrieve data from disk—Module 8

System service

Menu display and command choice—Module 2
Begin program execution—Module 1
Storage allocation and program initialization—Module 12
Program restart—Module 13
Exit—Module 14
Place variable name in symbol table—Module 15
Form list of names—Module 16
Collect product-moment matrix—Module 17
Error-handling—Module 18
Screen-handling—Module 19

Data Storage

A program can be regarded as a group of procedures acting on a set of data. The program modules can be regarded as communicating with one another through the changes they make in the program's data base. In this case the data base begins with the data observed by the program user. Suppose the user has n observations on each of k different variables. We'll store the data internally in an n by k matrix called X. Observations on variable i are stored as the ith column of matrix X. As it is frequently convenient to have a constant vector, the program will automatically set column zero of X to equal 1.

People think in names, not column numbers. Rather than require the user to number variables, we store the names of the variables, in a string array NAMES$, and let the computer make the connection between the user specified variable name and the numerical index for the appropriate column of X. NAMES$ can be thought of as a very simple symbol table. The first variable in the symbol table, "(CONST)", will always point to the ones in column zero.

Several other variable definitions are also useful. TRUE% and FALSE% are set to −1 and 0 respectively. NUMVAR is the number of variables the user has defined. MAXVAR is the maximum number of variables the system can hold, a number which depends on the available memory. NUMOBS is the number of observations on a variable. (Each variable must have the same number of observations.) A number of modules communicate through the array LISTV, which contains a list of the column numbers corresponding to a user specified list of variables. LISTLEN is the number of elements in LISTV. Finally, we adopt the convention that all BASIC variables beginning with a letter between I and N will be integer variables. All other variables are single precision unless a "%", "#", or "$" is appended to indicate integer, double precision, or string, respectively.

Module By Module

We undertake here a detailed, module-by-module explanation of the statistical analysis program. (Since each module is short, this isn't too difficult.) Along the way, we point out some places where the program could be made more flexible or more "idiot-proof," albeit at the expense of a lot more code. If you read through the code and the explanations here, you should find it easy to make your own additions or changes to the program.

We'll "walk through" the program modules in the order which makes it easiest to understand, rather than the order in which they appear in the code.

Menu Display—Module 2—Line 2000

This module displays the available commands and asks for the user's choice. The response must be an integer between 1 and 11. Given any other response, the program prompts for a new answer. Notice the simple trick to check whether a number is an integer. The program accepts any characters as ANSWER$. The VAL function sets ANSWER to zero if the response is not a number. We then set ANSW% = ANSWER. Since ANSW% must be an integer, the two will only be equal if ANSWER was an integer.

Once ANSW% is in hand, the routine does an ON ANSW% GOSUB to the appropriate module. After the program returns, the menu display module starts all over again. To add another command to the program, we need only add a PRINT line to the menu display, add a line number to the GOSUB list, and change the valid answer range from 1 through 11 to 1 through 12.

Catalog Data in Memory—Module 3—Line 3000

This module allows the user to catalog the system's internal data base. The module first prints out the number of observations per variable, the number of variables already defined, and the number remaining still open for definition.

After displaying the catalog, module 3 calls module 19, which asks the user to hit a key to return to the command menu. If the program didn't do this, the display would vanish from the screen without giving the user time to think.

Display Data—Module 4—Line 4000

This module displays the data in one or more user selected variables. Module 16 is called to collect the variable names from the user. Module 16 expects certain information. MAXNAMES is the maximum number of names the user is permitted to enter. In this case, the user can enter as many as have been defined. NEWNAMES = FALSE% tells module 16 not to enter the names in the symbol table. FORCE0% = FALSE% tells module 16 that it should not automatically include "(CONST)" in the list. On return from module 16, LISTV(0) through LISTV(LISTLEN − 1) has the column numbers of the matrix X holding the desired data. (If NAMEERR is true, then module 16 found an error it couldn't handle.)

The data display module prints up to five variables to a line, up to 20 lines to a screen. It then pauses (using module 19) to let the user look at the data. The program could be fancier here in several ways. We might want to display the data differently according to whether the screen displays 40 or 80 columns across. We might also want to allow the user to direct output to the printer rather than the screen. Finally, we could pretty up the display by using more graphics.

Enter Data—Module 5—Line 5000

This module allows the user to enter the data for a single variable. We again use module 16, though this time we only allow one name to be specified and we ask module 16 to place the name as a new entry in the symbol table. Once the variable name is entered, the user is prompted for the data sequentially. Notice that there is no way for the user to "get out" of the data entry sequence except to follow it through to the end.

Edit Data—Module 6—Line 6000

Even a "plain vanilla" program must allow the user some way to correct mistakes. First, we use module 16 to ask the user which variable he or she wishes. Once we know the variable, we ask for an observation number. After displaying the current value, the program asks the user to specify a new value. Then the program displays both the new and old value for the user. The program keeps prompting for new observation numbers until the user responds with the ENTER key alone.

Save Data to Disk—Module 7—Line 7000

Serious statistical work is rarely completed in a single sitting. Module 7 allows the user to dump the system's database to disk for later retrieval. (The user also gets some protection against lost time due to power failure in this way.) The disk storage format is chosen for simplicity rather than efficiency. On the first line we dump out MAXVAR, NUMVAR, and NUMOBS. The next NUMVAR lines contain the contents of NAMES$. Finally, we dump the first NUMVAR columns of X. This simple format makes it possible to access the saved data from another program or to use another program to create data which can be read into our Statistical Analysis Program.

What happens if the user specifies a file name that already exists? BASIC will merrily write over an existing file, but it would be better to provide the user with at least some degree of protection against inadvertently wiping out important data. We use the following program trick to provide some protection. Before OPENing the output file, the program tries "NAME FILENAME$ AS FILENAME$". This command gives a BASIC error message "File already exists" if FILENAME$ is on the disk and "File not found" if FILENAME$ is a new file. The error trapping module, 18, checks to see if either of these errors occurred. In case of "File not found," module 18 RESUMEs execution as if nothing had happened. If this is a duplicate file, then module 18 asks the user for confirmation before allowing execution to proceed.

After storing the data on disk, the program closes the file and prints a message to the user before returning to the command menu.

Retrieve Data From Disk—Module 8—Line 8000

The disk retrieval module complements the disk storage module. This module retrieves a data base that had previously been stored on a disk file. The module first OPENs for input the user specified disk file. (The error-handling module swings into operation if a non-existent file is specified, so that the program won't bomb.) Once MAXVAR, NUMVAR, and NUMOBS are known, module 12 is called to reinitialize the program and allocate storage. (A more complicated program might add the contents of the disk file to the existing database rather than reinitializing the program.) Setting the flag DISKFILE% = TRUE% lets module 12 know that it needn't prompt the user for NUMOBS.

Restart Program—Module 13—Line 13000

Restarting the program is easy. Module 13 sets appropriate flags and calls module 12, which does all the work.

Exit Program—Module 14—Line 14000

One can always let the user hit a Ctrl-Break to end a BASIC program, but it's a lot more graceful to provide a specific command. Module 14 checks with the user to be sure an exit is intended, thus preventing accidental loss of valuable information. Use of the END statement also ensures that all files have been closed properly.

Descriptive Statistics—Module 9—Line 9000

Modules 9, 10, and 11 actually do some "productive" work for the user. Module 9 requests a list of variable names, using module 16, and then prints the mean, standard deviation, and variance of each of the listed variables. The 8087 procedure SUM is used to collect the sum of each variable and the 8087 routine INPROD collects the sum of the squared observations for each variable. Using 8087 routines for these procedures is almost as efficient as writing the entire module in assembly language, since these are the only parts of the module whose execution time is proportional to the number of observations.

Correlation—Module 10—Line 10000

The correlation module accepts a list of variable names (via module 16 again) and calculates the correlation coefficient between every pair of names on the list. This requires the sum of X_i times X_j, for each pair, plus the sum of each variable. The easiest, though slightly inefficient, way to get the sum of a variable is to take an inner product with a vector of ones. Module 10 accomplishes this by setting FORCE0% = TRUE% in order to guarantee that "(CONST)" is the first variable in LISTV. Module 17 is called to collect the "product-moment matrix" (the name given to the matrix of inner products of variable i with variable j). Once all the hard work is done in module 17, the correlation module prints out the correlation coefficients, checking as it goes along to avoid a "Division by zero" error.

Multiple Regression—Module 11—Line 11000

The multiple regression module uses module 16 twice, first to get the number of the dependent variable and second to get a list of numbers of the independent variables. The matrix X′y and the sum of y^2 are formed using INPROD. (Note that "X" refers here to only those columns of the database specified by the user in the list of independent variables.) Module 17 is called to form the matrix X′X. Module 17 only fills in the upper triangle of X′X, since the matrix is symmetric. We copy the upper half into the lower half since the matrix inversion subroutine expects to see the entire matrix. The 8087 routine INV is called to invert X'X. REALERR is used to check that the inversion routine only produced normal numbers. Finally GINPROD is used to multiply $(X'X)^{-1}$ by X'y and to form several auxiliary statistics. Results are then printed. As with the correlation module, all the hard number crunching is done by module 17.

Begin Program Execution—Module 1—Line 1000

Module 1 is quite simple. Module 12 is called after flag FIRSTTIME% is set to indicate that this is the first time through the program and flag DISKFILE% is set to indicate that this is not a call from module 8. The latter flag is logically redundant, but keeps the call to module 12 consistent with other parts of the program. By and large, when programming, consistency is worth a little redundancy.

Some programmers prefer to place program initialization code at the beginning of a program. In fact, some programming languages require one to do so. (The IBM Personal Computer BASIC Compiler for example!) With the BASIC interpreter, the placement of initialization code is largely a matter of taste.

Allocation and Program Initialization—Module 12—Line 12000

This module needs to consider two questions: Is this the first time the program has been initialized? Is this initialization preparatory to loading a disk file?

Suppose that this is the first time through the program. We need to clear the BASIC workspace and set aside enough space to load in the 8087 routines. Then the 8087 routines must be loaded and calling addresses set. (On the book diskette, all the programs in Chapter 9 are grouped in a file named "VECTOR.SAV"; the programs from Chapter 10 are in file "MATRIX.SAV"; and "MATADV.SAV" has the programs from Chapter 11. The addresses listed below reflect this arrangement. If you group your routines differently, you should change the calling addresses.)

The exact address at which the 8087 routines ought to be loaded may depend on which version of BASIC you use and on how much memory your computer has. The addresses shown work for standard IBM-PC BASIC. If you are using another version of BASIC, for example IBM-PC BASICA or the version of Microsoft BASIC delivered with many "PC compatibles," you will probably have to adjust the address for loading the 8087 routines.

Next, the program offers the user the option of loading data from disk. If the user invokes this option, module 8 is called. Note that module 8 calls back to module 12, which is perfectly legal in BASIC, though it is not allowed in many other programming languages. If the user does not choose to load data from disk, the program asks for the number of observations in the data.

Next the module determines how many variables will fit in memory. Since the data is stored in single precision, the data itself will require 4*n*k bytes. Space must also be set aside for the regression and correlation modules, and for LISTV. The amount of storage needed for NAMES$ will vary according to the length of variable names chosen by the user. Our module figures out the amount of free space by using the FRE function. It then figures out the maximum number of variables that will fit in the available space, leaving some spare room as a "fudge factor," and allocates storage.

If this is not the first time through the initialization routine, then module 12 must take one of two actions, depending on whether it is acting as a service routine for module 8. If we are loading data from the disk, then NUMOBS, and so forth, is already known. Module 12 need only erase the old database and dimension storage afresh. If we are not loading data, then the job is almost the same as if this were the first time through the program, except that we can begin directly with asking the user for the number of observations.

Module 12 is very "implementation dependent." For example, if we wanted to use another 8087 assembly language routine, we would have to change this module. While a new module might be programmed to load its own routines, the initialization module needs to know how much space to leave in the CLEAR statement.

If we wanted to use the BASIC compiler in place of the interpreter, this module would have to be moved to the front of the program, because the BASIC compiler requires DIM and DEF statements to appear before executable operations. Unfortunately, the BASIC compiler also requires fixed size dimensions for all the matrices, so to use the compiler we would be forced to create our own storage allocation mechanism. This would affect data storage in the entire program, not only module 12.

Insert Name in Symbol Table—Module 15—Line 15000

Module 15 attempts to place the name in NAMEIS$ in the symbol table and return its symbol table location in NAMELOC. Two possibilities might prevent completion of this task. First, the symbol table might be full, indicating that there is no more room in the database. Second, the name might already be defined. In either of these cases, module 15 prints an error message, sets the flag NAMEERR to TRUE%, and returns. If neither error arises, the module places NAMEIS$ in the first open location in NAMES$, adds one to the variable count in NUMVAR, and returns the proper value in NAMELOC.

Collect Names From User—Module 16—Line 16000

We've called this module from many other modules. Essentially, its job is to collect a series of names from the user and return their symbol table locations in LISTV. Module 16 treats collecting one variable and more than one variable as different cases, mostly so that we can give the user more intelligent prompts.

In the first case, MAXNAMES equals 1. We ask the user for a name, and call module 15 if NEWNAMES is TRUE%. If an undefined name is entered improperly, the user is given the opportunity to re-enter the name or to give a null response. A null response, or an error, causes the module to return with NAMEERR set to TRUE%. When a correct name is given, LISTV(0) is set to the location of the name and module 16 returns with NAMEERR set to FALSE%.

The problem of module 16 is considerably more complicated when a series of names is called for. We could prompt the user for one name at a time. It's friendlier to allow the user to enter a series of names separated by spaces. (As a side issue, the module must set LISTV(0) = 0 if FORCE0% requires us to include the constant term.) We accept a "variable list" from the user in ANSWER$. The module scans ANSWER$ looking for a space. The substring from the beginning of the scan to the space is taken as a variable name. We start scanning for the next name after the space. The scanning process is complete when the end of the string is reached. We check the names one at a time either by running through NAMES$ or by using module 15, depending on the value of NEWNAMES. (Notice that in this way an entire list of variables can be entered into the symbol table at once, even though the program does not use this feature.) If an error is found in processing the list of names, the user is asked to re-enter the entire list.

Notice that the error message for an undefined name displays the offending string within quotes. This is more than a nicety. Suppose the user enters variables named "X" and "Y" and later tries to retrieve "X <non-printing character>Y". The string "X 'space'" doesn't match the string "X". By placing the string in quotes we increase the chances that the user will notice the presence of a nondisplaying character.

Module 16 could be usefully modified by putting some restrictions on the legal variable names. Since some other modules only print variable names of limited length, we might want to restrict name length at the time of definition. We also might want to modify this module to accept upper and lower case characters without distinguishing between them. Finally, notice that the user might well enter a string that "wraps around" the end of the line, which is perfectly acceptable, or a string that is longer than 255 characters, which will cause an error that is trapped by the error-handling module.

Collect Product-Moment Matrix—Module 17—Line 17000

Almost the entire computational time of the program is spent in this module. The module creates a double precision matrix named XPX#. Element i,j, in the upper triangle of XPX#, is set to the inner product of the ith and jth variables in LISTV. The 8087 routine INPROD really does all the work.

Error-handling—Module 18—Line 18000

Nothing is worse in a canned program, even a simple one like this, than getting a BASIC error message. The whole point of a program being "canned" is that the user needn't understand its innards. Our program doesn't offer quite this level of protection, but it does catch a few possible errors. For example, if the user enters too many characters in response to the name prompt in module 16, we'd like to allow him or her another shot rather than have the program die. In addition, this routine handles a couple of places where we induce deliberate "errors," such as in the specification of file names.

Notice that we are quite careful to check the line number on which the error occurred before handling the error. In this way, we avoid "fixing" an error the program isn't prepared to handle.

Screen-handling—Module 19—Line 19000

Since the computer can display text faster than we can read, it's very convenient to have a way to make the screen stand still. Module 19 accomplishes this by going round in circles until the user hits a key.

A Little More on Programming Strategy

Our "8087 Statistical Analysis Program" is a very heavy number cruncher. Did you notice that of the several hundred lines of code, 8087 routines are referenced only nine times!?! Such a ratio is not in the least unusual for a general purpose program. However, these few references are responsible for almost all the speed and accuracy advantage of using the 8087.

```
5     REM PROGRAM FOR STATISTICAL ANALYSIS
10    REM THE PRINCIPLE SECTIONS OF THIS PROGRAM BEGIN AT
          LINES:
20    REM 1000 PROGRAM EXECUTION BEGINS
30    REM 2000 MENU DISPLAY
40    REM 3000 DATA CATALOG
50    REM 4000 DATA DISPLAY
60    REM 5000 DATA INPUT
70    REM 6000 DATA EDITING
80    REM 7000 SAVE DATA
90    REM 8000 RETRIEVE DATA
100   REM 9000   DESCRIPTIVE STATISTICS
110   REM 10000  CORRELATION
120   REM 11000  MULTIPLE REGRESSION
130   REM 12000  ALLOCATE STORAGE AND INITIALIZE PROGRAM
140   REM 13000  RESTART PROGRAM
150   REM 14000  EXIT PROGRAM
160   REM 15000  INSERT NAME IN SYMBOL TABLE
170   REM 16000  ASK USER FOR LIST OF NAMES
180   REM 17000  COLLECT PRODUCT MOMENT MATRIX
190   REM 18000  HANDLE ERRORS
200   REM 19000  HOLD SCREEN SCROLLING
500   REM
510   REM
1000  FIRSTIME%=-1  'FLAG FIRST TIME THROUGH PROGRAM AS TRUE
1010  DISKFILE%=0   'NOT LOADING A DISKFILE
1020  GOSUB 12000
2000  CLS
2005  PRINT "COMMANDS OF THE 8087 STATISTICAL ANALYSIS
       PROGRAM"
2010  PRINT "1  CATALOG DATA IN MEMORY"
2020  PRINT "2  DISPLAY DATA"
2030  PRINT "3  ENTER DATA"
2040  PRINT "4  EDIT DATA"
2050  PRINT "5  SAVE DATA TO DISK"
2060  PRINT "6  RETRIEVE DATA FROM DISK"
2070  PRINT "7  MEANS, STANDARD DEVIATIONS, AND VARIANCES"
2080  PRINT "8  CORRELATIONS BETWEEN VARIABLES"
2090  PRINT "9  MULTIPLE REGRESSION"
2100  PRINT "10 RESTART PROGRAM"
2110  PRINT "11 EXIT PROGRAM TO BASIC"
2120  PRINT
2130  INPUT "ENTER DESIRED SERVICE (1-11) >";ANSWER
2140  ANSW%=ANSWER
2150  IF ANSW%=ANSWER AND ANSW%>=1 AND ANSW%<=11 THEN 2200
2160  PRINT "RESPONSE REQUIRES AN INTEGER BETWEEN 1 AND 11"
2170  GOSUB 19030:GOTO 2000
```

```
2200  ON ANSW% GOSUB 3000,4000,5000,6000,7000,8000,9000,
                     10000,11000,13000,14000
2300  REM RETURN HERE AFTER PERFORMING SERVICE
2400  GOTO 2000
3000  REM DATA CATALOG
3010  CLS
3020  PRINT "NUMBER OF OBSERVATIONS PER VARIABLE: ";NUMOBS
3030  PRINT "NUMBER OF DEFINED VARIABLES: ";NUMVAR
3040  PRINT "NUMBER OF REMAINING VARIABLES: ";MAXVAR-NUMVAR
3050  PRINT "DEFINED VARIABLES ARE:"
3060  FOR I=0 TO NUMVAR-1:PRINT NAMES$(I):NEXT I
3070  GOSUB 19000
3080  RETURN
4000  REM
4010  REM DATA DISPLAY
4020  CLS
4030  PRINT "DATA IN ONE OR MORE VARIABLES MAY BE DISPLAYED"
4040  MAXNAMES=NUMVAR:NEWNAMES=FALSE%:FORCED%=FALSE
4050  GOSUB 16000:IF NAMEERR THEN RETURN
4060  REM VARIABLE NUMBERS ARE IN LISTV 0 THROUGH LISTLEN-1
4070  REM PRINT 4 VARIABLES ON A LINE, 20 OBSERVATIONS PER
       SCREEN
4071  IF LISTLEN=0 THEN RETURN
4080  FIRSTVAR=0:LASTVAR=3:FIRSTOB=0:LASTOB=19
4090  IF LASTVAR>LISTLEN-1 THEN LASTVAR=LISTLEN-1
4100  IF LASTOB>NUMOBS-1 THEN LASTOB=NUMOBS-1
4110  CLS
4120  PRINT "OBSERVATION ";
4130   FOR I=FIRSTVAR TO LASTVAR
4140   PRINT USING "\          \";NAMES$(LISTV(I));
4150   NEXT I
4160  PRINT
4170  FOR I=FIRSTOB TO LASTOB
4180   PRINT I,
4190    FOR J=FIRSTVAR TO LASTVAR
4200    PRINT X(I,LISTV(J)),
4210    NEXT J
4220   PRINT
4230  NEXT I
4240  REM ONE SCREENFUL IS PRINTED
4250  GOSUB 19030
4270  IF LASTVAR=LISTLEN-1 AND LASTOB=NUMOBS-1 THEN RETURN
4280  IF LASTOB=NUMOBS-1 THEN 4300
4290  FIRSTOB=LASTOB+1:LASTOB=FIRSTOB+19:GOTO 4100
4300  REM NEXT SET OF VARIABLES
4310  FIRSTVAR=LASTVAR+1:LASTVAR=FIRSTVAR+3
4320  FIRSTOB=0:LASTOB=19
4330  GOTO 4090
5000  REM
5010  REM ENTER DATA
5020  CLS
5030  PRINT "ENTER NEW VARIABLE NAME"
```

```
5040  MAXNAMES=1:NEWNAMES=TRUE%:FORCE0%=FALSE%
5050  GOSUB 16000:IF NAMEERR THEN RETURN
5055  REM VARIABLE IN LISTV(0)
5060  PRINT "ENTER DATA - (<ENTER> ALONE MEANS 0)"
5070   FOR I=0 TO NUMOBS-1
5080   PRINT NAMES$(LISTV(0));"(";I;") >";
5090   INPUT "",X(I,LISTV(0))
5100   NEXT I
5110  RETURN
6000  REM
6010  REM EDIT DATA
6020  CLS
6030  PRINT "ENTER NAME OF VARIABLE TO BE EDITED"
6040  MAXNAMES=1:NEWNAMES=FALSE%:FORCE0%=FALSE%
6050  GOSUB 16000:IF NAMEERR THEN RETURN
6060  REM VARIABLE IN LISTV(0)
6070  LVAR=LISTV(0)
6080  CLS
6090  PRINT "OBSERVATION NUMBER TO BE CHANGED";
6100  INPUT " <ENTER> ALONE RETURNS TO MAIN MENU >";ANSWER$
6110  IF ANSWER$="" THEN RETURN
6120  ANSWER=VAL(ANSWER$):ANSW%=ANSWER
6130  IF ANSWER=ANSW% AND ANSW%>=0 AND ANSW%<NUMOBS THEN
       6160
6140  PRINT "OBSERVATION MUST BE INTEGER BETWEEN 0 AND
       ";NUMOBS-1
6150  GOTO 6090
6160  PRINT NAMES$(LVAR);"( "ANSWER;") = ";X(ANSW%,LVAR);
6170  INPUT "NEW VALUE?>",ANSWER
6180  PRINT NAMES$(LVAR);"( "ANSWER;") WAS ";X(ANSW%,LVAR);
6190  PRINT " IS NOW ";ANSWER
6200  X(ANSW%,LVAR)=ANSWER
6210  GOTO 6090
7000  REM
7010  REM SAVE DATA ON DISK FILE
7020  REM FIRST LINE HAS MAXVAR,NUMVAR,NUMOBS
7030  REM THEN THE VARIABLE NAMES IN ORDER
7040  REM THEN THE DATA IN EACH VARIABLE IN ORDER
7050  CLS
7060  INPUT "ENTER DISK FILE NAME> ",FILENAME$
7065  NAME FILENAME$ AS FILENAME$
7070  OPEN FILENAME$ FOR OUTPUT AS #1
7080  WRITE#1,MAXVAR,NUMVAR,NUMOBS
7090  FOR I=0 TO NUMVAR-1:WRITE#1,NAMES$(I):NEXT I
7100   FOR I=0 TO NUMVAR-1
7110    FOR J=0 TO NUMOBS-1
7120    WRITE#1,X(J,I)
7130   NEXT J,I
7140  CLOSE #1
7150  PRINT "DATA FILED IN ";FILENAME$
7160  GOSUB 19000:RETURN
8000  REM
```

```
8010  REM RETRIEVE DATA FROM DISK FILE
8020  CLS
8030  INPUT "ENTER DISK FILE NAME> ",FILENAME$
8040  OPEN FILENAME$ FOR INPUT AS #1
8050  INPUT#1,MAXVAR,NUMVAR,NUMOBS
8060  DISKFILE%=TRUE%
8090  GOSUB 12000
8100  FOR I=0 TO NUMVAR-1:INPUT#1,NAMES$(I):NEXT I
8110   FOR I=0 TO NUMVAR-1
8120    FOR J=0 TO NUMOBS-1
8130    INPUT#1,X(J,I)
8140   NEXT J,I
8150  CLOSE #1
8160  PRINT "DATA RETRIEVED FROM ";FILENAME$
8170  GOSUB 19000:RETURN
9000  REM
9010  REM PRINT MEANS, STANDARD DEVIATIONS, VARIANCES
9020  CLS
9040  MAXNAMES=NUMVAR:NEWNAMES=FALSE%:FORCED%=FALSE%
9050  GOSUB 16000:IF NAMEERR THEN RETURN
9060  REM VARIABLE NUMBERS ARE IN LISTV 0 THROUGH LISTLEN-1
9070  PRINT "VARIABLE","   MEAN   ","STANDARD DEVIATION",
       "VARIANCE"
9090  REM COLLECT SUM OF EACH VARIABLE IN SUM#
9100  REM COLLECT SUM-SQUARE OF EACH VARIABLE IN SUMSQ#
9110  FOR I=0 TO LISTLEN-1
9112  LI=LISTV(I)
9120  SUM#=0:CALL SUM%(X(0,LI),NUMOBS,SUM#)
9130  SUMSQ#=0:CALL INPROD%(X(0,LI),X(0,LI),SUMSQ#,NUMOBS)
9140  AVERAGE#=SUM#/NUMOBS
9150  VARIANCE#=(SUMSQ#-SUM#*SUM#/NUMOBS)/(NUMOBS-1)
9160  PRINT NAMES$(LI),AVERAGE#,SQR(VARIANCE#),VARIANCE#
9170  NEXT I
9180  GOSUB 19000
9190  RETURN
10000 REM
10010 REM PRINT CORRELATIONS
10020 CLS
10040 MAXNAMES=NUMVAR:NEWNAMES=FALSE%:FORCED%=TRUE%
10050 GOSUB 16000:IF NAMEERR THEN RETURN
10060 REM VARIABLE NUMBERS ARE IN LISTV 0 THROUGH LISTLEN-1
10080 CORRERR$= "\      \ \      \ WHOOPS CONSTANT
       VARIABLE"
10090 PRINT "VARIABLE-1 VARIABLE-2 CORRELATION COEFFICIENT"
10100 REM HAVE PRODUCT-MOMENT MATRIX COLLECTED IN XPX#
10110 GOSUB 17000
10120  FOR I=1 TO LISTLEN-1
10130  NM1$=NAMES$(LISTV(I))
10140   FOR J=I TO LISTLEN-1
10150   NM2$=NAMES$(LISTV(J))
10160   COV#=NUMOBS*XPX#(I,J)-XPX#(0,I)*XPX#(0,J)
10170   V1#=NUMOBS*XPX#(I,I)-XPX#(0,I)*XPX#(0,I)
```

```
10180     V2#=NUMOBS*XPX#(J,J)-XPX#(0,J)*XPX#(0,J)
10190     IF (V1#*V2#)<>0 THEN 10220
10200     PRINT USING CORRERR$; NM1$,NM2$
10210     GOTO 10230
10220     PRINT NM1$,NM2$,COV#/SQR(V1#*V2#)
10230   NEXT J,I
10240 GOSUB 19000
10250 RETURN
11000 REM
11010 REM MULTIPLE REGRESSION SECTION
11020 REM FIRST GET DEPENDENT VARIABLE
11030 REM THEN INDEPENDENT VARIABLES
11040 REM THEN GO TO WORK
11050 CLS
11060 PRINT "MULTIPLE REGRESSION"
11070 PRINT "ENTER DEPENDENT VARIABLE"
11080 MAXNAMES=1:NEWNAMES=FALSE%:FORCE0%=FALSE%
11090 GOSUB 16000:IF NAMEERR THEN RETURN
11100 REM DEPENDENT VARIABLE IN LISTV(0)
11110 DEPVAR%=LISTV(0)
11120 PRINT "ENTER INDEPENDENT VARIABLES"
11130 MAXNAMES=NUMVAR:NEWNAMES=FALSE%:FORCE0%=FALSE%
11140 GOSUB 16000:IF NAMEERR THEN RETURN
11150 REM VARIABLE NUMBERS ARE IN LISTV 0 THROUGH LISTLEN-1
11160 IF LISTLEN>=NUMOBS THEN 11600
11170 REM ALLOCATE REGRESSION STORAGE
11180 ERASE XPY#,XPXINV#,BETA#,SCRATCH,INDEX
11190 L1=LISTLEN-1
11200 DIM XPY#(L1),XPXINV#(L1,L1),BETA#(L1),SCRATCH(L1),INDEX(L1)
11210 REM NOW DO THE REGRESSION
11220 YSQR#=0:CALL INPROD%(X(0,DEPVAR%),
      X(0,DEPVAR%),YSQR#,NUMOBS)
11226 SUMY#=0:CALL SUM%(X(0,DEPVAR%), NUMOBS,SUMY#)
11230   FOR I=0 TO LISTLEN-1
11240   CALL INPROD%(X(0,DEPVAR%),X(0,LISTV(I)),XPY#(I),NUMOBS)
11250   NEXT I
11260 GOSUB 17000 'COLLECT XPX# - UPPER HALF
11263   FOR I=0 TO LISTLEN-1
11264     FOR J=I+1 TO LISTLEN-1
11265     XPX#(J,I)=XPX#(I,J)
11266   NEXT J,I
11270 IER=0:TYPEX%=8:L2=LISTLEN*LISTLEN
11280 CALL INV%(XPX#(0,0),XPXINV#(0,0),SCRATCH(0),INDEX(0),IER,
                           TYPEX%,LISTLEN)
11290 IF IER<>0 THEN 11700
11292 IFDEN=FALSE%:IFINF=FALSE%:IFNAN=FALSE%:ELEMENT%=0
11294 CALL REALERR%(XPXINV#(0,0),TYPEX%,L2,IFDEN,IFINF,
                           IFNAN, ELEMENT%)
11296 IF (NOT IFDEN) AND (NOT IFINF) AND (NOT IFNAN) THEN 11300
11298 PRINT "WARNING NUMERICAL RESULTS HIGHLY SUSPECT"
11300 REM NOW FORM XPXINV# TIMES XPY#
11310 IONE=1
11320   FOR I=0 TO LISTLEN-1
```

```
11330  CALL GINPROD%(XPXINV#(I,0),XPY#(0),BETA#(I),TYPEX%,
                          TYPEX%,LISTLEN,IONE,LISTLEN)
11340  NEXT I
11350 REM NOW FORM SUM SQUARE RESIDUALS AS Y'Y-BETA'X'Y
11360 TEMP#=0:CALL GINPROD%(BETA#(0),XPY#(0),TEMP#,
                            TYPEX%,TYPEX%,IONE,IONE,
                            LISTLEN)
11370 SSR#=YSQR#-TEMP#
11375 IF YSQR#=0 THEN PRINT "ZERO LHS VARIABLE???":GOTO
       11510
11380 CLS
11390 S2#=SSR#/(NUMOBS-LISTLEN)
11410 PRINT "VARIABLE","COEFFICIENT","S.E."" ,"T-STATISTIC"
11430  FOR I=0 TO LISTLEN-1
11440  SE#=SQR(S2#*XPXINV#(I,I))
11450 IF SE#<>0 THEN PRINT NAMES$(LISTV(I)),CSNG(BETA#(I)),
           CSNG(SE#),CSNG(BETA#(I)/SE#)
          ELSE PRINT NAMES$(LISTV(I)),CSNG(BETA#(I)),"-","-"
11460  NEXT I
11470 PRINT NUMOBS;" OBSERVATIONS ";LISTLEN;" VARIABLES"
11480 PRINT "STANDARD ERROR OF REGRESSION= ";SQR(S2#)
11490 PRINT "SUM SQUARE RESIDUALS= ";SSR#
11500 PRINT "R-SQUARED= ";1-SSR#/(YSQR#-SUMY#*SUMY#/NUMOBS)
11510 GOSUB 19000
11520 RETURN
11600 PRINT "MORE OBSERVATIONS THAN DEPENDENT VARIABLES
       REQUIRED"
11610 GOSUB 19000:RETURN
11700 PRINT "NUMERICALLY SINGULAR MATRIX"
11710 PRINT "EITHER VARIABLE INCLUDED TWICE OR TOO MUCH ";
11720 PRINT "MULTICOLLINEARITY"
11730 GOSUB 19000:RETURN
12000 REM
12010 REM ALLOCATE STORAGE AND INITIALIZE PROGRAM
12020 IF NOT FIRSTIME% THEN 12420
12030 CLEAR ,&H7F00 'SET ASIDE SPACE IF YOU HAVE LESS THAN
       96K
12040 DEFINT I-N
12045 ON ERROR GOTO 18000
12050 TRUE%=-1:FALSE%=0
12060 FIRSTIME%=FALSE%:WASFIRST%=TRUE%
12070 DEF SEG=&HEF0 'SUBROUTINE AREA
12075 VECTOR%=0:MATRIX%=&H420:MATADV%=&H790
12080 BLOAD "VECTOR.SAV",VECTOR%:BLOAD "MATRIX.SAV",
       MATRIX%
12085 BLOAD "MATADV.SAV",MATADV%
12090 INPROD%=MATRIX%+&H121:GINPROD%=MATRIX%+&H1A6
12091 INV%=MATADV%+&H4F3:SUM%=VECTOR%+0:
       REALERR%=VECTOR%+&H2DC
12095 CLS
12100 PRINT "DO YOU WISH TO LOAD DATA FROM A DISK FILE (Y/
       N)>";
12110 INPUT "",ANSWER$
```

```
12120 IF ANSWER$="Y" OR ANSWER$="y" THEN GOSUB 8000:GOTO
      12410
12130 INPUT "NUMBER OF OBSERVATIONS>"ANSWER$
12140 IF ANSWER$="" THEN RETURN
12150 ANSWER=VAL(ANSWER$)
12160 ANSW%=ANSWER
12170 IF (ANSW%=ANSWER) AND (ANSW%<>0) THEN 12210
12180 PRINT "POSITIVE INTEGER REQUIRED";
12190 PRINT "<ENTER> RETURNS TO COMMAND MENU"
12200 GOTO 12100
12210 NUMOBS=ANSW%
12220 REM FOR K VARIABLES NEED ABOUT
12230 REM     4NK FOR X
12240 REM     16K*K FOR XPX,XPXINV
12250 REM   AT LEAST 16K FOR NAMES
12260 REM   16K FOR XPY AND BETA
12270 REM BETTER LEAVE A LITTLE EXTRA FOR SAFETY, SAY
12280 REM USE 2000+K(4N+16K+32)
12285 ERASE X,NAMES$
12290 SPACE=FRE(0)-2000
12300 K=INT(SPACE/NUMOBS/4):K1=SQR(SPACE/16)
12305 IF K>K1 THEN K=K1 'FIRST ESTIMATE FOR K
12310 IF (4*K*(NUMOBS+4*K+8))>SPACE THEN K=K-1:GOTO 12310
12320 MAXVAR=K
12330 IF MAXVAR>1 THEN 12360
12340 PRINT "TOO MANY OBSERVATIONS"
12350 GO TO 12130
12360 REM NOTE THAT BASIC INITIALIZES EVERYTHING TO ZERO
12370 K1=K-1:N1=NUMOBS-1:NBYK=NUMOBS*MAXVAR
12380 ERASE NAMES$,X
12385 DIM NAMES$(K1),X(N1,K1)
12390 NAMES$(0)="(CONST)"
12395 FOR I=0 TO N1:X(I,0)=1.0:NEXT I
12400 NUMVAR=1
12410 IF NOT WASFIRST% THEN RETURN
12415 GOTO 2000 'FAKE RETURN, GOSUB WIPED OUT BY CLEAR
12420 REM NOT THE FIRST TIME INITIALIZED
12430 ERASE X,NAMES$
12440 IF NOT DISKFILE% THEN 12095
12450 K1=MAXVAR-1:N1=NUMOBS-1:NBYK=NUMOBS*MAXVAR
12460 ERASE NAMES$,X
12465 DIM NAMES$(K1),X(N1,K1)
12470 RETURN
13000 REM
13010 REM RESTART PROGRAM
13020 FIRSTIME%=FALSE%:DISKFILE%=FALSE%
13030 GOSUB 12000
13040 RETURN
14000 REM
14010 REM EXIT PROGRAM
14020 INPUT "ARE YOU SURE YOU WANT TO EXIT (Y/N)>";ANSWER$
14030 IF ANSWER$="y" OR ANSWER$="Y" THEN END
```

```
14040 RETURN
15000 REM
15010 REM INSERT NAME IN SYMBOL TABLE
15020 REM NAME TO BE INSERTED IS IN NAMEIS$
15030 REM IF SYMBOL TABLE IS FULL, PRINT MESSAGE AND SET
       NAMEERR
15040 REM IF NOT A NEW NAME, PRINT MESSAGE AND SET NAMEERR
15050 REM OTHERWISE PUT NAMEIS$ IN NEXT LOCATION IN NAMES$
15060 REM REPORT IT'S POSITION IN NAMELOC
15070 IF NUMVAR<MAXVAR THEN 15100
15080 PRINT "SYMBOL TABLE FULL!!!!NO NEW VARIABLES"
15090 NAMEERR=TRUE%:RETURN
15100 FOUNDIT%=FALSE%
15110  FOR I=0 TO NUMVAR-1
15120  IF NAMEIS$=NAMES$(I) THEN FOUNDIT%=TRUE%
15130  NEXT I
15140 IF NOT FOUNDIT% THEN 15170
15150 PRINT CHR$(34);NAMEIS$;CHR$(34);
                    " ALREADY DEFINED - NOT A NEW NAME"
15155 GOSUB 19000
15160 NAMEERR=TRUE%:RETURN
15170 NAMELOC=NUMVAR
15180 NUMVAR=NUMVAR+1
15190 NAMES$(NAMELOC)=NAMEIS$
15200 RETURN
16000 REM
16010 REM COLLECT A LIST OF NAMES AND RETURN LOCATIONS IN
       LISTV
16020 REM A SINGLE NAME IS A SPECIAL CASE
16030 NAMEERR=FALSE%
16040 IF MAXNAMES>1 THEN 16500
16050 INPUT "VARIABLE NAME IS?>",NAMEIS$
16060 IF NAMEIS$="" THEN NAMEERR=TRUE%:RETURN
16070 IF NOT NEWNAMES THEN 16100
16080 GOSUB 15000
16090 IF NAMEERR THEN RETURN ELSE 16180
16100 NAMELOC=-1
16110  FOR I=0 TO NUMVAR-1
16120  IF NAMES$(I)=NAMEIS$ THEN NAMELOC=I
16130  NEXT I
16140 IF NAMELOC<>-1 THEN 16180
16150 PRINT CHR$(34);NAMEIS$;CHR$(34);" NOT DEFINED"
16160 PRINT "RE-ENTER NAME OR <ENTER> TO RETURN TO COMMAND
       MENU"
16170 GOTO 16050
16180 REM PUT NAMELOC IN LISTV
16190 LISTLEN=1
16200 LISTV(0)=NAMELOC
16210 RETURN
16500 REM COME HERE TO COLLECT A SERIES OF VARIABLES
16501 REM IF FORCE0% THEN INCLUDE CONSTANT AUTOMATICALLY
16502 IF NOT FORCE0% THEN LISTLEN=0 ELSE LISTV(0)=0:LISTLEN=1
```

```
16510 INPUT "ENTER VARIABLE NAME(S) SEPARATED BY A SPACE>",
       ANSWER$
16520 IF ANSWER$="" THEN NAMEERR=TRUE%:RETURN
16530 FOR I=LISTLEN TO MAXNAMES-1:LISTV$(I)="":NEXT I
16540 LOOKFROM=1
16550 REM RETRIEVE A VARIABLE NAME
16560 SPACELOC%=INSTR(LOOKFROM,ANSWER$," ")
16570 IF SPACELOC%=0 THEN SPACELOC%=LEN(ANSWER$)+1
16580 NAMEIS$=MID$(ANSWER$,LOOKFROM,SPACELOC%-LOOKFROM)
16590 NAMELOC=-1
16600 IF NAMEIS$="" THEN 16730
16610 IF NOT NEWNAMES THEN 16630
16620 GOSUB 15000: IF NAMEERR THEN RETURN
16630  FOR I=0 TO NUMVAR-1
16640 IF NAMES$(I)=NAMEIS$ THEN NAMELOC=I
16650  NEXT I
16660 IF NAMELOC<>-1 THEN 16700
16670 PRINT CHR$(34);NAMEIS$;CHR$(34);" NOT DEFINED"
16680 PRINT "RE-ENTER LIST OR <ENTER> TO RETURN TO COMMAND
       MENU"
16690 GOTO 16500
16700 REM PUT NAMELOC IN LISTV
16710 LISTV(LISTLEN)=NAMELOC
16720 LISTLEN=LISTLEN+1
16730 LOOKFROM=SPACELOC%+1
16740 IF LOOKFROM>LEN(ANSWER$) THEN RETURN
16750 IF LISTLEN<MAXNAMES THEN 16560
16760 PRINT "TOO MANY NAMES"
16770 GO TO 16680
17000 REM
17010 REM COLLECT PRODUCT MOMENT MATRIX IN UPPER HALF OF
       XPX#
17020 ERASE XPX#:L1=LISTLEN-1:DIM XPX#(L1,L1)
17030  FOR I=0 TO LISTLEN-1
17040   FOR J=I TO LISTLEN-1
17050   CALL INPROD%(X(0,LISTV(I)),X(0,LISTV(J)),
                                    XPX#(I,J),NUMOBS)
17060  NEXT J,I
17070 RETURN
18000 REM
18010 REM HANDLE A FEW ERRORS HERE
18020 REM DID WE RUN OUT OF SPACE?
18030 IF ERR<>7 AND ERR<>14 THEN 18070
18040 PRINT "PROGRAM RAN OUT OF MEMORY IN LINE ";ERL
18050 PRINT "SORRY. . ."
18060 STOP
18070 REM DID WE TRY TO READ FROM A NON-EXISTENT FILE?
18080 IF ERR<>53 OR ERL<>8040 THEN 18120
18090 IF FILENAME$="" THEN RESUME 8170 'BACK TO MENU
18100 PRINT "CAN'T FIND ";FILENAME$
18110 RESUME 8030 'TRY AGAIN
18120 REM IS THIS A NEW OUTPUT FILE?
```

```
18130 IF ERR<>53 OR ERL<>7065 THEN 18150
18140 RESUME NEXT
18150 IF ERR<>58 OR ERL<>7065 THEN 18200
18160 PRINT "FILE ALREADY EXISTS, ARE YOU SURE? (Y/N)";
18170 INPUT "",ANSWER$
18180 IF ANSWER$="y" OR ANSWER$="Y" THEN RESUME NEXT
18190 RESUME 7060
18200 IF ERR<>5 OR (ERL<>12285 AND ERL<>12430 AND
       ERL<>11180 AND ERL<>17020 AND ERL<>12460 AND
       ERL<>12380) THEN 18220
18210 RESUME NEXT 'OK, WE JUST ERASED SOMETHING THAT WASNT
       THERE
18220 ON ERROR GOTO 0
18230 END
19000 REM HOLD SCREEN
19010 PRINT "HIT ANY KEY TO RETURN TO COMMAND MENU>";
19020 IF INKEY$="" THEN 19020 ELSE RETURN
19030 PRINT "HIT ANY KEY TO RETURN TO CONTINUE>";
19040 IF INKEY$="" THEN 19040 ELSE RETURN
```

15

Commercial Data Processing

The name "numeric data processor" naturally leads people to think of the 8087 as a tool for "scientific" rather than "business" applications. While the 8087's forte is certainly working with numbers, it does have important applications in business and commercial EDP (Electronic Data Processing).

The Cookbook—Chapter 15

Program:	**ADDSTR**
Purpose:	Add array of integer-valued strings.
Call:	CALL ADDSTR(A$(0),ISPACE(0),SUM,IER,N)
Input:	A$—N element string array. ISPACE—5 element integer array; scratch space. N—integer number of elements of A$.
Output:	SUM—single precision scalar; sum of VAL(A$(I)) IER—integer; −1 if error, 0 otherwise.
Language:	8087/8088 assembly language.

The 8087 is valuable in any application involving numbers. In the last chapter, we built a small statistical package out of the matrix routines of Chapters 10 and 11. Business people normally don't care about technical aspects of matrix inversion! However, mathematical tools such as regression analysis (which use matrix operations internally) are a regular part of the forecasting and planning function in every large company. The 8087 is an important tool for anyone building software for business people to use.

Typical commercial EDP applications (payroll programs and the like) do relatively little numerical computation. Such programs spend more time converting data from an external "ASCII" format to an internal binary format than they spend manipulating the numbers after the conversion. For this reason, commercial programs often avoid conversion costs by operating directly on data stored in decimal, rather than binary, representation. The 8087 supports such operations through its packed decimal instructions.

Almost all commercial data processing applications are written in high-level languages. Languages such as COBOL and PL/I allow you to operate on decimal data. The BASIC language offered on personal computers rarely provides a decimal data type. In order to show off the 8087's prowess at decimal operations, we've written a small assembly language routine that replaces part of a BASIC program.

Consider the following BASIC program which creates a string array filled with integers and then totals up the values in the strings.

```
10   DEFINT I-N
20   DIM A$(4999)
30   N=4999
40     REM FILL UP A$ WITH INTEGERS
50     FOR I=0 TO N:A$(I)=STR$(I):NEXT I
60   REM TIME THIS PART
70   T1$=TIME$
80   SUM=0
90     FOR I=0 TO N
100    SUM=SUM+VAL(A$(I))
110    NEXT I
120  T2$=TIME$
130  PRINT N+1,SUM,T1$,T2$
140  END
```

Most of the work in lines 90, 100, and 110 is in the function "VAL" which converts strings to single precision. (If you change the array of strings, A$, to a single precision array, A, you'll see the program's speed nearly triple.) Assembly language subroutine ADDSTR, below, adds up a vector of strings (representing integers) and returns a single precision sum. We can replace lines 90-100 with ADDSTR, as in the following program.

```
10   DEFINT I-N
20   DIM A$(4999),ISPACE(4)
30   N=4999
40     REM FILL UP A$ WITH INTEGERS
50     FOR I=0 TO N:A$(I)=STR$(I):NEXT I
60   REM TIME THIS PART
70   T1$=TIME$
80   SUM=0
90   IER=0
100    CALL ADDSTR(A$(0),ISPACE(0),SUM,IER,N)
110  T2$=TIME$
120  PRINT N+1,SUM,T1$,T2$
130  END
```

ADDSTR processes each string in three steps. First, it finds the string by untangling the string descriptor provided by BASIC. Second, ADDSTR converts the string's ASCII representation to packed decimal while doing some limited error checking. Third, ADDSTR uses the 8087 packed decimal instructions to add up the converted values.

```
;SUBROUTINE ADDSTR(A$(0),ISPACE(0),SUM,IER,N)
;      ASSUMPTIONS:  A$ - N LONG ARRAY OF STRINGS
;                    ISPACE - 10 FREE BYTES
;                    SUM - SINGLE PRECISION ANSWER
;                    IER - INTEGER, 0 ON RETURN FOR NO ERROR
;                                  -1 IF ERROR
;                    N - INTEGER NUMBER OF ELEMENTS OF A$
;
;                    ELEMENTS OF A$ ARE ASSUMED TO BE
                      INTEGERS NO MORE TAHN 18 BYTES LONG.

;
; ADDSTR ADDS UP VALUES IN A$
;
          PUBLIC     ADDSTR
CSEG      SEGMENT    'CODE'
          ASSUME     CS:CSEG
ADDSTR    PROC       FAR
          PUSH       BP
          MOV        BP,SP
          MOV        BX,[BP]+8          ;BX=ADDR(IER)
          MOV        WORD PTR [BX],0    ;ASSUME NO ERROR
          MOV        BX,[BP]+6          ;KEEP COUNT OF ARRAY
          MOV        CX,[BX]            ;IN CX AS USUAL
          FLDZ                          ;CLEAR OUT STACK TOP
          CMP        CX,0
          JG         NOTDONE            ;N=0?
          JMP        DONE

NOTDONE:
          MOV        BX,[BP]+14         ;BX=ADDR(A$(0))
;NOTICE BX KEEPS TRACK OF THE DESCRIPTORS OF THE STRINGS,
;          NOT THE STRINGS THEMSELVES
GET_DESCRIPTOR:
;UNFORTUNATELY, THE BASIC COMPILER AND THE BASIC INTERPRETER
;STORE STRINGS DIFFERENTLY
;THE COMPILER DESCRIPTOR HAS THE STRING LENGTH IN ONE WORD
;    FOLLOWED BY THE STRING ADDRESS IN A SECOND WORD
;THE INTERPRETER DESCRIPTOR HAS THE STRING LENGTH IN ONE
 BYTE
;    FOLLOWED BY THE STRING ADDRESS IN A WORD
;ASSUME THIS PROGRAM IS RUN WITH COMPILED BASIC
          MOV      AX,WORD PTR [BX]   ;ASSUME COMPILER
;         MOV      AH,0
;         MOV      AL,BYTE PTR [BX]   ;IF INTERPRETER
```

```
; AX IS NUMBER OF BYTES IN STRING
;CLEAR OUT WORKSPACE
          MOV     SI,[BP]+12            ;SI=ADDR(ISPACE)
          MOV     WORD PTR [SI],0
          MOV     WORD PTR [SI]+2,0
          MOV     WORD PTR [SI]+4,0
          MOV     WORD PTR [SI]+6,0
          MOV     WORD PTR [SI]+8,0
;
          MOV     DI,WORD PTR [BX]+2 ;DI=ADDR(STRING(I))
;         MOV     DI,WORD PTR [BX]+1 ; IF INTERPRETER
;
;CHECK FIRST CHARACTER FOR MINUS SIGN
          MOV     DL,BYTE PTR [DI]   ;DL IS FIRST CHARACTER
          CMP     DL,45              ;CHECK FOR MINUS
          JNE     NUMBER             ;SIGN
;IT'S NEGATIVE
          OR      BYTE PTR [SI],80H  ;SET SIGN BIT
          DEC     AX                 ;USED UP ONE BYTE
; CHECK STRING LENGTH
          CMP     AX,0               ;NULL STRING NOT
          JLE     ERROR              ;ALLOWED
          CMP     AX,18
          JG      ERROR
NUMBER:
;NOW START AT RIGHT END OF STRING AND WORK BACKWARD
          ADD     DI,AX              ;DI POINTS TO
          DEC     DI                 ;LAST BYTE OF STRING
          CMP     DL,45              ;BUT TEST IF WE HAD
          JNE     L1                 ;ALREADY SUBTRACTED
          INC     DI
L1:
;WE NEED TO REMEMBER WHETHER TO PLACE DIGIT IN
;LEFT OR RIGHT NIBBLE (HALF OF BYTE)
;KEEP FLAG IN DH, 0 MEANS RIGHT 1 MEANS LEFT
          MOV  DH,0
;NOW TRANSLATE EACH CHARACTER
NEXTNUM:
          MOV     DL,BYTE PTR [DI]   ;GET CHARACTER
          CMP     DL,32              ;IS IT A SPACE?
          JNE     NOT_A_SPACE
          MOV     DL,48              ;IF SO, MAKE IT ZERO
NOT_A_SPACE:
          CMP     DL,48              ;<0?
          JL      ERROR
          CMP     DL,57              ;>9?
          JG      ERROR
          SUB     DL,48              ;MAKE 0-9
          CMP     DH,0               ;RIGHT NIBBLE?
          JNE     LEFT
```

```
STOWIT:     OR      BYTE PTR[SI],DL     ;STORE DECIMAL
            XOR     DH,1                ;SWITCH NIBBLE
            JMP     NEXTCH
LEFT:       SHL     DL,1                ;GET IT TO LEFT
            SHL     DL,1                ;NIBBLE
            SHL     DL,1
            SHL     DL,1
            OR      BYTE PTR[SI],DL     ;STORE DECIMAL
            XOR     DH,1                ;SWITCH NIBBLE
            INC     SI                  ;NEXT BYTE
NEXTCH:
            DEC     DI                  ;NEXT CHARACTER
            DEC     AX                  ;DONE YET
            JG      NEXTNUM             ;MORE?
;NOW ISPACE HAS A NICE PACKED DECIMAL NUMBER IN IT
            MOV     SI,[BP]+12          ;POINT TO ISPACE
                                        ;AGAIN
            FBLD    [SI]                ;PUSH IT ONTO STACK
            FADDP   ST(1),ST            ;ADD INTO TOTAL
            ADD     BX,4                ;NEXT ARRAY ELEMENT
;           ADD     BX,3                ;IF INTERPRETER
            LOOP GOTO_GET_DESCRIPTOR
DONE:       MOV     SI,[BP]+10          ;SI=ADDR(SUM)
            FSTP    DWORD PTR [SI]      ;STORE AWAY SUM
            POP     BP
            FWAIT
            RET     10
GOTO_GET_DESCRIPTOR:  JMP GET_DESCRIPTOR
ERROR:      MOV     BX,[BP]+8           ;BX=ADDR(IER)
            MOV     WORD PTR [BX],-1    ;ERROR INDICATOR
            JMP     DONE
ADDSTR      ENDP
CSEG        ENDS
            END
```

Notice how we provide the scratch space that ADDSTR needs to store the packed decimal value. We could have set up a 10-byte area in an extra segment, as we have in other programs. Instead, we get BASIC to pass us a 10-byte array called ISPACE. (This was mostly just as an excuse to show an alternative technique for finding storage for an assembly language program.)

Table 15-1 provides some timing figures with and without ADDSTR.

Routine ADDSTR took over 100 lines of assembly language code to replace three lines of BASIC. In return for the extra work, we got a program that runs 50 times faster than interpreted basic and 12 times faster than compiled BASIC. In this example, the speed improvement for a commercial application is the same as we found for scientific applications earlier in the book.

While the 8087 may never become quite so indispensable in commercial work as it is in scientific programming, we can still expect its use to

Table 15-1. Speed benchmarks for packed decimal instructions (time in seconds).

Program	*Add 5,000 integer strings*
BASIC interpreter	64
BASIC compiler	15
8087 routine	1.25

become widespread, especially as 8087-compatible translators for commerical programming languages appear.

Postscript

I told you a little fib in the first chapter. I said you would use the 8087 to "turn minutes into seconds." The 8087 will indeed turn minutes into seconds, but I think you will find that the 8087's real value lies in its ability to extend your reach. Now that your machine is many times faster, you will find you will want to solve problems that are many times larger—and probably problems with more important answers. Solutions that could formerly be found only on a large computer—or that weren't available to you at all—are now within your grasp.

Appendix 1

Table A1-1. Instruction Set Reference Data. Courtesy of Intel Corporation.

FABS

FABS (no operands)
Absolute value

Exceptions: I

Operands	Execution Clocks		Transfers		Coding Example
	Typical	Range	8086	8088	
(no operands)	14	10-17	0	0	FABS

FADD

FADD //source/destination,source
Add real

Exceptions: I, D, O, U, P

Operands	Execution Clocks		Transfers		Coding Example
	Typical	Range	8086	8088	
//ST,ST(i)/ST(i),ST	85	70-100	0	0	FADD ST,ST(4)
short-real	105+EA	90-120+EA	2/4	4	FADD AIR_TEMP [SI]
long-real	110+EA	95-125+EA	4/6	8	FADD [BX].MEAN

FADDP

FADDP destination,source
Add real and pop

Exceptions: I, D, O, U, P

Operands	Execution Clocks		Transfers		Coding Example
	Typical	Range	8086	8088	
ST(i),ST	90	75-105	0	0	FADDP ST(2),ST

FBLD

FBLD source
Packed decimal (BCD) load

Exceptions: I

Operands	Execution Clocks		Transfers		Coding Example
	Typical	Range	8086	8088	
packed-decimal	300+EA	290-310+EA	5/7	10	FBLD YTD_SALES

FBSTP

FBSTP destination
Packed decimal (BCD) store and pop

Exceptions: I

Operands	Execution Clocks		Transfers		Coding Example
	Typical	Range	8086	8088	
packed-decimal	530+EA	520-540+EA	6/8	12	FBSTP [BX].FORECAST

FCHS

FCHS (no operands)
Change sign

Exceptions: I

Operands	Execution Clocks		Transfers		Coding Example
	Typical	Range	8086	8088	
(no operands)	15	10-17	0	0	FCHS

Table A1-1. Instruction set reference data (continued). Courtesy of Intel Corporation.

FCLEX/FNCLEX

FCLEX (no operands)
Clear exceptions

Exceptions: None

Operands	Execution Clocks		Transfers		Coding Example
	Typical	Range	8086	8088	
(no operands)	5	2-8	0	0	FNCLEX

FCOM

FCOM //source
Compare real

Exceptions: I, D

Operands	Execution Clocks		Transfers		Coding Example
	Typical	Range	8086	8088	
//ST(i)	45	40-50	0	0	FCOM ST(1)
short-real	65+EA	60-70+EA	2/4	4	FCOM [BP].UPPER_LIMIT
long-real	70+EA	65-75+EA	4/6	8	FCOM WAVELENGTH

FCOMP

FCOMP //source
Compare real and pop

Exceptions: I, D

Operands	Execution Clocks		Transfers		Coding Example
	Typical	Range	8086	8088	
//ST(i)	47	42-52	0	0	FCOMP ST(2)
short-real	68+EA	63-73+EA	2/4	4	FCOMP [BP+2].N_READINGS
long-real	72+EA	67-77+EA	4/6	8	FCOMP DENSITY

FCOMPP

FCOMPP (no operands)
Compare real and pop twice

Exceptions: I, D

Operands	Execution Clocks		Transfers		Coding Example
	Typical	Range	8086	8088	
(no operands)	50	45-55	0	0	FCOMPP

FDECSTP

FDECSTP (no operands)
Decrement stack pointer

Exceptions: None

Operands	Execution Clocks		Transfers		Coding Example
	Typical	Range	8086	8088	
(no operands)	9	6-12	0	0	FDECSTP

FDISI/FNDISI

FDISI (no operands)
Disable interrupts

Exceptions: None

Operands	Execution Clocks		Transfers		Coding Example
	Typical	Range	8086	8088	
(no operands)	5	2-8	0	0	FDISI

Table A1-1. Instruction set reference data (continued). Courtesy of Intel Corporation.

FDIV

FDIV //source/destination,source
Divide real

Exceptions: I, D, Z, O, U, P

Operands	Execution Clocks		Transfers		Coding Example
	Typical	Range	8086	8088	
//ST(i),ST	198	193-203	0	0	FDIV
short-real	220+EA	215-225+EA	2/4	4	FDIV DISTANCE
long-real	225+EA	220-230+EA	4/6	8	FDIV ARC [DI]

FDIVP

FDIVP destination,source
Divide real and pop

Exceptions: I, D, Z, O, U, P

Operands	Execution Clocks		Transfers		Coding Example
	Typical	Range	8086	8088	
ST(i),ST	202	197-207	0	0	FDIVP ST(4),ST

FDIVR

FDIVR //source/destination,source
Divide real reversed

Exceptions: I, D, Z, O, U, P

Operands	Execution Clocks		Transfers		Coding Example
	Typical	Range	8086	8088	
//ST,ST(i)/ST(i),ST	199	194-204	0	0	FDIVR ST(2),ST
short-real	221+EA	216-226+EA	2/4	6	FDIVR [BX].PULSE_RATE
long-real	226+EA	221-231+EA	4/6	8	FDIVR RECORDER.FREQUENCY

FDIVRP

FDIVRP destination,source
Divide real reversed and pop

Exceptions: I, D, Z, O, U, P

Operands	Execution Clocks		Transfers		Coding Example
	Typical	Range	8086	8088	
ST(i),ST	203	198-208	0	0	FDIVRP ST(1),ST

FENI/FNENI

FENI (no operands)
Enable interrupts

Exceptions: None

Operands	Execution Clocks		Transfers		Coding Example
	Typical	Range	8086	8088	
(no operands)	5	2-8	0	0	FNENI

FFREE

FFREE destination
Free register

Exceptions: None

Operands	Execution Clocks		Transfers		Coding Example
	Typical	Range	8086	8088	
ST(i)	11	9-16	0	0	FFREE ST(1)

Table A1-1. Instruction set reference data (continued). Courtesy of Intel Corporation.

FIADD

FIADD source
Integer add

Exceptions: I, D, O, P

Operands	Execution Clocks		Transfers		Coding Example
	Typical	Range	8086	8088	
word-integer	120+EA	102-137+EA	1/2	2	FIADD DISTANCE_TRAVELLED
short-integer	125+EA	108-143+EA	2/4	4	FIADD PULSE_COUNT [SI]

FICOM

FICOM source
Integer compare

Exceptions: I, D

Operands	Execution Clocks		Transfers		Coding Example
	Typical	Range	8086	8088	
word-integer	80+EA	72-86+EA	1/2	2	FICOM TOOL.N_PASSES
short-integer	85+EA	78-91+EA	2/4	4	FICOM [BP+4].PARM_COUNT

FICOMP

FICOMP source
Integer compare and pop

Exceptions: I, D

Operands	Execution Clocks		Transfers		Coding Example
	Typical	Range	8086	8088	
word-integer	82+EA	74-88+EA	1/2	2	FICOMP [BP].LIMIT [SI]
short-integer	87+EA	80-93+EA	2/4	4	FICOMP N SAMPLES

FIDIV

FIDIV source
Integer divide

Exceptions: I, D, Z, O, U, P

Operands	Execution Clocks		Transfers		Coding Example
	Typical	Range	8086	8088	
word-integer	230+EA	224-238+EA	1/2	2	FIDIV SURVEY.OBSERVATIONS
short-integer	236+EA	230-243+EA	2/4	4	FIDIV RELATIVE_ANGLE [DI]

FIDIVR

FIDIVR source
Integer divide reversed

Exceptions: I, D, Z, O, U, P

Operands	Execution Clocks		Transfers		Coding Example
	Typical	Range	8086	8088	
word-integer	230+EA	225-239+EA	1/2	2	FIDIVR [BP].X_COORD
short-integer	237+EA	231-245+EA	2/4	4	FIDIVR FREQUENCY

FILD

FILD source
Integer load

Exception: I

Operands	Execution Clocks		Transfers		Coding Example
	Typical	Range	8086	8088	
word-integer	50+EA	46-54+EA	1/2	2	FILD [BX].SEQUENCE
short-integer	56+EA	52-60+EA	2/4	4	FILD STANDOFF [DI]
long-integer	64+EA	60-68+EA	4/6	8	FILD RESPONSE.COUNT

Table A1-1. Instruction set reference data (continued). Courtesy of Intel Corporation.

FIMUL

FIMUL source
Integer multiply

Exceptions: I, D, O, P

Operands	Execution Clocks		Transfers		Coding Example
	Typical	Range	8086	8088	
word-integer	130+EA	124-138+EA	1/2	2	FIMUL BEARING
short-integer	136+EA	130-144+EA	2/4	4	FIMUL POSITION.Z_AXIS

FINCSTP

FINCSTP (no operands)
Increment stack pointer

Exceptions: None

Operands	Execution Clocks		Transfers		Coding Example
	Typical	Range	8086	8088	
(no operands)	9	6-12	0	0	FINCSTP

FINIT/FNINIT

FINIT (no operands)
Initialize processor

Exceptions: None

Operands	Execution Clocks		Transfers		Coding Example
	Typical	Range	8086	8088	
(no operands)	5	2-8	0	0	FINIT

FIST

FIST destination
Integer store

Exceptions: I, P

Operands	Execution Clocks		Transfers		Coding Example
	Typical	Range	8086	8088	
word-integer	86+EA	80-90+EA	2/4	4	FIST OBS.COUNT [SI]
short-integer	88+EA	82-92+EA	3/5	6	FIST [BP].FACTORED_PULSES

FISTP

FISTP destination
Integer store and pop

Exceptions: I, P

Operands	Execution Clocks		Transfers		Coding Example
	Typical	Range	8086	8088	
word-integer	88+EA	82-92+EA	2/4	4	FISTP [BX].ALPHA_COUNT [SI]
short-integer	90+EA	84-94+EA	3/5	6	FISTP CORRECTED_TIME
long-integer	100+EA	94-105+EA	5/7	10	FISTP PANEL.N_READINGS

FISUB

FISUB source
Integer subtract

Exceptions: I, D, O, P

Operands	Execution Clocks		Transfers		Coding Example
	Typical	Range	8086	8088	
word-integer	120+EA	102-137+EA	1/2	2	FISUB BASE_FREQUENCY
short-integer	125+EA	108-143+EA	2/4	4	FISUB TRAIN_SIZE [DI]

Table A1-1. Instruction set reference data (continued). Courtesy of Intel Corporation.

FISUBR

FISUBR source
Integer subtract reversed

Exceptions: I, D, O, P

Operands	Execution Clocks		Transfers		Coding Example
	Typical	Range	8086	8088	
word-integer	120+EA	103-139+EA	1/2	2	FISUBR FLOOR [BX] [SI]
short-integer	125+EA	109-144+EA	2/4	4	FISUBR BALANCE

FLD

FLD source
Load real

Exceptions: I, D

Operands	Execution Clocks		Transfers		Coding Example
	Typical	Range	8086	8088	
ST(i)	20	17-22	0	0	FLD ST(0)
short-real	43+EA	38-56+EA	2/4	4	FLD READING [SI].PRESSURE
long-real	46+EA	40-60+EA	4/6	8	FLD [BP].TEMPERATURE
temp-real	57+EA	53-65+EA	5/7	10	FLD SAVEREADING

FLDCW

FLDCW source
Load control word

Exceptions: None

Operands	Execution Clocks		Transfers		Coding Example
	Typical	Range	8086	8088	
2-bytes	10+EA	7-14+EA	1/2	2	FLDCW CONTROL_WORD

FLDENV

FLDENV source
Load environment

Exceptions: None

Operands	Execution Clocks		Transfers		Coding Example
	Typical	Range	8086	8088	
14-bytes	40+EA	35-45+EA	7/9	14	FLDENV [BP+6]

FLDLG2

FLDLG2 (no operands)
Load $\log_{10} 2$

Exceptions: I

Operands	Execution Clocks		Transfers		Coding Example
	Typical	Range	8086	8088	
(no operands)	21	18-24	0	0	FLDLG2

FLDLN2

FLDLN2 (no operands)
Load $\log_e 2$

Exceptions: I

Operands	Execution Clocks		Transfers		Coding Example
	Typical	Range	8086	8088	
(no operands)	20	17-23	0	0	FLDLN2

Table A1-1. Instruction set reference data (continued). Courtesy of Intel Corporation.

FLDL2E

FLDL2E (no operands)
Load $\log_2 e$

Exceptions: I

Operands	Execution Clocks		Transfers		Coding Example
	Typical	Range	8086	8088	
(no operands)	18	15-21	0	0	FLDL2E

FLDL2T

FLDL2T (no operands)
Load $\log_2 10$

Exceptions: I

Operands	Execution Clocks		Transfers		Coding Example
	Typical	Range	8086	8088	
(no operands)	19	16-22	0	0	FLDL2T

FLDPI

FLDPI (no operands)
Load π

Exceptions: I

Operands	Execution Clocks		Transfers		Coding Example
	Typical	Range	8086	8088	
(no operands)	19	16-22	0	0	FLDPI

FLDZ

FLDZ (no operands)
Load +0.0

Exceptions: I

Operands	Execution Clocks		Transfers		Coding Example
	Typical	Range	8086	8088	
(no operands)	14	11-17	0	0	FLDZ

FLD1

FLD1 (no operands)
Load +1.0

Exceptions: I

Operands	Execution Clocks		Transfers		Coding Example
	Typical	Range	8086	8088	
(no operands)	18	15-21	0	0	FLD1

FMUL

FMUL //source/destination,source
Multiply real

Exceptions: I, D, O, U, P

Operands	Execution Clocks		Transfers		Coding Example
	Typical	Range	8086	8088	
//ST(i),ST/ST,ST(i)'	97	90-105	0	0	FMUL ST,ST(3)
//ST(i),ST/ST,ST(i)	138	130-145	0	0	FMUL ST,ST(3)
short-real	118+EA	110-125+EA	2/4	4	FMUL SPEED_FACTOR
long-real'	120+EA	112-126+EA	4/6	8	FMUL [BP].HEIGHT
long-real	161+EA	154-168+EA	4/6	8	FMUL [BP].HEIGHT

occurs when one or both operands is "short"—it has 40 trailing zeros in its fraction (e.g., it was loaded from a short-real memory operand).

Table A1-1. Instruction set reference data (continued). Courtesy of Intel Corporation.

FMULP

FMULP destination,source
Multiply real and pop

Exceptions: I, D, O, U, P

Operands	Execution Clocks		Transfers		Coding Example
	Typical	Range	8086	8088	
ST(i),ST'	100	94-108	0	0	FMULP ST(1),ST
ST(i),ST	142	134-148	0	0	FMULP ST(1),ST

' occurs when one or both operands is "short"—it has 40 trailing zeros in its fraction (e.g., it was loaded from a short-real memory operand).

FNOP

FNOP (no operands)
No operation

Exceptions: None

Operands	Execution Clocks		Transfers		Coding Example
	Typical	Range	8086	8088	
(no operands)	13	10-16	0	0	FNOP

FPATAN

FPATAN (no operands)
Partial arctangent

Exceptions: U, P
(operands not checked)

Operands	Execution Clocks		Transfers		Coding Example
	Typical	Range	8086	8088	
(no operands)	650	250-800	0	0	FPATAN

FPREM

FPREM (no operands)
Partial remainder

Exceptions: I, D, U

Operands	Execution Clocks		Transfers		Coding Example
	Typical	Range	8086	8088	
(no operands)	125	15-190	0	0	FPREM

FPTAN

FPTAN (no operands)
Partial tangent

Exceptions: I, P
(operands not checked)

Operands	Execution Clocks		Transfers		Coding Example
	Typical	Range	8086	8088	
(no operands)	450	30-540	0	0	FPTAN

FRNDINT

FRNDINT (no operands)
Round to integer

Exceptions: I, P

Operands	Execution Clocks		Transfers		Coding Example
	Typical	Range	8086	8088	
(no operands)	45	16-50	0	0	FRNDINT

Table A1-1. Instruction set reference data (continued). Courtesy of Intel Corporation.

FRSTOR

FRSTOR source
Restore saved state

Exceptions: None

Operands	Execution Clocks		Transfers		Coding Example
	Typical	Range	8086	8088	
94-bytes	210+EA	205-215+EA	47/49	96	FRSTOR [BP]

FSAVE/FNSAVE

FSAVE destination
Save state

Exceptions: None

Operands	Execution Clocks		Transfers		Coding Example
	Typical	Range	8086	8088	
94-bytes	210+EA	205-215+EA	48/50	94	FSAVE [BP]

FSCALE

FSCALE (no operands)
Scale

Exceptions: I, O, U

Operands	Execution Clocks		Transfers		Coding Example
	Typical	Range	8086	8088	
(no operands)	35	32-38	0	0	FSCALE

FSETPM
287 only

FSETPM (no operands)
Set Protected Mode

Exceptions: none

Operands	Execution Clocks		Transfers		Coding Example
	Typical	Range	286	8088	
(no operands)	N/A	2-8	0	—	FSETPM

FSQRT

FSQRT (no operands)
Square root

Exceptions: I, D, P

Operands	Execution Clocks		Transfers		Coding Example
	Typical	Range	8086	8088	
(no operands)	183	180-186	0	0	FSQRT

FST

FST destination
Store real

Exceptions: I, O, U, P

Operands	Execution Clocks		Transfers		Coding Example
	Typical	Range	8086	8088	
ST(i)	18	15-22	0	0	FST ST(3)
short-real	87+EA	84-90+EA	3/5	6	FST CORRELATION [DI]
long-real	100+EA	96-104+EA	5/7	10	FST MEAN READING

Table A1-1. Instruction set reference data (continued). Courtesy of Intel Corporation.

FSTCW/FNSTCW	FSTCW destination Store control word				Exceptions: None
Operands	Execution Clocks		Transfers		Coding Example
	Typical	Range	8086	8088	
2-bytes	15+EA	12-18+EA	2/4	4	FSTCW SAVE CONTROL

FSTENV/FNSTENV	FSTENV destination Store environment				Exceptions: None
Operands	Execution Clocks		Transfers		Coding Example
	Typical	Range	8086	8088	
14-bytes	45+EA	40-50+EA	8/10	16	FSTENV [BP]

FSTP	FSTP destination Store real and pop				Exceptions: I, O, U, P
Operands	Execution Clocks		Transfers		Coding Example
	Typical	Range	8086	8088	
ST(i)	20	17-24	0	0	FSTP ST(2)
short-real	89+EA	86-92+EA	3/5	6	FSTP [BX].ADJUSTED RPM
long-real	102+EA	98-106+EA	5/7	10	FSTP TOTAL_DOSAGE
temp-real	55+EA	52-58+EA	6/8	12	FSTP REG_SAVE [SI]

FSTSW/FNSTSW	FSTSW destination Store status word				Exceptions: None
Operands	Execution Clocks		Transfers		Coding Example
	Typical	Range	8086	8088	
2-bytes	15+EA	12-18+EA	2/4	4	FSTSW SAVE_STATUS

FSUB	FSUB //source/destination,source Subtract real				Exceptions: I,D,O,U,P
Operands	Execution Clocks		Transfers		Coding Example
	Typical	Range	8086	8088	
//ST,ST(i)/ST(i),ST	85	70-100	0	0	FSUB ST,ST(2)
short-real	105+EA	90-120+EA	2/4	4	FSUB BASE_VALUE
long-real	110+EA	95-125+EA	4/6	8	FSUB COORDINATE.X

FSUBP	FSUBP destination,source Subtract real and pop				Exceptions: I,D,O,U,P
Operands	Execution Clocks		Transfers		Coding Example
	Typical	Range	8086	8088	
ST(i),ST	90	75-105	0	0	FSUBP ST(2),ST

Table A1-1. Instruction set reference data (continued). Courtesy of Intel Corporation.

FSUBR

FSUBR //source/destination,source
Subtract real reversed

Exceptions: I,D,O,U,P

Operands	Execution Clocks		Transfers		Coding Example
	Typical	Range	8086	8088	
//ST,ST(i)/ST(i),ST	87	70-100	0	0	FSUBR ST,ST(1)
short-real	105+EA	90-120+EA	2/4	4	FSUBR VECTOR[SI]
long-real	110+EA	95-125+EA	4/6	8	FSUBR [BX].INDEX

FSUBRP

FSUBRP destination,source
Subtract real reversed and pop

Exceptions: I,D,O,U,P

Operands	Executon Clocks		Transfers		Coding Example
	Typical	Range	8086	8088	
ST(i),ST	90	75-105	0	0	FSUBRP ST(1),ST

FTST

FTST (no operands)
Test stack top against +0.0

Exceptions: I, D

Operands	Execution Clocks		Transfers		Coding Example
	Typical	Range	8086	8088	
(no operands)	42	38-48	0	0	FTST

FWAIT

FWAIT (no operands)
(CPU) Wait while 8087 is busy

Exceptions: None (CPU instruction)

Operands	Execution Clocks		Transfers		Coding Example
	Typical	Range	8086	8088	
(no operands)	3+5n*	3+5n*	0	0	FWAIT

FXAM

FXAM (no operands)
Examine stack top

Exceptions: None

Operands	Execution Clocks		Transfers		Coding Example
	Typical	Range	8086	8088	
(no operands)	17	12-23	0	0	FXAM

FXCH

FXCH //destination
Exchange registers

Exceptions: I

Operands	Execution Clocks		Transfers		Coding Example
	Typical	Range	8086	8088	
//ST(i)	12	10-15	0	0	FXCH ST(2)

Table A1-1. Instruction set reference data (continued). Courtesy of Intel Corporation.

FXTRACT

FXTRACT (no operands)
Extract exponent and significand

Exceptions: I

Operands	Execution Clocks		Transfers		Coding Example
	Typical	Range	8086	8088	
(no operands)	50	27-55	0	0	FXTRACT

FYL2X

FYL2X (no operands)
$Y \bullet Log_2 X$

Exceptions:
P (operands not checked)

Operands	Execution Clocks		Transfers		Coding Example
	Typical	Range	8086	8088	
(no operands)	950	900-1100	0	0	FYL2X

FYL2XP1

FYL2XP1 (no operands)
$Y \bullet log_2(X+1)$

Exceptions:
P (operands not checked)

Operands	Execution Clocks		Transfers		Coding Example
	Typical	Range	8086	8088	
(no operands)	850	700-1000	0	0	FYL2XP1

F2XM1

F2XM1 (no operands)
2^X-1

Exceptions:
U, P (operands not checked)

Operands	Execution Clocks		Transfers		Coding Example
	Typical	Range	8086	8088	
(no operands)	500	310-630	0	0	F2XM1

Notes

1. The number of bus transfers given under the heading 8088 also applies to systems based on the 188. The number of bus transfers given under the heading 8086 also applies to systems based on the 186 or the 286. The precise number of transfers on these latter systems depends on whether data is stored on an even address (fewer transfers) or an odd address (more transfers).
2. Where EA is indicated under "Execution Clocks," between six and 14 clocks must be added to allow time for computation of the effective address for 8088, 8086, 188, and 186 systems. 286 based systems generally do not require extra time for effective address calculation.
3. Add approximately 4 clocks for each transfer.
4. Execution time can be calculated by dividing the number of execution clocks by the clock speed. For example, on a typical 5 megahertz PC, 120 clocks would use 24 microseconds. (IBM PC's and compatibles actually run at 4.77 megahertz, so a more accurate figure would be 25 microseconds.) On a 4 megahertz 287 as originally released with the IBM AT, the same 120 clocks would take 30 microseconds.

Appendix 2

Table A2-1. Exception conditions and masked responses. Courtesy of Intel Corporation.

Condition	Masked Response
Invalid Operation	
Source register is tagged empty (usually due to stack underflow).	Return real *indefinite*.
Destination register is not tagged empty (usually due to stack overflow).	Return real *indefinite* (overwrite destination value).
One or both operands is a NAN.	Return NAN with larger absolute value (ignore signs).
(Compare and test operations only): one or both operands is a NAN.	Set condition codes "not comparable".
(Addition operations only): closure is affine and operands are opposite-signed infinities; or closure is projective and both operands are ∞ (signs immaterial).	Return real *indefinite*
(Subtraction operations only): closure is affine and operands are like-signed infinities; or closure is projective and both operands are ∞ (signs immaterial).	Return real *indefinite*.
(Multiplication operations only): ∞ * 0; or 0 * ∞.	Return real *indefinite*.
(Division operations only): ∞ ÷ ∞; or 0 ÷ 0; or 0 ÷ pseudo-zero; or divisor is denormal or unnormal.	Return real *indefinite*.
(FPREM instruction only): modulus (divisor) is unnormal or denormal; or dividend is ∞.	Return real *indefinite*, set condition code = "complete remainder".
(FSQRT instruction only): operand is nonzero and negative; or operand is denormal or unnormal; or closure is affine and operand is −∞; or closure is projective and operand is ∞.	Return real *indefinite*.

Table A2-1. Exception conditions and masked responses (continued). Courtesy of Intel Corporation.

Condition	Masked Response
Invalid Operation	
(Compare operations only): closure is projective and ∞ is being compared with 0 or a normal, or ∞.	Set condition code = "not comparable"
(FTST instruction only): closure is projective and operand is ∞.	Set condition code = "not comparable".
(FIST, FISTP instructions only): source register is empty, or a NAN, or denormal, or unnormal, or ∞, or exceeds representable range of destination.	Store integer *indefinite*.
(FBSTP instruction only): source register is empty, or a NAN, or denormal, or unnormal, or ∞, or exceeds 18 decimal digits.	Store packed decimal *indefinite*.
(FST, FSTP instructions only): destination is short or long real and source register is an unnormal with exponent in range.	Store real *indefinite*.
(FXCH instruction only): one or both registers is tagged empty.	Change empty register(s) to real *indefinite* and then perform exchange.
Denormalized Operand	
(FLD instruction only): source operand is denormal.	No special action; load as usual.
(Arithmetic operations only): one or both operands is denormal.	Convert (in a work area) the operand to the equivalent unnormal and proceed.
(Compare and test operations only): one or both operands is denormal *or unnormal* (other than pseudo-zero).	Convert (in a work area) any denormal to the equivalent unnormal; normalize as much as possible, and proceed with operation.
Zerodivide	
(Division operations only): divisor = 0.	Return ∞ signed with "exclusive or" of operand signs.
Overflow	
(Arithmetic operations only): rounding is nearest or chop, and exponent of true result > 16,383.	Return properly signed ∞ and signal precision exception.
(FST, FSTP instructions only): rounding is nearest or chop, and exponent of true result > +127 (short real destination) or > +1023 (long real destination).	Return properly signed ∞ and signal precision exception.

Table A2-1. Exception conditions and masked responses (continued). Courtesy of Intel Corporation.

Underflow	
(Arithmetic operations only): exponent of true result <−16,382 (true).	Denormalize until exponent rises to −16,382 (true), round significand to 64 bits. If denormalized rounded significand = 0, then return true 0; else, return denormal (tag = special, biased exponent =0).
(FST, FSTP instructions only): destination is short real and exponent of true result <−126 (true).	Denormalize until exponent rises to −126 (true), round significand to 24 bits, store true 0 if denormalized rounded significand = 0; else, store denormal (biased exponent = 0).
(FST, FSTP instructions only): destination is long real and exponent of true result <−1022 (true).	Denormalize until exponent rises to −1022 (true), round significand to 53 bits, store true 0 if rounded denormalized significand = 0; else, store denormal (biased exponent = 0).
Precision	
True rounding error occurs.	No special action.
Masked response to overflow exception earlier in instruction.	No special action.

Appendix 3

Four of the programs below convert data back and forth between the Intel format used in the 8087 and the Microsoft format used in much pre-8087 software. Two programs, SM2I and DM2I, convert from Microsoft to Intel; two, SI2M and DI2M, convert from Intel to Microsoft. Two programs, SM2I and SI2M, convert single precision data; two, DM2I and DI2M, convert double precision data. Occasional minor loss of precision in the conversion process is unavoidable.

The fifth program, INIT8087, initializes the 8087.

The Cookbook—Appendix 3

Program:	**SM2I**
Purpose:	Convert single precision vector from pre-8087 Microsoft format to Intel 8087 format.
Call:	CALL SM2I(SOURCE(0),DESTINATION(0),N).
Input:	SOURCE—single precision n-vector. N—integer number of elements in SOURCE.
Output:	DESTINATION—single precision N-vector.
Language:	8088 assembly language.
Program:	**SI2M**
Purpose:	Convert single precision vector from Intel 8087 format to pre-8087 Microsoft format.
Call:	CALL SI2M(SOURCE(0),DESTINATION(0),N).
Input:	SOURCE—single precision n-vector. N—integer number of elements in SOURCE.
Output:	DESTINATION—single precision N-vector.
Language:	8088 assembly language.
Program:	**DM2I**
Purpose:	Convert double precision vector from pre-8087 Microsoft format to Intel 8087 format.
Call:	CALL DM2I(SOURCE(0),DESTINATION(0),N).

Input: SOURCE—double precision n-vector.
N—integer number of elements in SOURCE.
Output: DESTINATION—double precision N-vector.
Language: 8088 assembly language.

Program: **DI2M**
Purpose: Convert double precision vector from Intel 8087 format to pre-8087 Microsoft format.
Call: CALL DI2M(SOURCE(0),DESTINATION(0),N).
Input: SOURCE—double precision n-vector.
N—integer number of elements in SOURCE.
Output: DESTINATION—double precision N-vector.
Language: 8088 assembly language.

Program: **INIT8087**
Purpose: Initialize 8087.
Call: CALL INIT8087.
Input: none.
Output: none.
Language: 8087/8088 assembly language.

If you use a version of BASIC which does not store data in Intel format, you must use conversion routines before and after calling 8087 routines. The following BASIC code provides an example.

```
10  DEFINT I-N
20  DEFDBL D
30  N=100:N1=N-1
40  DIM A(N1)
50  FOR I=0 TO N1:A(I)=RND:NEXT I
60  CALL INIT8087
70  CALL SM2I(A(0),A(0),N)
80  CALL SUM(A(0),N,DSUM)
90  CALL SI2M(A(0),A(0),N)
100 I1=1:CALL DI2M(DSUM,DSUM,I1)
110 PRINT "THE SUM IS",DSUM
120 END
```

Conversion Routines

```
PUBLIC SM2I,SI2M,DM2I,DI2M,INIT8087

ESEG  SEGMENT   'DATA'
WS         DW   4 DUP(?)
ESEG ENDS

CSEG          SEGMENT    'CODE'
FIRST_INST EQU           THIS WORD
```

```
;SUBROUTINE SM2I(SOURCE,DESTINATION,N)
;CONVERT MICROSOFT TO INTEL
              ASSUME     CS:CSEG,ES:ESEG
SM2I          PROC       FAR
              PUSH       BP
              MOV        BP,SP

;
;SET UP EXTRA SEGMENT TAKING CARE OF RELOCATION
              PUSH       ES
              CALL       NEXT51
NEXT51:       POP        AX
              SUB        AX,(OFFSET NEXT51)-(OFFSET FIRST_INST)
              MOV        CL,4
              SHR        AX,CL
              MOV        BX,CS
              ADD        BX,ESEG
              SUB        BX,CSEG
              ADD        AX,BX
              MOV        ES,AX

;
;ROUTINE PROPER STARTS HERE
              MOV        BX,[BP]+6           ;ADDR(N)
              MOV        CX,[BX]             ;CX=N
              JCXZ       OUT
              MOV        SI,[BP]+10
              MOV        DI,[BP]+8
SM2ILOOP:     MOV        AX,[SI]             ;COPY SOURCE WORD 1
              MOV        [DI],AX
              MOV        DX,[SI]+2           ;MOVE WORD 2 INTO
                                              DX
              MOV        AH,DL               ;GET SIGN BIT
              AND        AH,80H
              SUB        DH,(129-127)
              JBE        Z1                  ;CHECK FOR ZERO OR
                                              CLOSE
              SHR        DH,1
              JC         SET1
              AND        DL,7FH              ;BIT 7 OFF
              JMP        L1
SET1:         OR         DL,80H              ;BIT 7 ON
L1:           AND        DH,7FH              ;SET SIGN
              OR         DH,AH               ;BIT
              MOV        [DI]+2,DX           ;STUFF ANSWER AWAY
              JMP        LOOPBOT1

Z1:           MOV        WORD PTR [DI],0     ;MAKE IT ZERO
              MOV        WORD PTR
                          [DI]+2,0
LOOPBOT1:     ADD        SI,4
              ADD        DI,4
              LOOP       SM2ILOOP
```

```
OUT:        POP     ES
            POP     BP
            RET     6
SM2I        ENDP

;SUBROUTINE SI2M(SOURCE,DESTINATION,N)
;CONVERT INTEL TO MICROSOFT
            ASSUME  CS:CSEG,ES:ESEG
SI2M        PROC    FAR
            PUSH    BP
            MOV     BP,SP

;
;SET UP EXTRA SEGMENT TAKING CARE OF RELOCATION
            PUSH    ES
            CALL    NEXT52
NEXT52:     POP     AX
            SUB     AX,(OFFSET NEXT52)-(OFFSET FIRST_INST)
            MOV     CL,4
            SHR     AX,CL
            MOV     BX,CS
            ADD     BX,ESEG
            SUB     BX,CSEG
            ADD     AX,BX
            MOV     ES,AX

;
;ROUTINE PROPER STARTS HERE
            MOV     BX,[BP]+6            ;ADDR(N)
            MOV     CX,[BX]              ;CX=N
            JCXZ    OUT2
            MOV     SI,[BP]+10
            MOV     DI,[BP]+8
SI2MLOOP:   MOV     AX,[SI]              ;COPY SOURCE WORD 1
            MOV     [DI],AX
            MOV     DX,[SI]+2            ;WORD 2 INTO DX
            MOV     AH,DH                ;GET SIGN BIT
            AND     AH,80H
            SHL     DH,1
            TEST    DL,80H               ;LOOK AT LSE BIT
            JZ      L2
            OR      DH,1                 ;SET LSE
L2:         CMP     DH,0                 ;CHECK FOR TRUE
                                          ZERO
            JE      Z2
            ADD     DH,(129-127)
            AND     DL,7FH               ;BIT 7 OFF
            OR      DL,AH                ;SET SIGN BIT
            MOV     [DI]+2,DX
            JMP     LOOPBOT2
Z2:         MOV     WORD PTR [DI],0      ;SET TO ZERO
            MOV     WORD PTR
                     [DI]+2,0
```

```
LOOPBOT2:   ADD      SI,4
            ADD      DI,4
            LOOP     SI2MLOOP
OUT2:       POP      ES
            POP      BP
            RET      6
SI2M        ENDP

;SUBROUTINE DM2I(SOURCE,DESTINATION,N)
;CONVERT MICROSOFT TO INTEL
            ASSUME   CS:CSEG,ES:ESEG
DM2I        PROC     FAR
            PUSH     BP
            MOV      BP,SP
;
;SET UP EXTRA SEGMENT TAKING CARE OF RELOCATION
            PUSH     ES
            CALL     NEXT53
NEXT53:     POP      AX
            SUB      AX,(OFFSET NEXT53)-(OFFSET FIRST_INST)
            MOV      CL,4
            SHR      AX,CL
            MOV      BX,CS
            ADD      BX,ESEG
            SUB      BX,CSEG
            ADD      AX,BX
            MOV      ES,AX
;
;ROUTINE PROPER STARTS HERE
            MOV      BX,[BP]+6         ;ADDR(N)
            MOV      CX,[BX]           ;CX=N
            JCXZ     AROUND3
            JMP      LL3
AROUND3:    JMP      OUT3
LL3:        MOV      SI,[BP]+10
            MOV      DI,[BP]+8
DM2ILOOP:   MOV      AX,[SI]           ;COPY SOURCE INTO
            MOV      ES:WS,AX          ;WORK AREA
            MOV      AX,[SI]+2
            MOV      ES:WS+2,AX
            MOV      AX,[SI]+4
            MOV      ES:WS+4,AX
            MOV      AX,[SI]+6
            MOV      ES:WS+6,AX

            MOV      DH,[SI]+6         ;GET SIGN BIT INTO
            AND      DH,80H            ;DH
            SUB      AX,AX             ;CLEAR AX REGISTER
            MOV      AL,[SI]+7         ;GET EXPONENT
            CMP      AL,0              ;CHECK FOR ZERO
            JE       Z3
            ADD      AX,(1023-129)     ;CORRECT BIAS
```

```
              SHR       DH,1                ;SHIFT SIGN BIT
                                             INTO
              SHR       DH,1                ;RIGHT POSITION
              SHR       DH,1
              SHR       DH,1
              OR        AH,DH               ;SET SIGN BIT
              AND       BYTE PTR ES:        ;CLEAR OLD SIGN BIT
                         WS+6,7FH
              SHR       AX,1
              JNC       L3
              OR        BYTE PTR ES:        ;TURN ON LSE BIT
                         WS+6,80H
L3:           MOV       BX,3
LA3:          SHR       AX,1
              RCR       BYTE PTR ES:
                         WS+6,1
              RCR       WORD PTR ES:
                         WS+4,1
              RCR       WORD PTR ES:
                         WS+2,1
              RCR       WORD PTR
                         ES:WS,1
              DEC       BX
              JG        LA3
              MOV       BYTE PTR ES:        ;ALL SET IN WORK
                         WS+7,AL             AREA NOW
              MOV       AX,ES:WS            ;STICK IN
                                             DESTINATION
              MOV       [DI],AX
              MOV       AX,ES:WS+2
              MOV       [DI]+2,AX
              MOV       AX,ES:WS+4
              MOV       [DI]+4,AX
              MOV       AX,ES:WS+6
              MOV       [DI]+6,AX
              JMP       LOOPBOT3
Z3:           MOV       WORD PTR [DI],0     ;STORE AWAY ZERO
              MOV       WORD PTR
                         [DI]+2,0
              MOV       WORD PTR
                         [DI]+4,0
              MOV       WORD PTR
                         [DI]+6,0
LOOPBOT3:     ADD       SI,8
              ADD       DI,8
              LOOP      DM2ILABEL
              JMP       OUT3
DM2ILABEL:    JMP       DM2ILOOP
OUT3:         POP       ES
              POP       BP
              RET       6
DM2I          ENDP
```

```
;SUBROUTINE DI2M(SOURCE,DESTINATION,N)
;CONVERT INTEL TO MICROSOFT
            ASSUME     CS:CSEG,ES:ESEG
DI2M        PROC       FAR
            PUSH       BP
            MOV        BP,SP
;
;SET UP EXTRA SEGMENT TAKING CARE OF RELOCATION
            PUSH       ES
            CALL       NEXT54
NEXT54:     POP        AX
            SUB        AX,(OFFSET NEXT54)-(OFFSET FIRST_INST)
            MOV        CL,4
            SHR        AX,CL
            MOV        BX,CS
            ADD        BX,ESEG
            SUB        BX,CSEG
            ADD        AX,BX
            MOV        ES,AX
;
;ROUTINE PROPER STARTS HERE
            MOV        BX,[BP]+6            ;ADDR(N)
            MOV        CX,[BX]              ;CX=N
            JCXZ       AROUND4
            JMP        LL4
AROUND4:    JMP        OUT4
LL4:        MOV        SI,[BP]+10
            MOV        DI,[BP]+8
DI2MLOOP:   MOV        AX,[SI]              ;COPY SOURCE INTO
            MOV        ES:WS,AX             ;WORK AREA
            MOV        AX,[SI]+2
            MOV        ES:WS+2,AX
            MOV        AX,[SI]+4
            MOV        ES:WS+4,AX
            MOV        AX,[SI]+6
            MOV        ES:WS+6,AX
            MOV        DH,[SI]+7            ;GET SIGN BIT INTO
            AND        DH,80H               ;DH
            MOV        AX,[SI]+6            ;GET EXPONENT
            AND        AX,0111111111110000B
            SHR        AX,1
            SHR        AX,1
            SHR        AX,1
            SHR        AX,1                 ;NOW EXPO IS IN
                                             RIGHT SPOT
            CMP        AX,(1023-129)        ;CHECK FOR ZERO
            JBE        Z4
            SUB        AX,(1023-129)        ;CORRECT BIAS
            MOV        BYTE PTR ES:         ;STORE AWAY
                        WS+7,AL              EXPONENT
            SHR        DH,1                 ;SHIFT SIGN BIT
                                             INTO
```

```
                SHR         DH,1                 ;RIGHT POSITION
                SHR         DH,1
                AND         BYTE PTR ES:         ;CLEAR OLD SIGN BIT
                             WS+6,0FH
                OR          BYTE PTR ES:         ;SET SIGN BIT
                             WS+6,DH
                MOV         BX,3
L4:             SHL         WORD PTR
                             ES:WS,1
                RCL         WORD PTR ES:
                             WS+2,1
                RCL         WORD PTR ES:
                             WS+4,1
                RCL         BYTE PTR ES:
                             WS+6,1
                DEC         BX
                JG          L4

                MOV         AX,ES:WS             ;STICK IN
                                                  DESTINATION
                MOV         [DI],AX
                MOV         AX,ES:WS+2
                MOV         [DI]+2,AX
                MOV         AX,ES:WS+4
                MOV         [DI]+4,AX
                MOV         AX,ES:WS+6
                MOV         [DI]+6,AX
                JMP         LOOPBOT4
Z4:             MOV         WORD PTR [DI],0      ;STORE AWAY ZERO
                MOV         WORD PTR
                             [DI]+2,0
                MOV         WORD PTR
                             [DT]+4,0
                MOV         WORD PTR
                             [DI]+6,0
LOOPBOT4:       ADD         SI,8
                ADD         DI,8
                LOOP        DI2MLABEL
                JMP         OUT4
DI2MLABEL:      JMP         DI2MLOOP
OUT4:           POP         ES
                POP         BP
                RET         6
DI2M            ENDP
;SUBROUTINE     INIT8087
INIT8087        PROC        FAR
                FINIT
                RET
INIT8087        ENDP
CSEG            ENDS
                END
```

Index

G

I

J

K

L

M

N

O

P

Diskette Files to Accompany *8087 Applications and Programming for the IBM PC and Other PCs*

The diskette files accompanying *8087 Applications and Programming for the IBM PC, XT, and AT* are described in this note. Complete descriptions of the programs and their operation appear in the text. This note is limited to a technical description of the diskette files.

If you have not already done so, please read the copyright notice, liability disclaimer, and the section on the inherent dangers in using machine language programs.

The programs require one single-sided disk drive, 64K of memory, a copy of the operating system version 1.1 or higher and, for the most part, an 8087. The programs are distributed on a "flippy diskette." (Each side of the diskette is equivalent to one regular single-sided diskette.) The diskette is not copy protected.

The assembly language programs in the text appear in the following files:

VECTOR.ASM	Chapter 9 programs—basic vector routines
MATRIX.ASM	Chapter 10 programs—basic matrix routines
MATADV.ASM	Chapter 11 programs—advanced matrix routines
TRANS.ASM	Chapter 12 programs—transcendental routines
BCD.ASM	Chapter 15 program—compiler version
BCDI.ASM	Chapter 15 program—interpreter version
CONVERT.ASM	Appendix programs—Intel/Microsoft conversion routines

These files are almost, but not exactly, identical to the programs appearing in the book. The differences are:

1. All 8087 mnemonics have been replaced with the equivalent 8088 mnemonics so that the programs can be assembled by assemblers which do not recognize the 8087 names. The 8087 mnemonics have a semicolon placed in front of them to turn them into comments. (For the information of IBM PC users, all these files can be assembled using version 1.0 of the IBM Macro Assembler.)
2. The programs from each chapter have been grouped together in one file. Slight rearrangements of CSEG/ENDS statements have been made. Some statement labels have been modified to eliminate duplicate definitions. For example, you will see labels "NEXT01",

"NEXT02", and so forth, instead of "NEXT", and "NEXT", and so forth.

Not everyone has an assembler program. As a convenience, each file above has been assembled into a program with the extension ".OBJ" replacing the extension ".ASM".

Since linking a machine language program for use with interpreted BASIC is time consuming, we have translated each of the files into a file with the extension ".SAV". These files can be loaded directly into interpreted BASIC using the BLOAD command. (Since program BCD can be used only with the interpreter, there is no ".SAV" version. Use "BCDI.SAV" instead.)

The memory map produced by the LINK program appears in files with extension ".MAP". Use the information in these files to find the offset of a particular routine. If you are going to load more than one file into BASIC, remember that the relocation scheme explained in the book requires the routines to be loaded at an address ending in hexadecimal zero. That is, you can say BLOAD "CONVERT.SAV",&H10, but you should not try BLOAD "CONVERT.SAV",&H11.

For an example of loading multiple assembly language programs into an interpreted BASIC program, see the program "STAT87.BAS".

Remember that the assembly language routines expect all data to be in INTEL format. If you are mixing these routines with pre-8087 programs, you must convert data. For an example of using conversion routines, see the program "STATPRE.BAS".

The "8087 Statistical Analysis Program" appears in two versions. STAT87.BAS is the program as it appears in the text. STATPRE.BAS includes calls to the conversion routines, so you can use the program immediately with pre-8087 versions of BASIC. Module 12 of these programs include "CLEAR" and "DEF SEG" statements that allow these programs to run in systems with 64K of memory. If you have more memory, you may want to change these statements to increase the space available for data storage. The programs are standard text files. If you load the program into BASIC and then SAVE it, the SAVEd version will LOAD much faster than the original. If you eliminate the REMark statements from the program, the space for data storage will increase.

The "DEF SEG" statements in the BASIC programs load the assembly language programs into a clear area of memory. If you use a version of BASIC other than standard IBM PC BASIC, you may have to adjust the DEF SEG statements. In particular, you will probably have to adjust these statements if you use IBM PC BASICA or the version of Microsoft BASIC delivered with many "PC compatibles."

The following BASIC programs also appear on the diskette. Remember to modify these programs to reflect your own data and functions.

CPP.BAS	Crout decomposition
GPP.BAS	Gauss decomposition
SOLP.BAS	Solution following Crout decomposition
DIFFER.BAS	numerical differentiation
INTEGRAT.BAS	numerical integration
ZERO.BAS	solve non-linear equation
MAX.BAS	maximize non-linear function

As a convenience for the user, a number of extra routines are included in the files TRANS.ASM, TRANS.OBJ, etc. These extra routines can be used from BASIC to call the routines written in Chapter 12 in order to transform an entire vector. For example, the routine VSINE(X(0),Y(0),TYPE%,N%) accepts as input the vector X and writes the sine of X into the vector Y. As with other routines in the book, TYPE% is an integer variable equaling 4 if X and Y are single precision and 8 if X and Y are double precision. N% is an integer variable giving the number of elements in X or Y.

Ten extra routines are provided. VY2THEX(X(0),Y(0),Z(0),TYPE%,N%) computes Z=Y^X. All the other routines accept four arguments using exactly the format shown above the VSINE. The nine remaining routines are:

Routine	**Use**
VLN	natural logarithm
VLOG10	common logarithm
VTWO2THEZ	2^X
VEXP	exp(x)
VTEN2X	10^x
VTANGENT	tangent
VSINE	sine
VCOSINE	cosine
VARCTAN	arctangent